Decision Making in Law Firms

IRYNA NIKITINA

Commissioning editor
Alex Davies

Managing director
Sian O'Neill

Decision Making in Law Firms
is published by

Globe Law and Business Ltd
3 Mylor Close
Horsell
Woking
Surrey GU21 4DD
United Kingdom
Tel: +44 20 3745 4770
www.globelawandbusiness.com

Decision Making in Law Firms

ISBN 978-1-83723-182-9
EPUB ISBN 978-1-83723-183-6
Adobe PDF ISBN 978-1-83723-184-3

Contents

Executive summary

Law firm partners are among the most analytically rigorous professionals on the planet – yet their firms struggle with decisions that drag on too long, build consensus that doesn't hold, and execute strategies that lose momentum before they take root. The problem is not a shortage of intelligence. It is a shortage of self-awareness – about how lawyers actually decide, how partnerships actually reach agreement, and how the timing and architecture of decisions shape the firm's trajectory for years. *Decision Making in Law Firms* is a practitioner's guide to all three.

Part one analyses the anatomy of decision making, with chapter one dismantling the mythology surrounding partnership decisions. The author identifies 13 pervasive illusions – about who decides, how rationality operates, and what "unanimous agreement" actually means – and distills them into four convenient fictions – the illusion of structure, the illusion of role, the illusion of action, and the illusion of progress. These are not signs of incompetence, but rather, natural defenses against the messy complexity of running a partnership. They are also the reason intelligent people so often fall short of their potential.

Chapter two maps the decision-making terrain accurately. It introduces a five-level decision pyramid – from operational to purpose-level decisions – and examines the real cast of characters, including managing partners and informal power brokers, and the informal conversations that often shape outcomes before formal discussion begins. The chapter shows how complexity, growth, and multidimensional firm structures compound the challenge of getting anything decided at all.

Chapter three examines the external and internal forces that shape decisions before partners are even aware of it. Market pressure, competitor signaling, and the personal cost of commitment all operate as silent inputs to every significant choice. Understanding these forces is the prerequisite for managing them.

Part two looks at why smart people make strange decisions. Chapter four introduces the psychology of individual decision making in legal partnerships. The author debunks the myth of the rational lawyer and presents five core decision-making styles – Rational, Intuitive, Dependent, Avoidant, and

Spontaneous – each with distinct strengths and predictable failure modes. Beyond style, the chapter examines the cognitive, emotional, and situational drivers that shape behavior in ways partners rarely acknowledge.

Chapter five reveals that pure styles are largely fictional. Through the DMA (Decision-Making Archetypes) framework – a 5×5 matrix generating 16 distinct archetypes – the author shows how lawyers actually operate, through hybrid combinations of dominant and secondary styles that shift depending on context, pressure, and stakes. The chapter profiles three archetypes in depth – the Logical Seer, the Instinctive Impulsive, and the Hesitant Conformist – demonstrating that no archetype is universally superior and that effectiveness depends entirely on situational fit.

Chapter six moves from individual to collective. It explores how different decision-making styles create synergies, generate predictable conflict patterns, and gradually crystallize into a firm's identity. Culture, the author argues, is not an atmosphere – it is accumulated consensus made habitual.

Part three then starts to deconstruct consensus. Chapter seven examines the mechanics of partner buy-in. "Consensus" is the most frequently invoked and most consistently misunderstood concept in partnership governance. The chapter shows how partners conflate consensus with unanimity – a confusion that either paralyzes firms or enables manipulation – and maps the real hierarchy of influence that determines whether agreement will survive beyond the meeting room.

Chapter eight reframes consensus entirely. Drawing on political theory from Cicero to contemporary social psychology, the author distinguishes genuine agreement from its many imitations and introduces the TRUE Consensus Framework. This has four markers – Trust, Rationale, Unity, and Engagement – that separate decisions built to last from decisions built to look good. The framework functions both as a preventative tool before decisions are finalized and as a diagnostic when implementation stalls.

Part four then examines strategic and architectural decisions. Chapter nine examines the decisions that define a firm's long-term competitive position – the layered architecture of market positioning, service model, organizational structure, and execution mechanics. The author explains why architectural decisions are so difficult to reverse – not because change is technically hard, but because everything built on top of those decisions must change simultaneously. The chapter explores foundational strategic tensions, including the Hunter vs Farmer philosophy and the Renter vs Investor orientation, which shape firm culture and partnership dynamics for decades.

Chapter ten focuses on the financial architecture of the partnership – specifically the compensation system as a strategic instrument. The author connects compensation design directly to decision-making behavior, showing how formulas that reward individual origination can undermine collective strategy, and how firms can calibrate their systems to align partner incentives with the decisions the firm actually needs to make.

Finally, part five looks at the decision-making timeline. Chapter 11 maps the life cycle of architectural decisions across the stages of firm development. It identifies four types of foundational decisions and traces the characteristic crises that emerge at each phase – the leadership crisis when founders become bottlenecks, the autonomy crisis when the partnership strains against its own systems, the bureaucratization crisis when process consumes purpose, and the relevance crisis when the market has moved on and the firm's positioning has not. The chapter provides principles for navigating each.

Chapter 12 addresses the real time of decisions – when they should happen, how to prepare for them, and how to organize authority over them. The author introduces a decision calendar framework and a decision-making matrix that maps roles, responsibilities, and levels of involvement across the partnership. The chapter closes with a practical approach to monitoring whether the firm's decision systems are actually working – before pressure reveals otherwise.

In her conclusion, the author returns to the book's founding premise – that decision-making challenges in law firms are not a talent problem or a personality problem. They are a systems problem – one that can be understood, diagnosed, and addressed with the right frameworks and a clearer understanding of how partnerships actually operate.

About the author

Iryna Nikitina is an organizational psychologist and strategic advisor specializing in law firm partnerships and decision-making. For over a decade, she has helped legal leaders navigate complex strategic transformations, optimize partnership structures, and enhance decision-making processes to drive firm success. With a background in law firm leadership and operations, Iryna brings deep expertise in the psychology of legal professionals – how they think, decide, and lead. Her research on decision-making styles within law firms explores how partners balance logic and intuition, structure and agility, independence and collaboration. A sought-after speaker and author, Iryna contributes to international publications, offering insights at the intersection of psychology, strategy, and law firm management.

Part I:
The Anatomy Of Decision Making

Chapter 1: Common illusions in the decision-making process

Dismantling the mythology – how decision making really happens in law firms

For as long as I can remember, partners in law firms have complained about how complicated decision making can be in their world. It's never as simple as picking a morning coffee. Each choice demands strategy, diplomacy, and consensus – ideally achieved without stepping on anyone's toes. Listening to their stories, you'd think every decision was a Herculean task.

But the more I hear these stories, the more I realize they reveal less about the decisions themselves and more about the mythology surrounding how decisions are made in law firm partnerships.

In practice, the process rarely matches the polished accounts shared in meetings or presented at firm retreats. It doesn't always follow the formal procedures in the rulebooks either. More often, it's shaped by what's most convenient, by who stands to gain, or by that familiar phrase: "Let's table this for next time."

It's time to have an honest look at how decisions really happen.

Debunking decision-making myths – the reality behind the façade

Below are 13 persistent myths that law firm partnerships lean on to project an image of logic and order. We all play along with these myths to some extent – the only question is how deeply we buy into them.

Myth 1: Decisions are always strategy-driven

In glossy annual reports, every choice seems perfectly aligned with the firm's strategy. In real life, convenience often wins.

Strategy in law firms is often a story crafted after the fact – a tidy explanation for decisions made on impulse, out of fear, habit, or to appease an influential partner. In many cases, "strategic" is more of a label than a guiding principle.

Myth 2: Procedures and regulations govern everything

On paper, rulebooks reign supreme. In reality, every situation somehow becomes an "exception". Formal procedures work until they inconvenience the wrong person. Rules are bent, interpretations stretched, and special cases made to deliver the desired outcome. Nothing undermines a policy faster than constant exceptions for the favored few.

Myth 3: Data drives our decisions

When the data supports the preferred outcome, it's praised. When it doesn't, it quietly disappears. Metrics and analytics are trendy tools, but in most law firms, they rarely lead the way. Decisions are often based on gut instinct, with data added later to make them look objective – or postponed until the numbers tell a friendlier story. That's not always a bad thing – a seasoned partner's intuition can often outshine a spreadsheet. The problem arises when firms pretend data, not instinct, is running the show.

Myth 4: Partners are the decision makers

In theory, absolutely. In practice? It's complicated. Law firm partnerships create an odd paradox – every partner has the formal right to decide, but not all are keen to exercise it. Some throw themselves into every decision, others hide behind the comfort of consensus, and a talented few manage to delegate responsibility while pulling strings from the shadows.

This is perfectly natural – any system develops informal hierarchies. The trouble starts when we pretend otherwise and cling to the fiction that "everyone decides everything".

Myth 5: Every partner's voice carries equal weight

On paper, yes. In the room? Not quite. A partner's actual influence depends on all sorts of things, including the size of their practice, personal charisma, how long they've been around, or simply their willingness to own a decision. This isn't scandalous – it's how partnerships naturally work.

The myth of absolute equality sounds noble, but it actually gets in the way of honest conversations about who does what. Acknowledging that some voices carry more weight isn't betraying partnership ideals – it's being realistic about how to govern effectively.

Myth 6: Decisions are made collectively

Collective decision making sounds wonderful. Reality is messier. The higher the stakes, the smaller the group actually making the call. Most "collective" decisions are rubber-stamped after the real work happens in private – over phone calls, dinners, or quiet side agreements. That "we discussed and agreed" narrative often masks a fair bit of behind-the-scenes horse-trading.

Myth 7: Partners focus on high-level strategy

"We focus on strategy, not the details" is a common line – until you watch what actually happens. Partners claim to prioritize big-picture thinking, then spend an hour debating presentation fonts, personally rewriting press releases, or signing off on firm-wide birthday messages. Meanwhile, genuinely strategic decisions – about talent, processes, or growth – drift for weeks without resolution. Micromanaging creates the illusion of leadership. Real strategic progress requires trust, which remains in worryingly short supply.

Myth 8: The back office is merely operational

HR, processes, marketing – just technical stuff, right? Not in law firms. The back office isn't simply support – it's where critical management decisions happen. Who gets hired? Who controls budgets? Who evaluates performance? Dismissing these as "technical" matters undermines a firm's ability to grow and adapt effectively.

Myth 9: Making a decision is half the battle

Decision made? Brilliant. Now, who's actually doing it? Law firms suffer from a chronic gap between decisions and delivery. Without clear ownership, deadlines, or accountability mechanisms, decisions fade into the operational ether – forgotten or quietly undermined. A decision is barely the starting point, let alone the finish line.

Myth 10: We can always revisit decisions

A wonderfully convenient excuse for doing nothing. Promising to "revisit" something usually means avoiding action altogether. It's a way to dodge accountability. Without finality, responsibility never sticks, leaving partnerships trapped in endless debate with no actual progress.

Myth 11: Slow decisions are thoughtful decisions

Sometimes. More often, they're just slow. Delay rarely signals careful consideration. It's usually a symptom of internal conflict, fear of owning the outcome, or hoping the issue will simply go away. These "thoughtful" delays have a nasty habit of killing initiative.

Myth 12: Decisions drive growth

In presentations, certainly. In practice, they often preserve the status quo. Many decisions are dressed up as transformative but actually aim to keep things comfortably familiar. Real progress requires discomfort, which partnerships instinctively resist. "Growth" often becomes a polished way of deferring actual change.

Myth 13: The market dictates, we adapt

A convenient way to avoid responsibility. Claiming "the market decided for us" is essentially surrendering strategic control. It's the posture of a passenger, not a driver. This mindset erodes competitive advantage and internal agency, while providing a tidy excuse for prolonged inaction.

Four illusions concealing the truth

Strip away the rhetoric, and these 13 myths come down to four convenient hiding places. Not just for partners – for all of us, really. These are the comforting stories we tell ourselves about how partnerships work.

1. *The illusion of structure.* Put your faith in strategies, procedures, and data – all those reassuringly official documents that look perfect on paper.
2. *The illusion of role.* The partner as master of the universe – decisive leader, skilled manager, everything firmly under control.
3. *The illusion of action.* Make the decision, announce it at the meeting, job done. Results will surely follow.
4. *The illusion of progress.* Every decision moves us forward – even when it's really just preserving what we already have, dressed up in progressive language.

These illusions aren't signs of weakness or incompetence. They're natural defenses against the messy complexity of running a partnership. The problem isn't that they exist – it's when we believe them so completely that we lose touch with what's actually happening.

But you can't build a functioning system on myths alone. To manage decisions effectively, you first need to understand them – where they come from, what level they operate at, who really owns them, and who lives with the consequences.

That's where we're heading next. No more myths. Just a clear map of decision making, and an honest look at why some decisions take ten minutes while others drag on for years.

Chapter 2:
A true map of the decision-making journey

The decision-making pyramid

Most law firm partnerships don't collapse from a lack of decisions. Quite the opposite – they're drowning in them.

The problem is that we treat every decision as if it's the same. We debate hiring a junior associate as though it's a strategic masterstroke. We try to reposition the firm without touching any of the underlying rules. We plan for the future while staying locked in this quarter's logic.

Everything gets labelled a "decision", then we wonder why some transform the firm while others barely register.

Five levels – from routine to purpose

Think of decision making as operating on five distinct levels – not ranked by importance, but by how deeply they affect the partnership. Understanding which level you're actually working at clarifies what you're really deciding.

Level 1: Operational decisions

These barely register as decisions at all. Reply or forward? Put a mid-level associate on the call or wait for someone senior? Use the standard NDA or customize it for this client?

Trivial? Not remotely. These choices set the firm's rhythm and reveal who's actually running things. Who drives the pace? Who slows it down? Who quietly becomes the gatekeeper? The operational level is the partnership's pulse. When it's erratic, the whole system starts to wobble.

Level 2: Tactical decisions

This is where planning starts – but strictly within existing rules. How to staff a matter. Who to bring to a pitch. When to schedule the firm retreat. How much to pay for new office space.

The danger here is the illusion of control. A partner hires someone for a project and calls it "investing in growth". They tweak the billing system and announce a "new business model". Really, they're just rearranging furniture in the same room.

Level 3: Managerial decisions

These focus not on what to do, but on how decisions get made in the first place.

Who has authority to hire? How is profit distributed? Which metrics actually matter? Where does practice autonomy end?

This is where partnerships typically stall. Managerial decisions mean limiting someone's freedom, so they get deferred with familiar excuses – "Not now," "Let's not formalize things," or "It's working fine as is" – until a crisis reveals that nobody actually knows the rules.

Level 4: Strategic decisions

These change not the mechanics, but the direction.

Open an office in a new jurisdiction. Merge with a competitor. Exit a profitable but toxic practice area. Fundamentally reshape the partnership model.

These decisions are always painful because they touch identity – who we are, where we're going, what we stand for. They can be delayed for years, dressed up as tactical moves. But eventually, reality forces the choice.

Level 5: Existential decisions

These are rarely spoken aloud, yet they determine whether a partnership has a soul.

Are we genuine partners, or just splitting profits? Do we actually trust each other? Is there something beyond money holding us together?

You can't resolve these with a vote. They mature over years and surface during crises – one partner leaves, saying "We want different things". Another stays, realizing – we're actually in this together.

See Table 2.1 overleaf.

Why it matters

Most partnerships don't fail because of wrong decisions. They fail because they make decisions at the wrong level. They fiddle with operations when strategy is what's needed. They shift strategy without fixing broken processes. They avoid existential questions until they explode into open conflict.

Understanding which level you're working at means recognizing what actually needs attention. Sometimes it's just keeping things running smoothly. Sometimes it's charting a completely new course. And sometimes it's having an honest conversation about why you're all in this together in the first place.

Table 2.1: The decision-making pyramid

Level	Focus	Key questions
5. Existential	Why we exist	Are we genuine partners? Do we trust each other? What holds us together beyond money?
4. Strategic	Where we are going	What markets to enter? Which practices to grow? What kind of firm do we want to become?
3. Managerial	How decisions get made	Who has authority? How is profit distributed? What are the actual rules?
2. Tactical	Planning within rules	How to staff matters? When to pitch? How much to spend on office space?
1. Operational	Daily execution	Who to assign? Which version to use? When to respond?

The internal conflict of partner roles

We've looked at the different levels of decision making – from operational to existential. Now for another layer of complexity. At every level, partners aren't deciding from a single perspective. They're juggling three competing roles.

Every partner contains three identities – lawyer, manager, and owner. These roles don't just complement each other, they actively clash, especially when decisions need making. Until we acknowledge this internal conflict, decisions will stay contradictory and their execution will be sabotaged from within.

Three competing logics

The lawyer is the service provider. Quality, depth, and professional integrity come first. They think in terms of client interests, personal involvement in matters, and professional reputation. For them, a good decision is one that deepens their expertise.

The practice manager sees things differently. They focus on team workload, process efficiency, meeting deadlines, and keeping clients flowing through the system. Their decisions follow an internal logic – what can we actually handle with current resources? Who's overworked? Who's underutilized? Where does reshuffling make sense?

The business owner operates from the logic of capital. They prioritize the firm's long-term sustainability, reputational risk, and growth potential. They ask forward-looking questions: how will today's choices affect the firm's value in three years?

Three competing logics within every partner is the key to understanding the internal tension. Every decision triggers all three logics simultaneously. The tension is a feature, not a bug. See Table 2.2.

Table 2.2: Partner role conflict matrix

Role	Primary focus	Decision logic	Typical question
The Lawyer	Quality and expertise	Professional integrity, client interests, personal reputation	"Will this deepen my expertise?"
The Practice Manager	Team and efficiency	Workload balance, deadlines, resource allocation	"Can we handle this with current resources?"
The Business Owner	Economics and growth	Profitability, market position, long-term value	"Does this make financial sense?"

How it plays out in practice

Case 1: The toxic but lucrative client
A client with serious reputational baggage but a hefty budget shows up.
Lawyer: "Fascinating case – completely novel legal ground!"
Manager: "This keeps the team busy for six months."
Owner: "This could seriously damage our reputation."

Case 2: Implementing a new CRM system
The firm is considering an expensive project management platform.
Lawyer: "Another distraction from actual work. And the interface is terrible."
Manager: "Finally – proper transparency and control."
Owner: "The return on investment is far from clear. Should we hold off?"

Case 3: Launching a new practice area
An opportunity emerges to start an ESG practice.
Lawyer: "I don't know this area. I'd be starting from scratch."
Manager: "We'd need to hire specialists and build everything from the ground up."
Owner: "This is where the market's going. If we don't move now, we'll miss it."

In each case, all three perspectives are legitimate. But you can only make one decision.

Conflict as a feature, not a bug

This internal conflict isn't a character flaw or a sign of muddled thinking. It emerges in every partner when significant decisions arise. In fact, partners who don't experience this tension are often less effective – they view everything through a single lens and ignore the others.

- A "pure lawyer" partner takes on brilliant cases that drain the firm's resources.
- A "pure manager" partner builds processes that strangle creativity.
- A "pure owner" partner chases profits while losing talent and clients.

The skill isn't eliminating the conflict. It's managing it.

Navigating role conflict

The key is learning to balance these competing roles deliberately. Here's a practical approach:

- *Recognize it exists.* Start by admitting, "Yes, I've got three competing logics running in my head, and that's completely normal". Acknowledging the conflict is half the battle.
- *Identify your default role.* Every partner has a natural leaning – some instinctively think like lawyers, others like owners. Knowing your default helps you recognize when you're operating on autopilot.
- *Switch roles deliberately.* Adapt to what the situation actually needs. With clients, think like a lawyer. When planning resources, think like a manager. For strategic decisions, think like an owner.
- *Use the partnership as a system.* The strongest partnerships distribute these roles across people. One partner excels as a lawyer, another as a manager, a third as a strategic owner. Together, they create something complete.

The best partnerships aren't full of generalists trying to do everything. They're full of specialists who understand their strengths and trust each other's.

Every decision is a choice of role

Every significant decision isn't just choosing between options A and B. It's choosing which role takes priority.

Problems emerge when:

- Partners don't realize which role they're speaking from.
- They try to satisfy all three roles at once.
- They think they're being "objective" while actually defending one particular logic.

Understanding role conflict doesn't make decisions easier. But it makes them honest. You stop pretending there's a "perfect" decision that satisfies everyone. Instead, you choose which logic matters most in this situation – and accept the consequences.

Who really makes decisions in a law firm

Now that we understand decision levels and the internal conflicts shaping them, let's look at who actually makes decisions in a law firm. Spoiler: it's not always the people with formal authority.

Law firms love talking about "firm decisions", "management decisions", or "partnership decisions". But behind these grand phrases are real people – not "the firm", not "management", not some abstract "board". A specific lawyer, partner, manager, or leader makes the call. Or pretends not to.

The hierarchy of decision-makers – who decides what (and what comes of it)

Here's who's actually making decisions:

- Junior lawyers and associates.
- Project leads.
- Practice heads.
- Functional managers (COO, HR, Marketing, Finance).
- Non-equity partners.
- Equity partners.

Each role works within certain boundaries of responsibility, authority, and limitations. What follows is who decides what, where their power ends, and the paradoxes that shape their actual impact.

Junior lawyers / associates

Decide: Operational tasks – how to structure a memo, which tasks to tackle first, whether to check with a senior.

Don't decide: Anything touching money, teams, or clients.

Paradox: Their "small" decisions shape how clients experience the firm day-to-day.

Project leads

Decide: Tactical choices – how to set up the team, who does what, how to communicate with the client.

Don't decide: Who's on the project, what it costs, or who gets bonuses.

Paradox: They – not the partners – are often the firm's actual face to clients.

Practice heads

Decide: Management matters – growth strategy, hiring, business development, practice direction.

Don't decide: Firm-wide strategy, bonus structures, or partnership formulas.

Paradox: Their decisions drive 80 percent of results but influence only 20 percent of overall strategy.

Functional managers
Decide: Infrastructure – support staff hiring, internal processes, systems, and tools.
Don't decide: The strategic "what" or "why" – only the "how".
Paradox: They build the systems that enable everything the firm does, but need approval for every step.

Non-equity partners
Decide: Client and project matters within their patch.
Don't decide: Their own future or how profits get divided.
Paradox: Maximum responsibility with minimum actual control.

Equity partners
Decide: Strategic and existential matters – anything that fundamentally reshapes the firm.
Don't decide: Day-to-day operations (unless they choose to meddle).
Paradox: Formally equal, but in practice some actually decide while others just turn up to meetings.

Decisions mapped to levels

Understanding who should decide what creates clarity. Table 2.3 (overleaf) maps the five decision levels to the roles best placed to handle them – keeping everyone in their lane while the partnership stays aligned.

In an ideal world, everyone sticks to their lane and decisions flow smoothly from vision to execution. In reality? Lines blur constantly. Partners debate font choices. Junior lawyers offer strategic opinions. That's where understanding role conflict matters – recognize when you're straying from your lane, switch perspective when needed, and use the partnership's collective strengths to keep things on track.

Why the system breaks down

Decisions ≠ authority
Often, the people who should decide don't – out of fear, indifference, or excessive deference. Meanwhile, people without formal authority push decisions through sheer force of personality, influence, or persistence.

Table 2.3: Decision authority map

Decision level	Examples	Who decides
Existential	Mergers, fundamental model changes, partner exits	Managing partner and key equity partners
Strategic	Budgets, new practices, partnership formulas	All equity partners
Managerial	Processes, hiring policies, practice development	Practice heads and functional managers
Tactical	Project setup, task allocation	Project leads
Operational	Task execution, document work	Lawyers at all levels

Invisible decisions
Who gets invited to the meeting. Who's mysteriously left off the email chain. Whose suggestion quietly disappears. These micro-decisions shape culture far more than any official policy.

Parallel power structures
Every firm has three levels:

- *Formal decision-makers:* The people on the org chart.
- *Real decision-makers:* The people everyone actually asks for advice.
- *Shadow decision-makers:* The people pulling strings behind the scenes.

This creates a dual reality – how decisions officially happen, and how they actually happen.

Decisions as a power indicator
Here's a simple rule – show me what you decide, and I'll tell you where you really stand.

- Deciding on stationery? You're nobody.
- Deciding on people? You're a manager.
- Deciding on money? You're a partner.
- Deciding on purpose? You're a leader.

What to do about it

Understanding who actually makes decisions in your firm is the first step toward effective management – not perfect management, not textbook management, but management that works for your specific people and circumstances.

You can draw all the org charts you like. But until you acknowledge who's really pulling the levers, you're managing a fantasy, not a law firm.

How decisions are made

Now that we know who makes decisions, let's look at how they're actually made – and why what appears to be chaos often follows a peculiar but predictable logic.

It all starts with consensus

In most law firm partnerships, decisions aren't made by vote or executive decree. They emerge through alignment – a process usually called consensus.

The formula is simple – a decision is made when no partner openly objects. It doesn't require everyone to support it actively – just that nobody explicitly opposes it.

Consensus is popular in law firms for good reasons. It minimizes conflict by ensuring nobody bears the full weight of defeat. It feels fair. It creates space for different perspectives, letting each partner contribute their view. This collective approach strengthens unity, reinforcing the idea that decisions are made together.

But consensus has a serious flaw – it obscures accountability. When decisions are collective, it's nearly impossible to trace who proposed what, who actually supported it, or who just went along for a quiet life. The result is a vague "we" that masks individual responsibility, making it difficult to pin down ownership when things go wrong later.

The shadow of the managing partner

In theory, all voices carry equal weight in consensus. In practice? Not remotely.

When the managing partner speaks first, others tend to fall in line. When they're visibly in favor of something, objecting feels less like challenging an idea and more like challenging authority.

"No one objects" might genuinely reflect agreement. Or it might reflect a strong reluctance to create conflict. Smart managing partners recognize this and speak last. But even their silence gets analyzed: "What do they actually want?"

The result is that consensus sometimes becomes "Everyone knows what the boss wants and nobody's brave enough to say otherwise".

Decisions as a journey, not a moment

In a law firm, a decision isn't a single event. It's a process. It doesn't arrive fully formed at the partnership meeting. It evolves, mutates, and adapts as it moves through the system.

A typical journey looks like this:

1. Someone floats an idea in a working group.
2. It comes up in a quiet conversation with the managing partner.
3. It gets tested informally with "key voices".
4. It's refined through discussions with HR or finance.
5. It finally reaches the partnership meeting – or quietly dies somewhere along the way.

At each stage, the decision shifts. What started the journey often bears little resemblance to what eventually gets adopted – if anything gets adopted at all. Sometimes the journey just stalls – no formal rejection, no explanation, just "We've moved on to other things".

The art of the minutes

Partnership meeting minutes aren't a record of what happened. They're an interpretation of what's deemed worth remembering.

"After discussion, partners reached consensus" – in reality, three people were strongly opposed, one walked out, and "consensus" emerged after an hour of attrition.

"Resolved to form a working group" – though nobody actually volunteered to lead it.

"Issue deferred for further review" – translation: nobody wants to touch this. Drafting minutes is political craft. The phrasing determines whether someone can later claim "That's not what we agreed".

Formally yes, practically maybe

A "made" decision doesn't automatically become an executed one. In law firms, there's often a substantial gap between the two.

What typically happens after "deciding":

- Key partners meet to "clarify the interpretation".
- The decision gets postponed "until conditions improve".
- Everyone waits for someone else to move first.
- Something more urgent comes up and the decision quietly fades away.

This isn't deliberate sabotage – it's just how the ecosystem works. A decision needs to fit the current balance of power and interests. Without active oversight, it simply dissolves.

Minutes don't guarantee action. Without someone owning it, a deadline attached to it, or any mechanism to track it, a decision enters a sort of hibernation – formally alive, practically dormant.

The cost of cancellation

Reversing a bad decision is harder than making a new one. Cancellation means admitting error, bruising egos, and setting what feels like a dangerous precedent.

It's far easier to work around it – adopt a new decision that quietly neutralizes the old one, stop implementing it without announcement, or reinterpret it until it means something completely different.

The result? Firms carry the weight of "dead" decisions for years. Everyone knows they don't work, but cancellation is a political act, not just a management one.

Collective responsibility means no responsibility

Group decisions are a partnership hallmark. Discussed together, decided together, accountable together. It sounds admirable. It works terribly.

Why collective responsibility fails:

- Nobody can trace where the idea actually came from.
- Everyone remembers the discussion differently.
- No single person is responsible for making it happen.

- When things go wrong, everyone claims: "I had doubts but didn't want to rock the boat".

Any group decision can be undone or reinterpreted: "We meant something different", "There were conditions attached", "Circumstances have changed". Without personal accountability, decisions belong to nobody – and nobody's decision is effectively no decision at all.

Decisions as compromise, not choice

Partnerships love compromise. It avoids giving offense, maintains balance, and sidesteps open conflict. But compromise has a cost – it rarely produces breakthrough results.

Strong decisions are inherently uncomfortable. They require:

- Shifting power.
- Abandoning what's familiar.
- Acknowledging someone got it wrong.
- Accepting conflict as necessary.

Instead, partnerships typically choose the "safe" option – adjust a little, adapt slightly, implement partially. The result? The status quo wearing different clothes.

Decisions as signals, not actions

Some decisions are never meant to be implemented. They're made to send a message.

To demonstrate activity. To reassure the team. To report progress to clients. To create the appearance of movement.

Examples of signal-only decisions:

- Forming an innovation committee (with no budget or authority).
- Approving new KPIs (with no way to measure them).
- Launching a wellbeing program (with no actual initiatives).

The trouble is that over time, people stop taking decisions seriously. Why invest energy if it's just another piece of theater?

The fatigue factor

When a decision gets made matters as much as what the decision actually is.

- Morning meeting: everyone's alert, ready to debate, drilling into detail.
- Late afternoon meeting: everyone's exhausted, keen to leave, willing to agree to almost anything.

Experienced operators know this and use it. Complex issues get placed early on the agenda. Contentious matters wait until opponents are worn down. "Must-pass" items slip into Any Other Business when attention has long since wandered. A decision made on tired minds is difficult to challenge later: "We all agreed to it!"

Decisions have an expiration date

In a law firm's shifting environment, decisions age fast. Contexts change. New factors emerge. Key people leave. What felt critical last week can be irrelevant today. Without a proper tracking system, decisions simply dissolve. Nobody formally cancels them, but everyone understands they're no longer in play. Then at the next meeting, the same issue comes up again. And again. And again.

Ghost decisions

Every firm has "decisions" that everyone knows about but nobody can recall actually making.

"We don't take on more than three major clients at once" – who decided that?

"We don't act against partners' business interests" – when was this agreed?

"New practices get 12 months to prove themselves" – where's that written down?

These ghosts emerge from:

- Offhand comments by the managing partner.
- One-off precedents that became rules.
- Collective assumptions nobody questioned.
- Convenient myths that serve someone's purpose.

Ironically, ghost decisions often work better than formal ones. They're flexible, adaptable, and can't be challenged by pointing to the minutes. But they also create space for manipulation – everyone interprets them however suits them best.

Informal alliances and backroom decisions in partnerships

We've examined the mechanics of decision making – consensus, compromise, ghost decisions. But there's another layer, rarely discussed openly, where real decisions get made before they ever reach the minutes.

In most law firm partnerships, decision-making runs on two tracks – formal and informal. The formal track involves meetings, agendas, minutes, and decisions communicated to everyone. The informal track consists of quiet conversations, pre-agreed positions, subtle signals to "park this for now", and outcomes known to key players well before any official discussion begins.

The structure of backroom deals

Formal partnership meetings are often the finish line, not the starting point. Decisions typically take shape long before they appear on any agenda.

How it actually looks:

- A call to the managing partner to "test the waters on something".
- A WhatsApp group of influential partners "exploring options".
- A conversation in the lift after a client meeting.
- Lunch among three partners where a new initiative gets "informally" discussed.
- A five-minute cigarette break that resolves what the boardroom will debate for two hours.

By the time formal discussions happen, the script's already written. Key players know where everyone stands. The meeting becomes theater – objections get raised for the record, arguments are performed for junior partners, and the decision gets formalized for legitimacy. But the outcome was settled elsewhere, earlier, quietly.

A function, not a dysfunction

It's tempting to dismiss backroom deals as murky politics, but that's too simplistic. Informal channels aren't conspiracies or manipulation. They're the natural result of a structure built on relationships, not just formal hierarchy. Partnerships are inherently fluid – influence always extends beyond official voting rights.

Why backroom deals emerge:

- *Fear of chaos:* Testing ideas privately avoids public rejection
- *Time efficiency:* Why debate for two hours when lunch can resolve it in 20 minutes?
- *Tension reduction:* Conflicts are easier to manage privately than in front of an audience.
- *Relationship preservation:* Some conversations work better one-to-one.

Informal alliances, oddly enough, help the formal system work. They act as lubrication in the machinery, reducing friction and enabling smoother progress.

When lubrication turns to sand

There is, however, a tipping point where this useful mechanism becomes destructive.

Sign #1: Alliances replace the system

Critical decisions can't proceed without the informal group's approval – not because the rules say so, but because "otherwise there'll be trouble". Formal processes become window dressing.

Sign #2: Politics over strategy

Backroom conversations shift from what's best for the firm to who wins and who loses; who needs backing, who needs containing, who owes whom. The focus moves from growing the firm to protecting positions.

When this happens, the partnership typically splits into two groups. On one side are the *Insiders* – those with access to information and real influence over decisions. On the other are the *Extras* – people performing their roles but with little actual say. Over time, those in the latter group start asking themselves, "If everything's decided without me, what exactly am I doing here?"

Two types of alliances

Not all informal groups are created equal. There's a crucial distinction.

- *Constructive alliances* form to strengthen decision making. They remain open to new members, work alongside formal processes, and focus on substance and outcomes. These groups make the partnership more effective.

- *Toxic alliances* exist to bypass the system. They stay closed to outsiders, replace formal mechanisms, and obsess over who holds power. While constructive alliances strengthen the partnership, toxic ones corrode it from within.

How can you tell the difference between constructive and toxic informal groups? Table 2.4 helps break this down.

Table 2.4: Alliance types comparison

Characteristic	Constructive alliances	Toxic alliances
Purpose	Strengthen decision-making effectiveness	Bypass the system and control outcomes
Membership	Open to new members who add value	Closed circle protecting power
Formal process	Works alongside formal mechanisms	Replaces formal mechanisms
Focus	Substance and outcomes	Who holds power
Partnership effect	Strengthens collective capacity	Corrodes trust and splits the firm

Trying to eliminate informal channels is pointless. The goal is to keep them constructive.

Maturity – acknowledge and integrate

Trying to eliminate informal channels in a law firm is like trying to abolish gravity – pointless. Mature partnerships recognize this and, rather than fighting backroom deals, choose to acknowledge and work with them. Some people need consulting before formal discussions. Some issues benefit from preliminary testing. Informal influence is inevitable and permanent.

The challenge isn't eliminating these dynamics – it's maintaining balance.

Formal processes must remain genuine spaces for decision making, where preliminary conclusions can be challenged, every voice genuinely matters, and participation means something beyond just showing up.

When this balance breaks down, the partnership splits into two realities – one for people who actually decide, another for people who simply attend meetings. These parallel worlds drift further apart until eventually someone calls it out and says what everyone already knows.

Multidimensionality – when partnerships have multiple layers

So far, we've talked about decision making as if all partners sit around one table, in one room, sorting out the same issues. Reality? Not even close. The moment a firm outgrows the "sitting around the kitchen table" phase, decision making gets exponentially messier.

A firm with one office and three to five partners is manageable. A firm with three offices spread across cities or countries, each running five practice areas, is a completely different animal. In the first scenario, decisions happen over lunch. In the second, they pass through so many hands that, by the time they emerge, nobody can remember who suggested what in the first place.

Offices – parallel universes

Opening a second office isn't just about getting a new address – it's the moment "us" and "them" enter the vocabulary.

Once you've got geographic spread, that lovely consensus model we talked about earlier? Fiction. Now you've got head office, regional offices, or just "the other lot".

The usual flashpoints:

- Should everyone work to the same standards, or do local offices get to do their own thing?
- Shared budget or office autonomy?
- One client base or territorial carve-ups?
- Rotate people between offices or let each office hoard its own talent?

Every decision now has to pass a double test – does it work for the firm as a whole? Does it work for each individual office? These two requirements are almost never compatible.

The video conference syndrome

Technology was supposed to make distance irrelevant. Instead, it just created a new pecking order.

When some partners are physically in the room and others are on screen, the real decisions get made by the people in the room. Everyone else is essentially watching theater.

"Colleagues from the Manchester office, can you hear us? Brilliant, let's crack on..." And then they proceed exactly as if the screen wasn't there.

Practices – feudal fragmentation

If offices create geographic tribes, practice areas create professional ones.

Every strong practice behaves like its own little kingdom:

- Its own clients (and God help anyone who wanders onto their territory).
- Its own standards ("This is how we've always done it").
- Its own jargon ("You lot in corporate wouldn't get it").
- Its own vision for where the firm should be heading (which, funnily enough, always puts their practice front and center).

Getting practices to work together – or even agree on anything – becomes like international diplomacy:

- Who pays when a client needs multiple practices? ("We brought them in!" versus "Yes, but we're doing all the actual work!")
- Whose standards apply on a joint piece of work? (Spoiler: neither – it just gets muddled through somehow.)
- Who takes responsibility when things go sideways? (Nobody – remember that bit about collective responsibility?)

The outcome is entirely predictable – officially, decisions apply "firm-wide". In reality, each practice reads them however suits them best, or just quietly ignores them. "We do things differently in our area."

Committees – another layer of complexity

When direct management gets too unwieldy, partnerships do what any sensible organization does – they create committees.

Compensation committee. Development committee. Risk committee. HR committee. Before long, the structure looks like one of those Russian dolls – open one up and there's another inside.

In theory, committees should:

- Spread the workload around.
- Tap into specialist expertise.
- Speed things up.

In practice, they:

- Add extra layers of approval.
- Become arenas for office politics.
- Turn into where good ideas go to die.

The classic journey of an initiative:

1. It gets discussed in the relevant committee.
2. It goes to the partnership meeting.
3. It's sent back to committee "for refinement".
4. It returns to the partnership with changes.
5. It's sent back again to "address some concerns".

By round three, nobody can remember what the original point was.

The political economy of committees

Of course, committees aren't just about getting work done. They're also about power, positioning, and occasionally, avoiding work altogether.

Here's how the game actually works:

- *Getting onto a key committee* = status upgrade (you're now "someone who matters").
- *Chairing a committee* = actual power (you set the agenda, you control what gets discussed, you decide when things are "ready").
- *Undermining a committee* = blocking decisions you don't fancy (just keep asking for "more analysis" or "broader consultation").
- *Creating a new committee* = a remarkably elegant way to bury a problem ("We're taking this seriously – we've formed a committee to look into it").

The beauty of committees is their flexibility. Need to show you're doing something? Form a committee. Need to delay a decision? Send it to committee. Need to kill an idea without openly opposing it? Let it die slowly in committee, where nobody's watching.

Some committees meet regularly and do genuine work. Others exist purely on paper, convening once a year to tick a governance box. And a few operate as inner circles – the real power centers where actual decisions get made before they're presented to anyone else.

The complexity matrix

Now picture all these layers stacked on top of each other.

Take something straightforward – say, updating the staff appraisal system. It needs to navigate:

1. *Geographic filter:* Get all offices onside.
2. *Practice filter:* Get sign-off from every practice area.
3. *Committee filter:* Get reviewed by the HR committee.
4. *Partnership filter:* Get final approval at the general meeting.

And that's the simple version. Add international offices, global network obligations, or local regulatory quirks, and the decision's route starts to resemble the Minotaur's labyrinth – except there's no thread to guide you out.

For more on this, see Appendix 1.

Attempts at simplification

When firms find themselves grappling with complexity, they usually try structural fixes to restore some clarity and get everyone pointing in the same direction. These efforts start with good intentions, but they tend to run into their own problems along the way.

The managing partner – traditionally just "first among equals" – increasingly ends up acting as orchestra conductor, trying to harmonize all the competing interests and priorities. The aim is to create at least the appearance of cohesive leadership, though there's always the risk of centralizing too much power if things aren't carefully balanced.

To bridge the management gaps, firms often establish a management committee made up of practice heads or office leaders, tasked with aligning everyone's perspectives. While this can help with coordination, it frequently just adds another layer of internal politics, making decision making more complicated rather than simpler.

Similarly, cross-functional teams get formed to tackle specific tasks. These can work well when they're kept small and focused. The trouble is, as they expand, they risk turning into yet another unwieldy committee, bogged down by bureaucracy and losing sight of what they were supposed to be doing in the first place.

Each of these efforts reflects a genuine attempt to wrangle the partnership's complexity into something manageable. But success really depends on maintaining discipline and clarity – otherwise your shiny new structure just becomes another obstacle.

The cost of complexity

Complexity doesn't just make organizational charts look messy – it creates real problems for getting anything decided.

Every extra layer eats up time. Partners and practice groups need aligning, priorities need negotiating, competing visions for the firm's future need reconciling. It's exhausting and slow. The more complicated things get, the more room there is for politics. Personal agendas creep in, factions form, and before long, people are advancing their own interests rather than the firm's. Trust takes a battering in the process.

The longer discussions drag on, the more the original point gets lost. What started as a clear proposal gets debated to death until nobody's quite sure what they're deciding anymore. The whole thing loses momentum – stalled by endless discussion, competing priorities, or just bureaucratic sludge.

In a simple structure, you might finalize a decision in a week and actually get something done. In a complex one, the same decision can take months, and by the time it emerges it's been so watered down that you wonder whether it was worth the bother.

Time, politics, dilution, inertia – these are the real costs of complexity. The only way to manage them is through disciplined, transparent processes that keep things clear, preserve the original purpose, and ensure decisions actually translate into action rather than simply more meetings. For a practical framework to calculate the full cost of your decisions, see Appendix 2.

The challenges of growth

Here's the paradox – if you want to avoid complexity, you have to give up on growth. You can't stay small and cozy while operating in the premium market. You can't serve major clients without offices in multiple locations. You can't compete effectively without specialist practices.

The choice isn't really between simplicity and complexity – it's between managing complexity well or letting it manage you.

What actually works:

- *Clear boundaries.* Work out which decisions genuinely need the full partnership process, and which don't. Not everything requires everyone's input.
- *Fast tracks.* Create simpler routes for operational matters that don't need elaborate approval chains.
- *Regular pruning.* Keep clearing out redundant approval steps that have accumulated over time. They pile up faster than you'd think.

- *The right mindset.* Structure should serve the business, not the other way round. The moment your processes become ends in themselves, you've lost the plot.

Ultimately, having multiple dimensions to your firm isn't fatal. It's just the reality of playing at this level. The skill that separates genuine leaders from administrators is the ability to simplify without breaking things – and to see the whole system rather than just your bit of it.

Partners and managers – two worlds, one decision

Multidimensionality is tricky enough. But what happens when you bring in people who aren't just from another office or practice area, but from a completely different world? Professional managers – people who've never drafted a contract in their lives but know how to manage the people who do.

For years, law firms operated on a straightforward principle – lawyers handled the legal work and everything else. Then it dawned on everyone that "everything else" actually required its own expertise. In came professional managers, and decision making was never quite the same again.

Clash of worlds

Remember that section on partners juggling multiple roles? Now add someone from outside that equation entirely. Partners are already spinning four plates at once – expert lawyer, team leader, practice manager, business owner. It's exhausting, frankly. Something usually drops – and it's typically the management plate.

Professional managers arrive to pick up that plate. But then the obvious question emerges: whose plate is it now? Who decides where it goes? And why should a partner trust someone who "isn't even a lawyer"?

The classic standoff goes something like this:

Partners think:

"They don't understand how law firms actually work."
"We managed perfectly well for ten years without them."
"This is our firm – we know how to run it."
"Why are we paying a manager when any partner could do this?"

Managers think:

"Partners confuse strategy with day-to-day operations."
"They make decisions based on gut feeling, not evidence."

"Everything here is untouchable, apparently."
"Every partner seems to think they're a management guru."

Both sides have a point – they're just operating from completely different frames of reference.

The issue of trust

Remember how we talked about trust binding the "insiders" who shape decisions? Well, trusting an "outsider" – like a professional manager – is a different matter entirely.

In a law firm, trust is worth more than money. Partners spend years building it with clients, weighing every word and action to maintain their credibility.

But when it comes to internal managers – say, a CFO or HR director – that same trust mysteriously evaporates. It's a curious contradiction – partners will happily pay eye-watering fees to external consultants for advice they'd dismiss immediately if it came from their own finance or operations team.

The reason is simple perception. External experts turn up with their competence taken for granted. Internal managers have to prove themselves daily, while navigating all the firm's politics and peculiarities.

Firms typically try to solve this in one of two equally flawed ways.

1. *The "one of us" approach:* Promote someone who already knows the firm – the long-serving assistant becomes HR director, the familiar accountant takes on finance. The logic is that they understand the culture and all its quirks. The reality is they often get stuck between their old role and their new one, unable to properly assert authority because everyone still sees them as they were.
2. *The "expensive pro" approach:* Hire a heavyweight from outside with an impressive CV. Then either give them carte blanche and hope for the best, or second-guess their every decision. The first option leads to chaos when they misread the firm's dynamics. The second leads to a demoralized manager whose expertise gets stifled by constant interference.

Both approaches miss the point. What's needed is a way to value genuine expertise while respecting what makes the partnership tick – but that balance turns out to be remarkably difficult to strike.

Turf wars

The most painful question of all: who actually decides what? Remember the decision-making pyramid in Table 2.1 and who actually decides? Add professional managers into the mix, and it turns into a battlefield.

Zones of relative clarity:

1. *Strategy:* Partners decide (though managers provide all the data and analysis).
2. *Operations:* Managers handle the day-to-day (though partners can't resist interfering).
3. *Clients:* Partners own the relationships (though managers build and run the CRM system).
4. *Processes:* Managers design them (though partners routinely ignore them).

Perpetual conflict zones are where the real fights happen, because there's no obvious answer to who should be in charge:

1. *Budgeting:* Who controls spending – the people who bring in the money, or the people who understand how finance actually works?
2. *Hiring:* Who decides whether someone's right for the role – a practicing lawyer with no HR training, or an HR professional who's never practiced law?
3. *Growth strategy:* Who sets the direction – visionary partners with client relationships, or analytical managers with market data?
4. *Pricing:* Who knows what to charge – the partner who understands the market, or the marketing team with the competitive intelligence?

There's no neat answer to any of these. Each firm muddles through in its own way, usually with a fair bit of friction.

The bias barrier

There's a familiar pattern in law firms – managers put together well-researched proposals, backed by solid data, and they go absolutely nowhere.

A manager spends weeks on detailed analysis, prepares a presentation with charts and benchmarks, proposes a solution that could boost efficiency by 30 percent. Partners listen politely, nod along, say "Very interesting" and then carry on exactly as before.

The problem isn't the quality of the work – it's that managers and partners are filtering the same information through completely different lenses – see Table 2.5 overleaf.

Table 2.5: Manager to partner "translation" matrix

What the manager says	What the partner hears
"A CRM system will increase lead conversion by 25 percent."	"More bureaucracy that'll get in the way of actual work."
"We need standardized processes across practices."	"They want to force everyone into the same rigid box."
"The data shows significant inefficiency."	"They don't understand how our work actually happens."

It's not deliberate obtuseness on either side. Managers genuinely believe efficiency improvements will help. Partners genuinely believe their way of working has evolved for good reasons. Both are partly right.

The trouble is, without someone who can translate between these two worldviews – someone who understands both the value of professional management and the realities of legal practice – proposals just bounce off each other like ships passing in the night. Good ideas stall, frustration builds on both sides, and everyone ends up wondering why nothing ever changes.

The COO – diplomat between worlds

The chief operating officer sits in a unique position – part manager, part diplomat, translating between two groups who often speak entirely different languages.

A good COO doesn't just present technical proposals. They reframe them in terms that actually resonate with partners, building trust while navigating all the firm's unwritten rules and cultural quirks. The skill lies in translation:

- Turn KPIs into client value.
- Turn efficiency into professional development.
- Turn change into opportunity.

What actually works:

- Start with how it benefits clients, then mention efficiency as a bonus.
- Find partner champions for each initiative – things move much faster with internal advocates.

- Demonstrate quick wins to build credibility.
- And whatever you do, don't cite "industry best practice" – partners are convinced their firm is completely unique.

What kills your credibility:

- Forcing "the correct way" of doing things down people's throats.
- Building your own little empire within the firm.
- Playing political games and setting partners against each other.
- Acting superior with the attitude of "I know better than you lot".

The COO role requires real finesse – balancing professional management expertise with an understanding of how partnerships actually work. Frame everything around client outcomes. Cultivate partner support before you need it. Build credibility through results, not authority.

Ultimately, whether a firm can bridge the partner–manager divide comes down to whether the COO can get these two groups working together rather than past each other. It's not easy, and plenty of COOs fail. But when it works, it's what allows firms to actually implement the changes they need rather than just talking about them endlessly.

Framework for collaborative authority

To stop partners and managers constantly treading on each other's toes, you need clear boundaries about who decides what – not rigid demarcation lines that nobody crosses, but sensible divisions that play to each group's strengths.

Here's how it tends to work best:

1. *Strategic level:*
   What to do: Partners decide the direction.
   How to measure success: Managers propose the metrics.
2. *Tactical level:*
   Priorities: Partners set what matters most.
   Resources: Managers work out how to allocate them.
3. *Operational level:*
   Professional standards: Partners define what good work looks like.
   Support processes: Managers design how things actually get done.

The underlying principle is straightforward – partners own the "what" and "why" (the firm's purpose, direction, and standards). Managers own the "how" and "how efficiently" (the systems, processes, and metrics that make it all happen).

This isn't about rigid territories. It's about recognizing that partners understand the business of law, while managers understand the business of running an organization. When you blur these lines – partners micromanaging processes, or managers trying to set strategic direction – things go sideways quickly.

The framework only works if both sides respect it. Partners need to genuinely let managers manage, rather than second-guessing every decision. Managers need to accept that certain decisions will always rest with the partnership, even when they've got data suggesting a different approach.

Get this balance right, and you reduce the constant friction that exhausts everyone. Get it wrong, and you end up with turf wars, paralysis, or both.

Stages of acceptance

Building a proper working relationship between partners and managers doesn't happen overnight. It's a journey, and most firms get stuck somewhere along the way. Here's how it typically unfolds:

- *Stage 1: Rejection.* "Why are we paying for expensive overhead? We've managed perfectly well on our own."
- *Stage 2: Testing.* "Fine, let them handle something that doesn't really matter. We'll see how they get on."
- *Stage 3: Acknowledgment.* "They're quite useful, actually. But let's not pretend they understand the business like we do."
- *Stage 4: Partnership.* "Honestly, we couldn't do this without them now – though obviously we're still ultimately in charge."
- *Stage 5: Synergy.* "We're one team. Different expertise, shared goals."

Most firms get stuck around stages 2 or 3, where skepticism and the need to stay in control dominate everything. Getting to genuine partnership – let alone synergy – requires a real cultural shift. Partners have to be willing to admit they don't know everything and that managers bring genuinely valuable expertise, not just administrative support.

That's harder than it sounds. It requires a degree of vulnerability that doesn't come naturally in a partnership structure built on professional authority. To assess where your partnership currently stands on this maturity spectrum, see Appendix 3.

Competitive advantage

The firms that crack this – the ones that genuinely blend legal expertise with professional management – gain an advantage that's remarkably hard to copy. It's not about having better processes or flashier org charts. It's about the chemistry that develops when people from completely different professional worlds learn to trust each other and build something together.

Competitors can hire managers. They can copy your structures. What they can't replicate is years of built trust and genuine collaboration. That's what actually moves the needle.

New rules of the game

When professional managers arrive, they don't just take on some admin work – they fundamentally change how decisions get made. What used to run on partner instinct starts requiring data and processes. It's a shift, and not everyone welcomes it.

Before managers:

- Decisions ran on experience and gut feeling.
- Every partner managed their own patch their own way.
- Client service was everything; efficiency was for accountants.

After managers:

- Decisions need data and justification.
- There are actual shared processes and standards.
- Client service still matters, but so does doing it efficiently.

This isn't about replacing one approach with another – it's about blending them. The old way had genuine strengths – deep client relationships, professional judgment, flexibility. The new way brings rigor, consistency, and the ability to scale without falling apart.

Firms that actually manage to combine these approaches – partner expertise plus professional management – end up with something competitors struggle to copy. You can poach their managers. You can mimic their processes. What you can't replicate is the years of trust and collaboration that make it all actually work.

The firms that reject managers entirely stay nimble but hit a ceiling. The firms that let managers take over lose what made them good in the first place. The firms that get the balance right? They're the ones that pull ahead.

Chapter 3: External and internal forces influencing decisions

External pressure – when the market dictates decisions

We've dissected the internal mechanics – decision levels, role conflicts, backroom deals, structural complexity, partner–manager tensions. You might think that's everything you need to understand how decisions get made. But there's one force that can override all your internal agreements in an instant – the outside world.

Partnerships like to think of themselves as captains of their own ship – meet, discuss, decide, set sail. Reality is rather less flattering. Often, you're more like a raft on a fast-moving river, with the current dictating direction far more than your oars do. That current is the external environment, and it shapes your decisions whether you acknowledge it or not.

Clients – the invisible meeting participants

Remember that decision-making pyramid? At every level, there's an unseen participant – the person who's actually paying.

In law firms, clients aren't just revenue sources – they're silent architects of everything you do. Most firms make a distinction, even if they don't say it aloud, between clients (small "c") who contribute to day-to-day income, and Clients (capital "C") whose expectations can reshape your entire strategy.

When someone at a partnership meeting says "Our key Client expects..." something remarkable happens. Debate stops. The discussion immediately shifts from "Should we?" to "How quickly can we?".

This is where the consensus model we discussed earlier gets interesting. Consensus isn't just among partners – it extends beyond your walls. You're not really reaching agreement among yourselves – you're aligning yourselves with what the Client wants, or what you think they want.

The Client's preferences – whether they've actually expressed them or you're just anticipating them – become the deciding factor. Internal disagreements that might drag on for weeks suddenly evaporate when someone invokes the Client's expectations.

This can be useful. It cuts through endless debate and forces decisions. But there's a risk – you can end up so closely aligned with one Client's vision that you lose your independence. You stop asking "What's right for our firm?" and start asking "What does the Client want?".

The anchor client phenomenon

When one client generates 20-30 percent of your revenue, they stop being just a client. They become an invisible board member, shaping every strategic decision you make.

This "anchor client" exerts a kind of gravitational pull on everything. Their needs, their direction, their priorities – all of it ends up defining your firm's path, often without anyone explicitly deciding that should happen.

You're discussing whether to open an office in a new city. Someone asks, "Does our Client have interests there?". That becomes the deciding factor, not whether it makes strategic sense for your firm.

You're considering developing a new practice area. The question isn't, "Is there market demand?", it's "Will our Client find this useful?".

You're debating whether to hire an expensive lateral partner. Somebody raises the concern, "How will our Client react to this?".

Even small decisions – adopting a new case management system, say – get filtered through, "Will this work for our Client?".

Formally, partners are deciding. In reality, you're all just trying to work out what the person paying 30 percent of your bills would want.

This warps your entire decision-making process. The firm stops evolving according to its own strategy and starts following the Client's trajectory instead. Their industry becomes your specialism. Their geographic footprint becomes your expansion plan. Their problems become your priorities.

In the short-term, this feels sensible. You're aligning with your biggest revenue source, keeping them happy, securing that income.

The danger emerges later. What happens when that Client shifts industries? When they consolidate their legal panel and you're suddenly one of five instead of the main adviser? When they hit financial trouble or get acquired?

You've built a firm shaped around one client's needs, and now you're misaligned with the broader market. You've got expertise nobody else particularly needs, offices in locations that made sense for them but not for anyone else, and a cost base built for revenue that's evaporated.

Convenient in the moment? Absolutely. Dangerous long-term? Extremely.

RFPs as external arbiters

"The RFP requires it" is one of the most powerful phrases in any partnership meeting. It stops debate dead.

Requests for Proposals from clients act like external referees, overriding internal resistance and pushing through decisions that might otherwise drift for months. They bring data and requirements from outside, and somehow those external demands become gospel in a way that internal analysis never does.

Remember those myths about decision making we discussed earlier? How firms claim to be data-driven but actually rely on gut instinct? Here's the curious bit – when data arrives via an RFP, it suddenly becomes sacred. The same partners who'd dismiss your carefully researched proposal will immediately accept something because "It's in the RFP".

Client wants ISO certification? "The RFP requires it, we'll get it sorted." Never mind that you've been debating ISO internally for two years – now it's happening.

Competitors mentioned legal tech in their bid? "They've listed it, so we need it too." Even though you've resisted that exact technology investment for months.

Major RFPs asking about ESG credentials? "Right, we're launching an ESG practice." Doesn't matter that half the partnership thinks it's a passing fad.

RFPs become a remarkably convenient way to push through unpopular decisions. Why waste energy convincing skeptical partners when you can just point to tender requirements? External pressure legitimizes what would face endless internal resistance.

It's effective, certainly. But there's a risk – you end up building your firm based on what clients are asking for in RFPs this quarter, rather than what makes strategic sense for you, long-term. You're letting the market's current preoccupations dictate your direction, which is fine until those preoccupations shift and you're left with capabilities nobody wants anymore.

Panel dependency

Getting onto a major corporation's legal panel is both a dream and a nightmare. Steady work and prestige on one side, a mountain of demands that can reshape your entire firm on the other.

Panels aren't just client relationships – they're formalized arrangements where the client's standards become your obligations. What they want, you provide. How they want it, that's how you do it. Reporting? Forget your familiar systems – you're now reporting in their format, on their schedule, through their portal. Billing? Wave goodbye to your standard rates and terms. You're using their pricing model now, whether it suits you or not. Diversity targets? They've got social responsibility goals, which means you've now got hiring quotas to meet. Insurance requirements? They want higher coverage limits, which means unexpected – and often substantial – additional costs. Communication standards? That memo format you've refined over years might as well be binned. You're using their templates now.

Now imagine you're on multiple panels. Bank A wants fixed fees. Corporation B insists on hourly rates. Company C demands you don't work for their competitors. Holding Company D is fine with you advising others. You end up trying to satisfy everyone, making contradictory decisions that cancel each other out. Internal logic gets sacrificed for external compliance. Staff get confused about which rules apply to which client. Systems get patched together to accommodate conflicting requirements.

Panels secure business, no question. But they can also trap you in reactive mode, constantly adapting to different clients' demands. You're spending so much energy conforming to external requirements that you lose sight of what your firm actually stands for. What happens to your strategy when it's being pulled in six different directions by six different panels? What happens to your culture when every practice area operates under different rules because they serve different panels? You end up with a firm that's brilliant at compliance but unclear on its own identity – efficient at meeting everyone else's standards while struggling to define its own.

Small details, big impact

Remember those operational decisions we discussed earlier? The ones that seem trivial but actually set your firm's rhythm and culture? Now imagine those decisions being made not by you, but by your clients' preferences.

Client "preferences" have a remarkable way of quietly reshaping your entire culture. It happens gradually, almost imperceptibly, until one day you realize you're not really running your own firm anymore.

One major client loves short, punchy emails. Before long, bullet points become your firm-wide standard. Your communication style – previously thoughtful and detailed – shifts to accommodate their preference. Another client prefers calls over email. Suddenly your email culture withers. Everyone's on the phone constantly because that's what this client expects, even though half your other clients would rather have things in writing. A key client operates in Asia. Your workday now starts at 6am to catch their business hours. What began as accommodation for one client becomes the new normal for everyone. A client demands responses within an hour, any time, any day. Work–life balance becomes a quaint memory. The expectation of constant availability seeps into everything you do.

Individually, each adaptation seems perfectly reasonable. You're being responsive, flexible, client-focused – all good things, surely? But collectively, these small changes erode who you are. Your communication style isn't yours anymore. Your working hours aren't set by what makes sense for your team. Your responsiveness expectations aren't based on genuine urgency – they're based on whoever shouts loudest.

The real damage isn't immediately obvious. It's the slow accumulation – burnout creeping up because nobody ever switches off, innovation dying because you're too busy responding to immediate demands, your distinctive approach disappearing because you've adapted it out of existence. And once you've drifted this far, getting back is remarkably difficult.

Corporate Stockholm Syndrome

The most dangerous trap is when you start confusing the client's interests with your own. It's a sort of corporate Stockholm syndrome – you've internalized their priorities so completely that you've lost sight of yours.

"It's what the client needs" becomes the universal justification for decisions that don't serve your firm at all. Hiring a lawyer who doesn't fit your culture? "The client likes them." Taking a loss-making project? "We can't upset the client." Dropping other opportunities? "The client has a conflict." The firm shifts from independent adviser to captive unit – formally separate, practically their outsourced legal department.

Breaking this pattern requires conscious effort to step back and ask, are we serving the client, or have we *become* the client? Client service should enhance your firm's identity, not replace it.

The art of balance

Healthy client relationships need you to keep some distance while staying close – a delicate balance that preserves your independence while delivering exceptional service.

What actually works? Diversification, for starters – no single client should be critical to your survival. A clear identity helps too – knowing who you are and what you won't do, regardless of the money on offer. Being willing to say no, even to a major client, when something contradicts your principles. And having an internal compass that guides your growth by your own strategy, not the client's trajectory.

Here's the curious bit – clients actually respect firms that hold boundaries. Independence is part of what makes an adviser valuable. When you become a compliant executor, you lose what made you worth hiring in the first place. Clients don't want a legal department they have to pay external rates for – they want independent judgment, fresh perspective, challenge when needed. That only comes from maintaining some separation.

Speed vs deliberation

Client-driven decisions are the fastest to execute – no lengthy debates, no internal resistance, no messy compromises. The client says jump, you ask how high. This speed can feel wonderfully efficient in a competitive market.

However, they're also the most dangerous for long-term health. Building your strategy around someone else's priorities is like navigating by their compass. It works perfectly well for a while – until you realize you're nowhere near where you actually wanted to go.

This raises an uncomfortable question. Who really runs your firm – the partners, or the people paying the bills? Answering honestly requires stepping back and reclaiming some autonomy. Client influence should enhance your strategy, not replace it. See Table 3.1 overleaf.

The mature response is neither automatic compliance nor automatic resistance – it is strategic choice.

Competitors – the race no one declared

Clients dictate what you do. Competitors dictate how fast. If client pressure shifts your direction, competitor pressure pushes you to sprint – often in completely the wrong direction.

The legal market is a club where everyone knows each other, smiles at conferences, and watches every move. One firm makes a bold step, and the rest rush to follow – not because it makes sense, but because "we can't be left behind".

The domino effect – geography of panic

Remember that discussion about multidimensionality – how strategic decisions require balancing internal logic with external pressure? This is where it all falls apart. Firms open new offices driven purely by fear of what competitors are doing, with no real strategy behind it.

Table 3.1: Client pressure decision tree

Situation	Decision framework
Anchor client request	Ask: Does this align with our strategy? YES? Accommodate with clear boundaries NO? Negotiate or decline (high risk of dependency)
RFP requirement	Ask: Is this defensible to the partnership? YES? Adapt if strategic value warrants NO? Decline and explain why
Panel position threat	Ask: Are we truly at risk of removal? YES? Assess if panel is worth keeping NO? Hold ground and educate client
Scope creep	Ask: Is this a one-off or a pattern? ONE-OFF? Accommodate with expectation-setting PATTERN? Formal discussion required
Fee pressure	Ask: What is our leverage position? STRONG? Negotiate from value delivered WEAK? Consider strategic alternatives
Unreasonable timeline	Ask: Can we deliver quality work? YES? Agree with resource commitment NO? Push back or bring in help
Process change demand	Ask: Does this improve service or just compliance? IMPROVES? Test and implement COMPLIANCE? Assess cost vs relationship value

Here's how it typically plays out. Monday, a market leader announces a new office in Dubai. Tuesday, the news ripples through every major firm's back channels. Wednesday, managing partners face urgent questions: "What about us?" Thursday brings emergency meetings about "our regional presence". Friday, someone's tasked with finding a local partner or alliance. Six months later, half the top 20 firms have Dubai offices.

Here's what nobody stops to ask. Are our clients actually in Dubai? Will this investment pay off? Can we genuinely operate effectively there? The only logic driving it is fear – "If they're opening there, they must know something we don't. We can't afford to lag behind."

The predictable outcome, carefully hidden behind glossy press releases? Two years later, half these offices quietly shut down, having failed to generate anything close to sustainable business.

The salary spiral – a race without a finish line

Remember that discussion about decision-making authority and how choices driven by internal needs can be tricky? Well, when fear of losing talent takes over, decisions become purely reactive – and expensive.

The mechanics are painfully simple. A top firm raises salaries by 20 percent. The news spreads market-wide within a day. Your senior associates start getting offers. HR sounds the alarm: "We're losing people!" An urgent decision follows: "Right, we're raising salaries too."

Nobody stops to ask the obvious questions. Can we actually afford this? Will it improve productivity? Are clients prepared to pay higher rates? The only thing driving it is fear: "Our people will jump ship otherwise".

Result? The entire market raises salaries. Everyone's relative position stays exactly the same, but costs have shot up across the board. A spiral driven by panic rather than strategy, burdening everyone without improving anyone's competitive position.

The talent war – from strategy to panic

A competitor poaches your star partner and their entire team. Panic ensues and strategic thinking goes out the window.

The sequence is depressingly predictable. Morning brings "How did we let this happen?" Midday, a crisis meeting: "What do we do now?" Evening, emergency measures get rolled out. Deferred bonus schemes to lock people in. Accelerated partnership tracks to keep them motivated. Revised compensation packages. Wellbeing initiatives to show you care.

Never mind that your existing system worked perfectly well for years. Never mind that the departure might have been purely personal. Fear of losing more people triggers frantic activity. Six months later, half these initiatives have quietly stalled. But the decisions have created expectations that are remarkably difficult to walk back, disrupting long-term stability in ways nobody anticipated.

The tech race – prestige over sense

Remember how we talked about decisions as signals? The legal tech race is all signal, precious little substance.

A competitor adopts AI for due diligence. Suddenly it feels essential – regardless of whether your M&A practice represents only five percent of revenue, the technology is still buggy, nobody's trained to use it, or the return on investment is distinctly negative.

The only concern is not looking like you're behind the times. Legal tech becomes a status competition. Who's first with blockchain for smart contracts? Who's got the slickest client portal? Whose machine learning is cleverest?

Whether it's actually useful comes a distant second to looking innovative.

The talent poker game – rising stakes

A competitor hires a former minister as of counsel. Game on. You respond with a retired Supreme Court judge. They counter with a renowned law professor. Someone else brings in a high-profile international arbitrator.

Whether there's sufficient work for these people? Whether they'll generate fees that justify their cost? Irrelevant. The goal is signaling to the market: "We're serious players. We're not second-tier. We're in the game."

These hires rarely deliver direct financial returns, but they're justified by reputational gains – keeping score in a competition where perception matters as much as profit, even when the costs far outweigh the tangible benefits.

FOMO – a corporate epidemic

Fear of Missing Out drives firms to chase every trend without any real strategic thinking, creating a cycle of purely reactive decisions.

Everyone's launching fintech practices? We launch a fintech practice. Everyone's into ESG? We establish an ESG practice. Everyone's talking compliance? We hire a compliance officer. Everyone's adopting agile? We implement agile methodologies.

The problem isn't the initiatives themselves – it's that there's no deep understanding behind them, insufficient resources to see them through, and wavering commitment once the initial excitement fades. You end up chasing every trend without mastering any, spreading yourself thin and draining resources on half-baked initiatives that go nowhere.

FOMO systematically undermines strategic coherence, leaving firms stretched across poorly executed projects that exist mainly so you can tick a box saying "We're doing this too".

Herd regulation

Sometimes the pressure to conform comes not from direct competitors but from the broader market ecosystem – a sort of soft coercion that's remarkably effective.

Professional associations or market leaders issue guidelines on remote work standards, pricing principles, approaches to developing junior lawyers, diversity and inclusion policies. Formally, these are recommendations. Practically, they become requirements.

Not following them risks positioning your firm outside the mainstream, which feels dangerous even when the standards don't particularly suit your context or needs. So you adopt them anyway, even when they don't make perfect sense for you.

This herd mentality stifles genuine innovation. Everyone ends up doing roughly the same things in roughly the same way, because deviating feels too risky. Conformity becomes the safest option, even when it means abandoning what made your firm distinctive in the first place.

Global pressure – foreign standards

For firms with international ambitions, there's another layer of pressure – global standards that often bear little relation to local realities.

The Magic Circle adopts a particular practice? That becomes the benchmark. Wall Street firms work round the clock? That sets the norm. London firms hit 50 percent women partners? That becomes the target everyone's aiming for.

These standards come from different markets, different cultures, different contexts entirely. But they get adopted without question because you need to meet "international benchmarks". Never mind whether they actually make sense for your market, your culture, your clients. The pursuit of global credibility can create real cultural dissonance, as foreign practices struggle to take root while diverting focus from strategies that might actually suit your specific environment.

The cost of the endless race

This relentless pursuit of whatever competitors are doing distorts decision making in some fairly fundamental ways. Your firm's unique identity erodes. You become increasingly similar clones, all chasing the same trends. Tactical reactions replace strategic planning – you're constantly responding rather than leading. Resources get drained trying to do everything, spreading yourself impossibly thin. Foreign practices, adopted wholesale without adaptation, create awkward cultural misfits that never quite work properly.

The greatest cost? Losing your own path entirely. When every decision is a reaction to what competitors are doing, building something genuinely distinctive becomes impossible. You're perpetually playing catch-up in a race where the finish line keeps moving, imitating rather than innovating, following rather than leading.

At some point, you have to ask: Are we building our firm, or just trying not to look worse than theirs?

A mature approach to competition

Monitoring the market and learning from competitors makes sense. But there's a world of difference between deliberate choice and panicked reaction.

A mature firm makes careful distinctions. What's genuinely important versus what's just loud? What's a lasting trend versus a passing fad? What works universally versus what works for us specifically? Where are we actually going versus where they happen to be headed?

These aren't always easy calls, but they're essential ones.

Competitor-driven decisions are inevitable – you can't operate in a vacuum. But the proportion matters enormously. If more than half your decisions are reactions to what others are doing, you're not running your own firm – you're playing their game on their terms.

A mature approach means filtering external pressures through your own strategic lens. Not ignoring the market, but not being driven by it either. Distinguishing between meaningful shifts and temporary noise. Conserving resources for what actually matters to your firm rather than spreading them across every initiative that looks impressive in someone else's press release.

The firms that succeed long-term aren't the ones copying everyone else. They're the ones that have worked out what they're genuinely good at, who they're really serving, and where they're actually trying to go – then making decisions that advance that path, whether or not it matches what competitors happen to be doing this quarter.

Table 3.2: Competitive pressure assessment

Competitive move	Panic response	Strategic response	Key questions
Salary increases	Match immediately to avoid losing people	Assess retention risk, market position, and affordability	Are we actually losing talent? Can we afford it? What is our value proposition?
Talent poaching	Counter-offer everyone or raid them back	Build culture and development pathways	Why are people leaving? What can we genuinely offer? Is this a pattern?
Technology adoption	Buy the same tools for prestige	Identify actual client needs and workflow gaps	Will clients value this? Does it solve real problems? What is the ROI?
New office opening	Open same location to match	Evaluate market opportunity and client demand	Do our clients need this? Can we compete there? What is the real cost?
New practice area	Hire laterals to copy them	Assess strategic fit and sustainable advantage	Does this align with our strategy? Can we build credibility? Is there genuine demand?

Table 3.2 above highlights the strategic response vs reactive panic. FOMO drives poor decisions. Mature firms ask, "Should we?" not just, "Can we?".

The decision and its cost – who goes all in

We've examined every factor shaping decisions – internal conflicts, structural complexity, clashing worlds, external pressures. One question remains. Why, despite understanding all this, do partnerships delay critical decisions for years?

This final section looks at the cost of delay – and the cost of action.

Two years to the obvious

The signals are obvious – resources are running out, the old market's disappearing, a key partner's checked out, the managing partner's drowning, the team's demoralized.

Everyone sees the signs. Everyone reads them. But nobody says them aloud. Speaking them forces a choice, and choice means commitment – and consequences.

There's an almost mystical pattern in law firm partnerships – decisions that should've been made yesterday take roughly two years to materialize. Regardless of how big or small they are. Especially if they're genuinely important.

The timeline plays out with remarkable consistency:

- *First six months:* It gets discussed obliquely, hinted at, danced around – never named directly.
- *Next six months:* The "let's not rock the boat" phase. Things are working well enough, aren't they? Best not to disturb what's functioning.
- *One year:* A chorus of "not now" – wrong timing, wrong market conditions, wrong moment in the partnership cycle.
- *Eighteen months:* Crisis symptoms become impossible to ignore, though people still try.
- *Two years:* The situation hits a wall. You can't pretend anymore. Something has to give.

Only then does movement actually begin – usually driven by necessity rather than choice, by crisis rather than strategy.

The cost no one wants to pay

This isn't weakness or deliberate sabotage. It's a protective reflex in a system where risk carries real consequences.

In a law firm partnership, any major decision lands multiple blows:

- *To status:* Someone loses position, influence, or symbolic capital. In partnerships where status often matters more than money, this cuts deep.
- *To balance:* Power gets redistributed, established relationships disrupted, unspoken agreements broken.
- *To comfort:* It means confrontation, saying things that have been carefully left unsaid, possibly damaging relationships you've spent years building.
- *To self-perception:* Admitting the old approach failed, that you got it wrong, that you missed the moment to act.

Even people who clearly see the need for change hold back. Not because they lack courage, but because they hope, maybe it'll sort itself out. Maybe the market will shift back. Maybe that difficult partner will come round. Maybe clients will return. Hope is remarkably persistent, especially when the alternative is painful.

The flexibility of motivation

Here's where motivation becomes wonderfully elastic. What looked like an urgent reason to act yesterday can be reframed as a reason to wait today:

"We're losing market share" becomes "It's just a temporary correction".

"Key people are leaving" becomes "Natural turnover, happens everywhere".

"Clients are unhappy" becomes "They've got unrealistic expectations".

"Competitors are pulling ahead" becomes "Their model isn't sustainable long-term".

The higher the cost of getting it wrong, the easier it becomes to redefine "urgent" as merely "desirable" – especially when things still look relatively stable on the surface. Especially when you can do something less painful instead – a rebrand, perhaps, or a working group, or some temporary measures that show you're doing something without actually changing anything fundamental.

When the wall comes into view

But external pressure keeps mounting. The market shifts faster than you adapt. Clients drift to more agile competitors. The team grows weary of waiting for change that never comes. Revenue drops, costs rise, tension becomes unbearable.

Then the decision gets made – often the exact same one you were discussing two years ago. But now it's rushed, made under time pressure, with no room for careful consideration. Not as a strategic choice, but as a forced reaction.

The difference is stark:

- Choice allows for preparation, proper communication, damage control.
- Reaction demands immediate action, often on significantly worse terms.

Maturity as willingness to pay

This is what distinguishes a mature partnership – not deciding faster necessarily, but recognizing when now is actually the best time you're going to get.

Internal signals matter as much as external pressures. Delaying doesn't reduce the cost – it just makes it harder to manage when it finally arrives.

A mature partnership understands some uncomfortable truths: There's no perfect moment coming. Full consensus is a fantasy. Success isn't guaranteed no matter when you move. And, crucially, the cost of delay often exceeds the cost of getting it wrong. For a diagnostic checklist of warning signs, see Appendix 4.

Decision as an act of acceptance

A decision isn't always an act of will or vision. Sometimes, it's just being ready to step into territory without guarantees. Without unanimous agreement. Without a clear way back. Only with an honest understanding of the price you're willing to pay.

Partnerships that grasp this make difficult decisions, not because it's comfortable, but because they recognize that delaying is also a decision – one with equally serious, often worse, consequences.

If you're going to pay a price either way, better to pay it consciously, on your terms, while you still have control. Not when circumstances have backed you into a corner and stripped away your options.

Ultimately, what matters isn't the decision itself. It's whether the partnership is genuinely ready to commit fully. To pay the full cost. Without endlessly second-guessing what you could've done differently. Without blaming circumstances or each other. Just move forward.

Part II:
Why Smart People Make Strange Decisions

Chapter 4: The psychology of how lawyers decide

Individual psychology and decision-making styles in partnerships

For as long as I can remember, the legal world has been grumbling about decision making in law firms. Partners moan about it as if choosing between two options is more torturous than a three-week trial. We're not talking about picking what to have for lunch here – every decision apparently requires strategic planning, endless consultation, and the sort of delicate consensus-building that would make a UN diplomat weep. Listen to their war stories, and you'd think every choice was a Herculean task. But here's the thing – the more I listen, the clearer it becomes that these tales reveal far more about the mythology partners create around decisions than about the decisions themselves.

It all started back in 1993, when Dr Larry Richard[1] dropped his groundbreaking study on lawyer personalities – finally giving us a proper look at what makes these people tick. Nearly a decade later,[2] his legendary article about managing lawyers introduced that perfect phrase about "herding cats". It struck such a chord that it became legal industry gospel, and you still hear it echoed in partnership meetings today. Reading his work, I couldn't help wondering, if we've figured out what makes lawyers unique, what can we learn about how they actually make decisions? How do their styles shape their careers, their firms, and – let's be honest – their ability to get along with each other?

These days, decision making feels like walking a tightrope, and nowhere is this more obvious than in law firms. Lawyers don't just make choices for clients – they're constantly making calls that affect their entire firm. Strategic planning, resource allocation, sorting out internal squabbles – it all lands on their desks. The result? They're expected to be brilliant legal minds *and* shrewd business operators, often at exactly the same time. And frankly, it's getting harder. McKinsey found[3] that while 72 percent of leaders agree decisions drive business results, only 20 percent actually trust their decision-making processes. Lawyers know this pain intimately – Thomson Reuters[4] reveals that 68 percent report their workload has become more complex and demanding in recent years.

As a former operations director and consultant, I've watched partners tackle these challenges – some with grace, others flailing about spectacularly.

Bonus allocations? One day it's all spreadsheets and data analysis, the next it's pure gut instinct.

Opening a new office? Sometimes it's calculated strategy, sometimes it feels like throwing darts at a map.

This contradiction fascinates me – and not just as an observer, but as someone determined to dig deeper. Every decision reveals something about personal style, and understanding that could transform a weakness into a strength.

The psychology of leadership decisions has been thoroughly explored. Kahneman and Tversky[5] mapped our cognitive blind spots. Janis[6] showed us how groups can think themselves into disasters. Simon[7] gave us "bounded rationality". Epstein[8] tackled decision making under uncertainty. The research is extensive. Yet law firm partners remained mysteriously absent from these studies. Hardly surprising – this is an exclusive, tight-knit group that's naturally suspicious of outsiders poking around their business. The reputational risks are simply too high for them to open their doors to researchers.

So we're left with solid theory about leadership in general, but a glaring gap when it comes to legal partnerships. Years of legal training create a very particular mindset – hunting for precedents, weighing risks, scrutinizing facts, building logical arguments. It becomes second nature. But here's the problem – this powerful toolkit gets used for everything, even when it's completely wrong for the job. The result? Lawyers over-analyze when they should trust their instincts, or get completely stuck when faced with something that doesn't fit their usual patterns.

The problem goes beyond professional habits. Lawyers genuinely believe they're rational about everything. "We're lawyers," they tell themselves, "we analyze, we weigh evidence, we think logically." They apply this confidence to every aspect of life. You've probably seen it – a partner who can untangle the most complex legal puzzle spends two years dithering over a straightforward staffing decision. Or a managing partner who handles million-pound strategies with ease but freezes when choosing an office contractor. Masters of argument spend hours bickering over trivial budget items – not because the money matters, but because winning the debate does.

You're about to get an inside look at how lawyers' minds work when they're making decisions. Spoiler alert: it's rarely the neat, rational process they'd have you believe. Prepare for some surprises. Understanding the psychology behind these choices isn't just interesting – it's genuinely useful for:

- Predicting how partners will behave in a crisis.
- Making sense of apparently irrational decisions.
- Designing processes that work with human nature, not against it.
- Reducing friction when the going gets tough.
- Improving decision quality by avoiding common mental traps.

In the pages ahead, we'll take apart the psychology of how lawyers decide – with real evidence, hard data, and insights you can actually use.

The myth of the rational lawyer

Beyond the stereotype – a diverse reality

Let's be honest from the start. That cherished image of lawyers as paragons of pure logic – coolly analytical, methodically reasoned, delivering perfectly measured judgments – simply doesn't hold water. It's the sort of picture firms love to paint in their glossy brochures and client presentations, but the reality is far messier. The research[9] tells a different story – only 59 percent of lawyers actually prefer making decisions rationally. That's a majority, sure, but it's hardly the universal truth we've been fed.

So what about the other 41 percent? Well, they're doing something completely different:

- 21 percent trust their gut and go with experience.
- 16 percent want everyone else's input before deciding anything.
- 13 percent avoid making tough decisions entirely.
- 14 percent just wing it and see what happens.

These numbers blow apart the stereotype completely. The legal profession is far more psychologically diverse than anyone wants to admit.

The origins of the rationality myth

The idea of the "rational lawyer" didn't just appear overnight. It goes back to the 1990s, when Dr Larry Richard's groundbreaking research[10] showed that 76 percent of lawyers score as "Thinking" types on personality tests[11] – meaning they're naturally wired for logical analysis and healthy skepticism. From this came the archetype – lawyers as pure rationalists, masters of reason. But here's the problem – being capable of logical thinking is completely different from actually preferring to use it when making decisions.

Think about the contradictions you see every day – a partner who can dissect a complex commercial agreement with surgical precision, then chooses the firm's Christmas party venue because "it feels right". Or someone who builds watertight courtroom arguments but spends months agonizing over a simple hiring decision because they're terrified of upsetting anyone.

The myth persists because there's a grain of truth to it – but only a grain.

Why the myth endures

So why does this myth have such staying power? Several things keep it alive. First, there's confusion between two completely different things – analytical thinking and rational decision making. Being analytical is a skill – spending hours poring over case law, building bulletproof arguments, spotting holes in the other side's logic. But rational decision making is a preference, a natural inclination. The same analytically brilliant mind might hire a new associate based purely on gut feeling or because they "just clicked" in the interview.

Then there's professional performance. The legal world demands that everything looks rational – saying, "My decision is based on hard facts" carries far more weight than admitting you went with your instincts. So lawyers adapt accordingly. A partner might follow a hunch on a deal, then dress it up with supporting data to convince the room. Another might go along with the group consensus but present it as "logical considerations". Or someone delays a decision because they hate conflict, but frames it as "needing more thorough analysis".

Finally, there's who the profession attracts in the first place. Law draws people with sharp analytical minds – but that doesn't mean they make decisions rationally. One lawyer might love untangling complex problems but decide everything on impulse. Another, methodical as anything when analyzing cases, might need the whole team's input before making any choice.

The cost of the myth

This belief that all lawyers are rational decision makers damages partnerships badly. When you expect every partner to think the same way, you're setting yourself up for disappointment. "What sort of partner can't make a straightforward decision?" comes the complaint, completely missing that the partner simply operates differently. An intuitive type wastes time gathering data they don't need; someone who thrives on consensus struggles alone with decisions that would be better made as a group.

Worse still, it wastes competitive advantage. Each style brings genuine strengths – intuition cuts through uncertainty quickly, consensus builds team commitment, caution prevents costly mistakes, spontaneity grabs opportunities others miss. Forcing everyone into the same rational mold means firms never tap into these natural assets.

The truth about "irrational" lawyers

Here's what might surprise you – those 41 percent who don't follow the rational playbook aren't inferior lawyers. They're not less intelligent, less successful, or less professional – they just think differently. An intuitive partner might spot something wrong with a deal before the numbers reveal it. Someone who seeks consensus can rally the entire team behind a difficult change. The cautious type prevents rash decisions that could backfire, while the spontaneous one jumps on market opportunities first.

The problem isn't their approach – it's our failure to use it properly. These "non-rational" lawyers aren't the issue; our inflexible expectations are.

A fresh look at the legal profession

The evidence is clear – the legal world isn't some uniform army of rational analysts. It's a collection of individuals who share certain skills but think in completely different ways. Yes, lawyers stand out from other professions – they're more analytical, more skeptical, more fiercely independent. But they're still human beings with the full range of human psychology.

Some love numbers and logic. Others trust their instincts and years of hard-won experience. Some need the team's voice; others prefer to mull things over quietly. Still others just act and see what happens. The 59 percent who prefer rational approaches are a significant force, but they're not the whole story – and the other 41 percent aren't oddities. They're the natural diversity that makes the profession richer and stronger.

Lawyers are people – brilliant, trained, and highly skilled people, but people nonetheless, not walking logic machines. Recognizing this is the first step towards managing legal teams and partnerships far more effectively.

Five decision-making styles – who is who

I've sat through enough partnership meetings to recognize the patterns. There's always that moment when you look around the table and think, "How did we end up with five completely different species in the same room?" You've got one partner frantically scribbling calculations, another tapping their fingers impatiently because they "just know" what the right call is, someone else polling the room for the third time to make sure everyone's comfortable, and the person in the corner who's been "reviewing the situation" for the past six months without reaching any conclusions. Meanwhile, the fifth person is practically bouncing in their chair, ready to make a decision before anyone's even finished explaining the problem.

It's like watching a nature documentary, except instead of lions and zebras, it's lawyers with fundamentally different approaches to making choices. And every single one of them is convinced their way is the only sensible approach.

This isn't just partnership politics or personality quirks – there's actually some science behind it. Back in the 1990s, a couple of psychologists named Scott and Bruce[12] figured out that people basically fall into five distinct decision-making categories. Other researchers have refined their work over the years, and what they discovered explains a lot about why partnership meetings can feel like diplomatic summits between warring nations.

These aren't abstract academic theories. These are your actual colleagues – the ones who drive you crazy because they can't see what's blindingly obvious to you, and who probably think you're equally mad for not seeing what's blindingly obvious to them. Let's meet them.

The Data Devotee: "Show me the spreadsheet or show me the door"

Let's start with the rational decision makers – the ones who treat every choice like a mathematical equation waiting to be solved. These are the people who genuinely believe that if you just gather enough information and apply enough logic, every decision becomes self-evident. They're not being difficult when they ask for the third cost-benefit analysis; they literally cannot comprehend making a choice without it.

Their world revolves around evidence, benchmarks, and systematic evaluation. They want to see every option laid out, every risk quantified, every assumption tested. Give them a spreadsheet and they're happy. Ask them to make a gut call and you might as well ask them to perform surgery blindfolded.

In legal practice, these are often your most methodical partners. They're the ones who'll spend weeks researching precedents before advising a client, who build detailed financial models for every deal, and who approach risk assessment like it's rocket science. Which, to be fair, sometimes it is.

Why the rational approach actually works

Here's the thing about data devotees – when they're right, they're really right. Their decisions can withstand scrutiny because they've already scrutinized everything themselves. There's no favoritism, no emotional baggage, no mysterious "leadership intuition" that nobody can explain afterward. Everything's transparent, logical, and defensible.

I've watched rational decision-makers save firms from disasters that everyone else was ready to walk into. They're the ones asking uncomfortable questions like, "Has anyone actually calculated what this will cost us?" or, "What happens if our assumptions are wrong?". Not exactly crowd-pleasers, but often necessary reality checks.

Their firms tend to run smoothly because the rules are clear and consistently applied. When bonus time comes around, nobody's wondering whether the managing partner's favorites got special treatment – the formula's right there for everyone to see.

Where logic meets its limits

But here's where rational decision makers drive the rest of us up the wall – they can turn every choice into a research project. Markets don't wait for your analysis to be complete. Clients don't pause their crises while you build another model. Sometimes "good enough" information combined with quick action beats "perfect" information that arrives too late.

I've seen opportunities disappear while rational decision makers were still gathering data. Competitors move faster because they're willing to act on 80 percent certainty instead of waiting for 100 percent. The pursuit of perfect information becomes the enemy of timely action.

And let's be honest – some decisions really don't need a full forensic analysis. When the team's debating whether to order sandwiches or pizza for the working lunch, and someone starts asking about cost per calorie and nutritional benchmarks, you know the rational approach has jumped the shark.

Portrait of a number-cruncher in action

Take John Johnson – he's the kind of guy who probably has a spreadsheet for his personal grocery shopping. At 45, he's spent two decades in banking law, starting in regulatory work where getting the capital adequacy calculations wrong could cost clients millions. His office looks like mission control – multiple monitors displaying different data sets, documents organized with military precision, and a calendar that's planned down to 15-minute intervals.

John's fundamental belief is simple: "Every decision should be driven by facts, not feelings. Numbers don't have hidden agendas." You can see this philosophy in everything he does, from client advice to internal firm decisions.

When it's time for the annual bonus discussion – always a partnership minefield – John comes prepared. He's got revenue figures, cost allocations, billable hour calculations, client feedback scores, and business development metrics. "Look," he'll say, pulling up his master spreadsheet, "here's our performance data. Revenue divided by time invested, adjusted for matter complexity and client value. It's mathematics, not politics."

You'll hear John asking questions like, "What objective evidence supports this decision?" or insisting, "We need to properly evaluate all available options before proceeding". When colleagues start talking about "feeling good" about a particular direction, he'll counter with, "Where's the financial modelling to support that intuition?" He's not trying to be difficult – he genuinely doesn't understand how anyone can be comfortable making important choices without comprehensive analysis.

Making peace with the analytical mind

The rational decision-making style isn't going anywhere, and that's probably for the best. Every partnership needs someone who'll slow things down long enough to ask whether the emperor's actually wearing clothes. The key is recognizing when exhaustive analysis adds value and when it's just expensive procrastination.

Smart firms learn to channel their rational decision makers effectively – letting them loose on the big, complex choices where getting it wrong is genuinely costly, while gently steering them away from turning every minor decision into a dissertation project. It's about matching the tool to the task, not trying to force every problem into the same analytical framework.

As we'll see with the other decision-making styles, the real magic happens when you understand how different approaches complement each other – and when you know which one to deploy when the stakes are high and time is short.

The Gut-Feeling Brigade: "Trust me on this one"

So, we've covered the spreadsheet devotees. Now let's talk about their natural enemies – the people who make decisions based on what they "feel" is right. I'm not talking about emotional decision making here, though that's how it often gets dismissed. I'm talking about the partners who can walk into a room, size up a situation in 30 seconds, and somehow know exactly what needs to happen next.

These are the lawyers who drive rational decision makers absolutely mental because they can't explain their reasoning in a way that fits into a PowerPoint slide. Ask them why they chose a particular strategy and you'll get something like, "It just felt right" or, "My experience told me this was the way to go". Try to pin them down for specifics and they'll start talking about "reading between the lines" and "sensing the client's real needs". To John and his spreadsheets, this sounds like complete nonsense. To them, it's the most natural thing in the world.

The magic of pattern recognition

Here's what's actually happening when someone makes an "intuitive" decision – their brain is processing massive amounts of information that their conscious mind can't articulate. They're drawing on years of similar situations, reading micro-expressions, picking up on subtle cues that don't show up in any data analysis. It's pattern recognition at lightning speed, the kind that comes from doing the same thing thousands of times until you can spot the outliers without thinking about it.

In legal practice, these are often your most effective client handlers and dealmakers. They can sense when a negotiation is about to go sideways, or when a client is holding back crucial information, or when opposing counsel is bluffing. They're the ones who suggest pivoting strategy mid-trial because something "doesn't feel right" about how the judge is responding – and they're usually correct.

I've watched intuitive decision makers spot market opportunities that looked crazy at the time but turned out to be brilliant moves. They're the ones who said, "We should get into data privacy law" back when everyone else was still focused on traditional corporate work. They couldn't prove it with market research, but they sensed something shifting in the business world. Three years later, everyone else was scrambling to catch up.

Why gut instinct actually works (sometimes)

The thing about intuitive decision makers is that they're often right in ways that are impossible to predict or replicate. They have this uncanny ability to cut through complexity and focus on what really matters. While everyone else is debating the details, they're already seeing the bigger picture.

They're also incredibly adaptable. When circumstances change – and in legal practice, they always do – intuitive decision makers don't get stuck trying to force reality to match their original plan. They adjust on the fly, trusting their ability to navigate whatever comes up. This makes them invaluable in crisis situations where there's no time for extensive analysis.

Their firms benefit from a culture of experimentation and quick response. Instead of endless committee meetings and feasibility studies, decisions get made and tested in real time. When markets are moving fast or client needs are evolving rapidly, this agility can be the difference between leading the pack and playing catch-up.

Where gut feelings go wrong

But here's the problem with intuitive decision making – it's really hard to quality-control. When someone makes a choice based on "feeling", how do you evaluate whether it was a good decision or just a lucky guess? And, more importantly, how do you prevent disasters when their intuition leads them astray?

I've seen intuitive decision makers champion ideas that seemed brilliant but collapsed under scrutiny. They get excited about opportunities without fully thinking through the risks, or they make strategic moves based on incomplete information. When their colleagues ask perfectly reasonable questions like, "What's our evidence for this?" or "How do we know this will work?", they get frustrated because they can't translate their insight into the kind of logical framework everyone else needs.

This creates real tension in partnerships. Other partners start feeling like they're being asked to trust blindly, especially when previous "gut feelings" haven't panned out. The lack of transparency can erode confidence over time, particularly when high-stakes decisions seem to be made on the basis of hunches rather than hard evidence.

Portrait of an instinct-driven decision maker

Meet Alex Alexon – she's the kind of lawyer who left BigLaw because she felt "suffocated by all the process and procedures". At 38, she's built a thriving wealth management practice by trusting her ability to read people and situations. Walk into her office and you'll see what I mean about intuitive thinkers – it's organized chaos. Case files mixed with strategy sketches on whiteboards, books on negotiation psychology scattered around, and sticky notes with random insights covering every surface.

Alex's fundamental belief is that "experience beats analysis every time". She'll tell you that working with high-net-worth families is about understanding the emotional undercurrents, not just the financial structures. "You can't spreadsheet your way to understanding what really matters to these people," she says. "It's about reading between the lines, sensing what they're not telling you."

When a new client came in with a complex inheritance situation, Alex took one look at the family dynamics during their first meeting and immediately knew the standard approach wouldn't work. "Forget the template," she told her team afterward. "This isn't about tax optimization – they want family unity. We're going to propose a trust structure with a unique governance component that gives everyone a voice. I can't prove it yet, but they'll love it."

You'll hear Alex saying things like, "I've got a strong feeling about this direction" or, "My gut's telling me we need to take a different approach". When colleagues push for more concrete reasoning, she'll say, "This isn't about the numbers – it's about understanding what these people really need". In negotiations, she's constantly emphasizing that, "This situation requires a more nuanced touch than our usual playbook".

Making peace with the mystery

The intuitive decision-making style drives analytical types crazy because it seems to operate outside the normal rules of evidence and logic. But here's the thing – some of the best strategic moves in legal practice come from recognizing patterns and opportunities that don't show up in traditional analysis.

The trick is learning when to trust intuitive insights and when to demand more rigorous evaluation. Smart partnerships find ways to harness their intuitive decision-makers' pattern recognition while building in safeguards to catch potential blind spots. It's about creating space for hunches while maintaining accountability for results.

As we'll see, every decision-making style has its place in the partnership ecosystem. The challenge isn't eliminating approaches that make us uncomfortable – it's learning to deploy the right approach at the right time, and understanding when someone's "gut feeling" might actually be processing information that your spreadsheets are missing entirely.

The Consensus Seekers: "Has everyone had their say?"

Now we come to what might be the most politically correct decision-making style in modern law firms – the people who genuinely believe that every choice should be a group effort. These are the partners who can't order office supplies without forming a committee, who turn every strategic decision into a consultation exercise, and who seem physically incapable of saying, "I've decided" without adding, "after extensive discussions with the team".

If you've ever sat through a three-hour meeting to decide something that should have taken five minutes, you've probably encountered a consensus-driven decision maker in their natural habitat. They're not being difficult or indecisive – they genuinely believe that better decisions emerge from collective wisdom, and that excluding people from the process is worse than taking forever to reach a conclusion.

These are the partners who grew up believing that teamwork makes everything better, that diverse perspectives lead to superior outcomes, and that buy-in matters more than speed. They're democracy enthusiasts in a profession that often rewards autocratic leadership, and they're convinced that if everyone has a voice, everyone will be happier with the result.

Why the collective approach actually works

Here's the thing about consensus builders – when they get it right, the results are remarkably durable. Decisions that emerge from genuine consultation and discussion tend to stick because everyone's had input into shaping them. There's no post-decision griping about "if only they'd asked me" or "this was obviously the wrong choice" because everyone was part of the process.

I've watched consensus-driven leaders build incredibly loyal teams because people feel genuinely valued and heard. When your managing partner regularly asks for your opinion and actually incorporates your feedback into final decisions, you develop a level of investment in outcomes that you simply don't get with top-down leadership.

Their firms often avoid the personality conflicts and political infighting that plague more hierarchical organizations. When decisions are made transparently through inclusive processes, it's harder for people to claim favoritism or feel excluded from the inner circle. Everything's out in the open, everyone knows how choices were reached, and the potential for resentment is significantly reduced.

Plus, let's be honest – some decisions really do benefit from multiple perspectives. Complex strategic choices, major policy changes, anything that affects how people work together – these are areas where consulting widely can prevent expensive mistakes and unintended consequences.

Where democracy becomes paralysis

But here's where consensus-driven decision making drives everyone else up the wall – sometimes you need someone to just make a choice and move on. Markets don't wait for your focus groups to report back. Clients don't pause their crises while you survey the partnership about the best response strategy. Opportunities have a nasty habit of disappearing while you're still building alignment around whether to pursue them.

I've seen firms lose competitive advantages because their consensus-building processes took so long that competitors moved first. By the time they'd consulted everyone, formed working groups, gathered feedback, and reached agreement, the window had closed. The pursuit of perfect consensus becomes the enemy of timely action.

And let's talk about consultation fatigue – that point where people stop engaging with the process because they're tired of being asked their opinion about everything. When every decision becomes a group project, even simple choices start feeling like major undertakings. Partners begin avoiding consensus builders because they know that asking a simple question will trigger a full consultation exercise.

There's also the dirty secret that not every opinion is equally valuable. When you're deciding on litigation strategy, the views of your most experienced trial lawyers probably matter more than the thoughts of your newest corporate associate. But consensus-driven leaders often struggle to weight inputs appropriately because doing so feels exclusionary.

Portrait of a consultation champion

Meet Simon Smith – the kind of guy who probably held family meetings to decide what to have for dinner when he was growing up. At 42, he's the head of corporate practice at a major firm, and if you visit his office, you'll immediately understand his approach to leadership. The space is dominated by an enormous conference table that seems to be in constant use, with people wandering in and out for impromptu discussions and scheduled consultations.

Simon's background explains a lot about his style. He grew up in a diplomatic family where every disagreement was treated as a negotiation opportunity and every decision involved extensive consultation. "Conflict was never about winning," he'll tell you. "It was about finding solutions that everyone could live with."

His fundamental belief is that "the best decisions emerge from dialogue, not isolation". He's convinced that collective wisdom consistently outperforms individual brilliance, and that excluding people from decision-making processes is both inefficient and disrespectful. "Everyone needs to feel heard," he says. "That's not just good politics – it's good management."

When the firm needed to update its HR policies – always a sensitive topic – Simon's approach was predictably thorough. "Right," he announced at the partnership meeting, "we're forming a task force with representatives from every practice group. We'll survey all staff, run focus groups with different seniority levels, and benchmark against comparable firms. This decision affects everyone, so everyone gets input."

You'll hear Simon constantly asking questions like, "What do our colleagues think about this approach?" or insisting, "We need to consider all perspectives before moving forward". When debates get heated, his go-to response is, "Let's put this to a vote after everyone's had a chance to weigh in". His favorite phrase is probably "Consensus drives our success" – he genuinely believes that decisions with broad support are inherently superior to those imposed from above.

Finding the sweet spot

The consensus-driven decision-making style serves an important function in partnership environments, but like every approach, it needs to be deployed strategically. The key is recognizing which decisions genuinely benefit from extensive consultation and which ones just need someone to make a choice and move on.

Smart partnerships learn to channel their consensus builders effectively – letting them lead on major strategic initiatives and sensitive internal issues while gently steering them away from trying to democratize every operational decision. It's about matching the process to the stakes and the timeline.

The real value of consensus-driven leaders isn't that they always make better decisions – it's that they create environments where people feel invested in outcomes. In a profession where talent retention and internal politics can make or break firms, that's not a trivial contribution. The challenge is learning when inclusion matters more than speed, and when speed matters more than making everyone happy.

The Professional Procrastinators: "Let's circle back on this"

Then there are the partners who have elevated "let's table this for now" to an art form. These are the people who can find a reason to delay virtually any decision, no matter how straightforward it seems to everyone else. They're masters of phrases like, "We need more time to assess the situation", "The timing isn't quite right", and my personal favorite, "Let's revisit this when we have more clarity".

Don't mistake this for laziness or incompetence – these are often highly experienced lawyers who've learned that rushed decisions can be spectacularly expensive. They've seen colleagues charge ahead with brilliant ideas that turned into costly disasters, and they've concluded that patience is not just a virtue, it's a survival strategy. Their instinct is always to wait, to see how things develop, to let situations mature before committing to any particular course of action.

If you've ever been in a meeting where someone suggests postponing a decision "until we have all the facts", you've encountered an avoidant decision maker doing what they do best. They're not being obstructive – they genuinely believe that time reveals information that rushed judgment misses, and that most problems either solve themselves or become much clearer if you just wait long enough.

The wisdom of strategic delay

Here's what drives action-oriented people crazy about avoiders – sometimes they're absolutely right to wait. I've watched avoidant decision makers save firms from disasters by simply refusing to be rushed into choices that everyone else thought were urgent. While their colleagues were ready to charge ahead, they were the ones asking uncomfortable questions about potential downsides and unintended consequences.

These are often your best risk managers, the partners who spot the hidden pitfalls that everyone else missed. They have an almost supernatural ability to sense when a situation isn't quite what it appears to be, when there are complications lurking beneath the surface that will only emerge if you move too quickly.

Their firms benefit from stability and careful deliberation. Major strategic decisions get the time and consideration they deserve, rather than being rushed through because someone's impatient to see results. Expensive mistakes get avoided because someone insisted on thinking things through properly before committing resources.

In high-stakes environments like legal practice, where a single misjudgment can cost millions or destroy reputations, having people who naturally lean toward caution can be invaluable. They're the ones who prevent firms from chasing every shiny new opportunity or pivoting strategy every time the market hiccups.

When caution becomes paralysis

But here's where avoidant decision makers drive their colleagues to distraction – sometimes waiting is the worst possible strategy. Markets move, opportunities disappear, problems compound, and competitors act while you're still "gathering more information" or "waiting for the right moment".

I've seen firms lose major clients because they couldn't make timely decisions about staffing changes or strategic direction. While the avoidant leaders were still "assessing the situation", their clients got tired of waiting and found more decisive counsel elsewhere. The pursuit of perfect timing becomes the enemy of any timing at all.

There's also the psychological toll on teams when decision making gets stuck in endless deferral loops. People need closure, they need direction, they need to know where the firm is heading so they can plan their own work and careers accordingly. When every significant choice gets postponed indefinitely, it creates an atmosphere of uncertainty that can be more damaging than making the occasional wrong decision.

And let's be honest – some decisions really don't benefit from extended deliberation. When the office coffee machine breaks down, you don't need a feasibility study to determine whether replacement is appropriate. When clients are calling with urgent questions, "Let's think about this for a few weeks" isn't the response they're looking for.

Portrait of a master delayer

Meet Jon Johnson – not to be confused with John Johnson from the rational decision-making camp, though they'd probably get along well in their shared distrust of hasty choices. At 52, Jon has three decades of experience in dispute resolution, much of it earned in the high-pressure world of tax consulting where a single miscalculation could cost clients millions.

Jon's office tells you everything about his approach to decision making – it's a sanctuary of calm in the chaotic world of legal practice. Soft lighting, family photos, documents organized in neat stacks that suggest methodical consideration rather than urgent action. Everything about the space says, "Take your time, think it through, don't rush".

His philosophy is simple: "Hasty decisions breed expensive problems. It's better to wait until the dust settles and you can see the situation clearly." He's fond of saying that "time is the wisest counsellor" – a belief that's been reinforced by decades of watching colleagues make brilliant-seeming choices that turned into costly disasters.

When a major client allocation dispute erupted between two practice groups – the kind of internal conflict that can tear firms apart if handled poorly – Jon's response was characteristically measured. "Look," he told the management committee, "emotions are running high right now. Nobody's in the right frame of mind for rational discussion. Let's step back, let people cool down, and revisit this with clear heads next month when we can focus on solutions rather than grievances."

You'll hear Jon saying things like, "We need more time to properly assess all the implications here" or, "I don't think we have complete visibility into all the relevant factors yet". When colleagues push for immediate action, his standard response is, "Let's not rush into something we might regret" or, "This situation requires very careful handling – we don't want to make things worse by moving too quickly".

Finding the balance between prudence and paralysis

The avoidant decision-making style serves an important function in any partnership – it provides a natural brake on impulsive choices and ensures that major decisions get proper consideration. But like every approach, it needs to be calibrated to the situation and the stakes involved.

Smart partnerships learn to leverage their avoidant decision-makers' risk-sensing abilities while preventing them from grinding important processes to a halt. It's about distinguishing between decisions that genuinely benefit from extended consideration and those that just need someone to make a choice and move forward.

The real value of avoidant decision makers isn't that they're right to delay everything – it's that they force everyone else to slow down long enough to consider whether they're about to make a mistake. In a profession where the pressure to act quickly can lead to expensive errors, having someone who asks, "Are we sure about this?" isn't just useful – it's essential. The trick is knowing when their caution is wisdom and when it's just fear dressed up as prudence.

The Light Speed Brigade: "Let's do this right now"

Finally, we come to the partners who make everyone else look like they're moving in slow motion – the ones who can assess a situation, make a decision, and start implementing it while their colleagues are still figuring out what questions to ask. These are the people who treat every opportunity like it has an expiration date of about five minutes, who'd rather make a quick choice and adjust course later than spend time perfecting a plan that might be irrelevant by the time it's finished.

If you've ever been in a meeting where someone says, "Let's just do it and see what happens", you've encountered a spontaneous decision maker in their element. They're not being reckless or impulsive – they genuinely believe that speed trumps perfection, that opportunities vanish while you're still analyzing them, and that it's better to be roughly right and moving forward than precisely correct and standing still.

These are the partners who thrive in crisis situations, who volunteer for the impossible projects, and who somehow always seem to be three steps ahead of whatever's happening in their practice area. They're energizing to work with and exhausting in equal measure, because they operate at a pace that leaves most people feeling slightly dizzy.

Why "ready, fire, aim" sometimes works

Here's what drives methodical people crazy about spontaneous decision makers – they're often spectacularly successful precisely because they don't overthink things. While everyone else is still debating whether an opportunity is worth pursuing, they've already pursued it, learned from the experience, and moved on to the next challenge.

I've watched spontaneous decision makers capture market advantages that more cautious firms completely missed. They're the ones who said "yes" to cryptocurrency clients when everyone else was still trying to figure out the regulatory implications, who jumped into data privacy work before GDPR became a household acronym, who started building artificial intelligence practices while their competitors were still forming committees to study the issue.

Their clients absolutely love them because they get immediate responses to urgent requests. When a crisis hits and a client needs legal counsel who can act quickly, spontaneous decision makers are the ones picking up the phone and saying "We'll handle it" before they've even fully understood what "it" involves. This responsiveness builds incredibly strong client relationships because people feel like their lawyers are genuinely engaged with their business realities.

These partners also bring an infectious energy to their teams. They're idea generators, always spotting new possibilities and getting excited about unconventional projects. Their enthusiasm can inspire colleagues to take on challenges they might otherwise avoid, creating a culture of innovation and experimentation that keeps firms ahead of the curve.

When speed kills quality

But here's where spontaneous decision makers drive their colleagues to despair – sometimes their rapid-fire approach creates more problems than it solves. They have a tendency to overcommit, saying "yes" to projects without fully considering whether the firm actually has the resources or expertise to deliver what they've promised.

I've seen spontaneous decision makers enthusiastically commit their firms to complex matters that required months of careful preparation, only to realize halfway through that they'd fundamentally misunderstood what was involved. Their colleagues end up scrambling to meet impossible deadlines or deliver results that were never actually feasible in the first place.

There's also the whiplash factor – spontaneous decision makers change direction so frequently that their teams can't keep up. One week they're all-in on a new practice area, the next week they've spotted a different opportunity and want to pivot completely. This constant shifting can frustrate colleagues who need stability and predictability to do their best work.

And let's be honest – some decisions really do benefit from careful analysis. When you're making strategic choices that will affect the firm for years to come, or when you're dealing with high-stakes matters where mistakes could be catastrophic, "Let's figure it out as we go" isn't always the optimal approach.

Portrait of a perpetual motion machine

Meet Jessica Dixon – she's the kind of person who probably makes decisions about what to have for lunch while she's eating breakfast. At 34, she's a partner in the firm's technology practice, having made the jump from an in-house counsel role at a fast-moving tech company where hesitation was essentially a career-limiting condition.

Visit Jessica's office and you'll immediately understand her approach to work and decision making. Her desk looks like a creativity explosion – multiple monitors displaying different projects, sticky notes with random insights covering every surface, files stacked in what appears to be organized chaos but somehow makes sense to her. She's rarely actually sitting at that desk anyway – she's usually on her phone while walking to another meeting, typing emails while having conversations, or sketching out new ideas on whatever surface is handy.

Jessica's fundamental philosophy is simple: "Opportunities don't wait for you to get organized. While other people are still forming committees to study the situation, the market has already moved on." She's convinced that analysis paralysis is a bigger risk than making the occasional wrong choice, and that it's better to try things and adjust based on real-world feedback than to perfect theoretical plans that might be irrelevant by the time you implement them.

When a major client called with an urgent request involving emerging technology that the firm had never handled before – the kind of situation that would send most lawyers running for their risk management policies – Jessica's response was immediate: "Yes, we can absolutely help with that. It's uncharted territory and there are definitely risks involved, but that's exactly why you need us. I'll pull together a team this afternoon, and we'll figure out the details as we go. The key thing is saying yes now, before you start shopping around to our competitors."

You'll hear Jessica constantly urging action with phrases like, "We need to move on this immediately" or, "We can work out the specifics as we go along". When colleagues start raising concerns about risks or logistics, her typical response is, "While we're sitting here debating, our competitors are already out there doing". Her favorite reminder to hesitant colleagues is that, "Risk is just the price of staying relevant in a fast-moving market".

Harnessing lightning in a bottle

The spontaneous decision-making style brings tremendous value to any partnership – it provides energy, responsiveness, and the kind of agility that can make the difference between leading markets and following them. But like every approach, it needs to be deployed strategically rather than universally.

Smart firms learn to channel their spontaneous decision-makers' energy while building in safeguards to prevent them from overcommitting the organization. It's about creating space for quick responses and experimental approaches while maintaining enough structure to ensure that rapid decisions don't create long-term problems.

The partnership puzzle – making sense of the mix

So there you have it – the five-person zoo that constitutes most law firm partnerships. John with his spreadsheets, Alex with her hunches, Simon with his committees, Jon with his delays, and Jessica with her lightning-fast decisions. Each one absolutely convinced that their approach is obviously the right one, each one occasionally frustrated by everyone else's inability to see what's clearly the best way forward.

Reading through these descriptions, you've probably recognized yourself somewhere in the mix. Maybe you're nodding along with one particular style, or maybe you're thinking, "I do a bit of all of these depending on the situation". That's completely normal – most people have a dominant style but can flex into others when circumstances require it.

Here's the thing that took me years to figure out – there is no "correct" decision-making style. Each approach brings real strengths to the table, and each one has blind spots that can create problems if left unchecked. The magic happens when you understand not just your own natural tendencies, but how to work effectively with people who operate completely differently.

The most successful partnerships aren't the ones where everyone thinks alike – they're the ones that have learned to harness the strengths of different approaches while compensating for their individual limitations. They know when to deploy John's analytical rigor, when to trust Alex's pattern recognition, when to use Simon's consensus-building skills, when to embrace Jon's cautious deliberation, and when to unleash Jessica's rapid response capabilities.

The secret isn't changing who you are – it's understanding who everyone else is, and learning when your natural approach is exactly what the situation needs and when you need to step back and let someone else take the lead. Sometimes the best decision is recognizing that someone else should be making the decision. Table 4.1 overleaf explains the five decision-making styles at a glance.

Table 4.1: Five decision-making styles at a glance

Style	Core drive	How they decide	Signature phrase	Strength	Blind spot
Rational	Need for data and logic	Demand evidence, analysis, spread-sheets	"Give me the data"	Rigorous, evidence-based	Analysis paralysis
Intuitive	Trust in pattern recognition	Read the room, trust gut, see connec-tions	"I just know"	Fast, holistic vision	Cannot always explain why
Dependent	Need for consensus	Seek input, build agreement, avoid isolation	"What does everyone think?"	Strong buy-in	Slow, risk of group-think
Avoidant	Fear of conse-quences	Postpone, gather more info, wait for clarity	"Let's think about it more"	Cautious, thorough	Missed opportuni-ties
Spontan-eous	Bias for action	Act quickly, trust instinct, adapt on the fly	"Let's just do it"	Speed, momen-tum	Hasty mistakes

What drives decisions beyond styles

So we've figured out that there are five basic ways lawyers make decisions, and you've probably spotted yourself somewhere in that lineup. But here's the thing that nobody talks about in those glossy management consulting presentations – knowing someone's decision-making style tells you absolutely nothing about what they'll actually do when the pressure's on and their reputation is at stake.

Because what really happens in partnership meetings isn't some pristine exercise in rational analysis or collaborative consensus-building. It's a bunch of highly educated primates trying to navigate the same social dynamics that have been driving human behavior since we were huddled around fires debating whether to hunt in the dangerous valley or stick to the safe meadows.

Ancient wiring, modern problems

Picture our ancestors 50,000 years ago, sitting around that fire trying to decide where to hunt tomorrow. On the surface, it's a logical discussion about animal tracks and weather patterns. But underneath, there's a young hunter who's spotted better hunting grounds but won't speak up because he's afraid the elders will think he's getting above himself. There's a seasoned warrior backing the chief's risky plan not because it makes sense, but because challenging leadership could mean exile – and exile meant death.

Fast-forward to today's boardrooms, and the same psychological machinery is running the show. That partner who stays silent despite having crucial insights? They're making the exact same calculation as that prehistoric hunter: "Is speaking up worth the risk to my standing in the group?" The senior associate who doesn't ask the obvious question? They're worried about the modern equivalent of tribal rejection – being seen as incompetent or not belonging.

The stakes have changed, but the wiring hasn't. We're still social creatures whose survival depends on maintaining our place in the group, and that ancient programming doesn't care whether we're debating mammoth migration patterns or merger strategies.

The real forces running the show

When I watch partnership meetings, I'm constantly struck by how much of the "decision-making process" is really just elaborate theater. The PowerPoints and financial models and strategic frameworks are all window dressing for what's actually happening – a bunch of people trying to figure out how to make choices that won't damage their relationships or threaten their position in the pecking order.

There are two psychological forces that drive most of what actually happens in these meetings, and they have almost nothing to do with legal analysis or business strategy. The first is what researchers call external validation dependency – our desperate need to have our choices approved and our status confirmed by the people around us. The second is the acceptance drive – our deep-seated terror of being rejected or excluded from the group.

These aren't character flaws or signs of professional weakness. They're hardwired survival mechanisms that kept our ancestors alive when being cast out from the tribe was literally a death sentence. The problem is that these same mechanisms can be disastrous in modern professional settings where independent thinking and rigorous analysis actually matter more than social harmony.

When smart people do dumb things

Let me give you a perfect example. I watched a partnership vote on a major technology upgrade – the kind of decision that would shape how the firm operated for years. The presentation was polished, the business case looked solid, and the managing partner was clearly enthusiastic. But I could see several partners shifting uncomfortably, obviously having concerns they weren't voicing.

The corporate practice head had serious doubts about the budget and timeline, based on similar projects he'd managed before. But he also knew that challenging the managing partner's pet project would be seen as undermining leadership. So he stayed quiet.

A senior associate who'd worked with similar systems at her previous firm knew they had integration problems that nobody was discussing. But she was still establishing herself at the new firm, and raising technical objections might make her look like a know-it-all or troublemaker. So she kept her mouth shut.

The IT practice head understood the technical challenges better than anyone and was privately skeptical about whether the system would deliver the promised benefits. But she valued her relationship with the managing partner, who'd been a mentor throughout her career. Publicly questioning his judgment felt like betrayal. So she nodded along.

Result? Unanimous approval for a technology upgrade that, six months later, was over budget, behind schedule, and causing exactly the problems that people in the room could have predicted. But in the moment, everyone felt good because nobody had to risk their standing by being the person who raised uncomfortable questions.

The validation trap

Here's what's really insidious about external validation dependency – it disguises itself as good judgment and professional responsibility. When that corporate partner decided not to challenge the technology proposal, he probably told himself he was being supportive of leadership and avoiding unnecessary conflict. When the senior associate stayed quiet, she likely rationalized it as being respectful of her new colleagues' expertise. When the IT head went along with the plan, she probably framed it as loyalty to a mentor.

But what was really happening is that all three prioritized maintaining their social standing over contributing their professional judgment. They let their need for approval override their responsibility to make the best decision for the firm. And because everyone else was making the same calculation, the group developed a collective blind spot that led to expensive mistakes.

This isn't unusual – it's the norm. The pressure to maintain relationships and avoid conflict consistently trumps the commitment to rigorous analysis and honest discussion. Partners who would fearlessly challenge opposing counsel in litigation become remarkably deferential when the stakes involve their own professional relationships.

The rankings game – when reputation becomes currency

The legal profession has turned this psychological vulnerability into an entire industry. We've got Legal 500, Chambers and Partners, Best Lawyers, IFLR1000 – a whole ecosystem of rankings and awards that feed directly into lawyers' need for external validation. Partners spend hours obsessing over why a competitor made the top tier while they landed in the second band. They memorize every phrase, every client comment, every media mention, knowing that prospective clients will choose between them and rivals based on exactly this information.

Firms invest tens of thousands of dollars chasing awards like "Lawyer of the Year" or "Deal of the Year", with entire marketing departments working year-round on submissions and promotions. This isn't just vanity – it's a manifestation of deep-seated psychological needs amplified by market pressure. The drive for recognition compels lawyers to play by rules they often view as arbitrary, but can't afford to ignore.

I know partners who routinely Google themselves, set up alerts for their names, and react viscerally to any criticism in professional outlets. They'll spend entire evenings analyzing comments about their firm, looking for hidden criticism or signs that their reputation is slipping. Major decisions get filtered through the lens of external perception – "How will this affect my chances of making the rankings?"

The demographics of decision making

What makes this even more complicated is that these psychological forces don't affect everyone equally. Your age, gender, position in the firm hierarchy, and practice area all influence how strongly you feel the pull of validation dependency and acceptance needs.

Take gender differences. Despite persistent stereotypes about women being "more emotional", research shows[13] that female lawyers are just as rational as their male counterparts – 59 percent of both men and women prefer rational decision-making styles. But women are 14 percent more likely to rely on intuitive approaches, which isn't about being less logical – it's about being better at integrating analytical thinking with emotional intelligence and pattern recognition.

Women are also more likely to seek consensus and consider colleagues' opinions, which often gets dismissed as weakness but frequently proves to be a safer approach in high-stakes environments. And women show avoidant decision-making styles more frequently, which may reflect the reality that their mistakes are judged more harshly than their male colleagues.

The hierarchy effect

Your position in the firm dramatically shapes how these forces affect you. Partners are 20 percent[14] less susceptible to external validation dependency than non-partners, which makes sense – they're the ones doing the evaluating rather than being evaluated. Their reputation is established, their competence proven.

Non-partners, however, live under constant scrutiny. Their work gets regularly reviewed, their career progression depends on subjective judgments from senior colleagues, and they have much less control over their professional destiny. They're 11 percent more likely to rely on others' opinions when making decisions and more likely to defer complex choices, hoping issues resolve themselves.

Age matters too. Young lawyers under 30 experience 13 percent[15] greater validation dependency than those over 46. They're still forming their professional identity, eager for recognition, desperate to prove they belong. With age comes perspective – other people's opinions still matter, but they don't define your worth in the same way.

The stress amplifier

Here's where things get really interesting. Stress doesn't change your fundamental decision-making style, but it amplifies all its worst tendencies. The rational partner doesn't become irrational under pressure – they become obsessed with how their analysis will be perceived rather than focusing on its quality. The consensus-seeking partner doesn't abandon collaboration – their need for approval becomes compulsive. The cautious partner doesn't suddenly become decisive – they become even more paralyzed by fear of making the wrong choice.

This is crucial for understanding colleague behavior. When you see someone making seemingly out-of-character decisions under pressure, you're not seeing their true nature – you're seeing their normal tendencies cranked up to 11 by stress and anxiety.

The paradox of power

Here's something counterintuitive – partners experience 25 percent[16] less stress than non-partners, despite having more responsibility and making higher-stakes decisions. The reason is control – partners feel they shape their professional destiny, while non-partners are at the mercy of others' choices.

Litigators experience significantly higher stress than transactional lawyers, not because litigation is more complex, but because it's more public. Every courtroom appearance is scrutinized by judges, opponents, and clients. A single weak argument can damage a reputation that took years to build. Transactional work is more collaborative, errors can often be corrected, and outcomes depend more on the quality of legal work than on external variables.

The acceptance imperative

The second major force – the need for acceptance – operates slightly differently but with equally powerful effects. While validation dependency is about getting approval for our choices, acceptance drive is about avoiding rejection altogether. It's the voice saying, "Don't rock the boat" or, "Maybe I should just go along with the group".

In large firms with 40+ lawyers, this need becomes 16 percent stronger.[17] In smaller firms, relationships feel more like family and belonging emerges naturally. In big firms, you might go months without interacting with colleagues from other practice areas. Everything becomes more formal, more distant, and you have to work actively to maintain visibility and relationships.

This creates what researchers call "groupthink" – cohesive groups prioritizing consensus over critical evaluation. People suppress doubts, avoid challenging questions, and conform to perceived group preferences, all to maintain harmony and their place in the organization. The tragedy is that this often happens precisely when diverse perspectives and rigorous debate would be most valuable.

Breaking the cycle

Understanding these forces isn't about blame or criticism – it's about recognizing that even brilliant, well-intentioned people are subject to psychological pressures that can lead them away from optimal decision making. The question isn't whether these forces exist – they do, in every human group. The question is whether we're going to acknowledge them and find ways to work with them constructively, or keep pretending our decisions are purely rational while these hidden drivers pull the strings behind the scenes.

The first step is simply awareness. When you find yourself staying quiet in a meeting despite having important insights, ask yourself, "Am I holding back because I genuinely think my input isn't valuable, or because I'm worried about how people will react?" When you see colleagues making choices that seem obviously wrong, consider whether they might be responding to social pressures rather than professional judgment.

The goal isn't to eliminate these psychological forces – that's impossible. It's to recognize when they're operating and create systems that allow for better decision making despite their influence. Because once you understand that the ancient wiring is still running the show, you can start designing modern processes that account for our very human need to belong while still getting to the best answers for the business.

References

1 Richard, L. (1993). Personality types of lawyers: Implications for counseling. *The American Bar Association Journal*, 79(6), 92–94.

2 Richard, L. (2002). Herding Cats: The Lawyer Personality Revealed. *Report to Legal Management by Altman Weil*, August 2002, Volume 29, Number 11.

3 McKinsey & Company (30 April 2019). *Decision making in the age of urgency*. McKinsey & Company. Retrieved from www.mckinsey.com/capabilities/people-and-organizational-performance/our-insights/decision-making-in-the-age-of-urgency

4 Thomson Reuters (2022). *2022 State of US Small Law Firms*. Thomson Reuters. Retrieved from www.thomsonreuters.com/en-us/posts/wp-content/uploads/sites/20/2022/11/State-of-Small-Law-Firms-2022.pdf

5 Kahneman, D., Tversky, A. (1979). Prospect Theory: An Analysis of Decision under Risk. *Econometrica*, 47(2), 263–291. doi:10.2307/1914185

6 Janis, Irving L. (1972). Victims of Groupthink. New York: Houghton Mifflin.

7 Simon, H. A. (1982). Models of bounded rationality: Empirically grounded economic reason (Vol. 1). MIT Press.

8 Epstein, S. (1994). Integration of the cognitive and the psychodynamic unconscious. *American Psychologist*, 49(8), 709–724.

9 These findings are based on the author's own survey of 237 lawyers from law firms across the CEE region, conducted in 2023-2024. The study explored decision-making styles, stress levels, and factors influencing decision-making within firms of various sizes. The battery of four standardized questionnaires (GDMSI, PSS, FNE, and NTB) was used for this research.

10 Richard, L. (1993). Personality types of lawyers: Implications for counseling. *The American Bar Association Journal*, 79(6), 92–94.

11 The Myers-Briggs Type Indicator (MBTI) is a personality system developed by Isabel Briggs Myers and Katharine Briggs, based on Carl Jung's theories. It identifies 16 personality types, including "Thinkers" who tend to make decisions through logical analysis rather than emotions.

12 Scott, S. G., Bruce, R. A. (1995). Decision-making style: The development and assessment of a new measure. *Educational and Psychological Measurement*, 55(5), 818–831.

13, 14, 15, 16, 17 See endnote 9.

Chapter 5:
When decision making gets complicated

The myth of the pure type

We've mapped out the five basic decision-making styles, explored the hidden psychological forces that really drive choices, and you're probably thinking you've got a handle on how your colleagues operate. Well, here's where things get interesting – and a lot more realistic.

Because here's the uncomfortable truth about human psychology – we don't actually fit into neat little boxes. That partner you've pegged as a pure "spreadsheet devotee" probably has moments when they throw caution to the wind and make gut decisions. The colleague you're convinced is all about consensus-building might suddenly become surprisingly decisive when the stakes are high enough. And that person who seems to procrastinate on everything? They might shock you by making lightning-fast choices when they're backed into a corner.

It's tempting to look around the partnership table and assign everyone a nice, clean label: "Sarah's our rational decision-maker, Tom's the intuitive one, and Lisa always seeks consensus". It makes the world feel more predictable and manageable. But real people are messier than that, and real decision making is far more complex than choosing one approach and sticking with it forever.

Think about your own decision making for a minute. Are you exactly the same when you're choosing a litigation strategy as when you're deciding on office space? Do you approach a client crisis in the same way you handle partnership disputes? Probably not. Most of us have a dominant style that feels most natural and comfortable, but we're constantly adapting based on the situation, the stakes, and what's worked for us in similar circumstances before.

A banking partner who normally demands three different financial models before making any decision might rely purely on instinct during a client crisis when there's no time for analysis. A wealth management lawyer known for trusting her gut might suddenly want extensive team input before making a high-stakes strategic decision. These aren't inconsistencies or character flaws – they're signs of psychological sophistication and adaptability.

The DMA Matrix – where styles collide and combine

When I started digging deeper into how people actually make decisions in real-world situations, I discovered something fascinating[1] – instead of five distinct types, what emerged was more like a spectrum of 16 different Decision-Making Archetypes (DMAs) – see Figure 5.1. Each represents a unique combination of a dominant style and a complementary style that emerges when circumstances demand it.

Figure 5.1: DMA (Decision-Making Archetypes) Matrix

	Dominant decision-making style				
Complementary decision-making style	**Rational**	**Intuitive**	**Dependent**	**Avoidant**	**Spontaneous**
Rational	Pure Rationalist	The Creative Architect	The Methodical Diplomat		
Intuitive	The Logical Seer	Pure Intuitive	The Empathic Ally	The Cautious Procrastinator	The Instinctive Impulsive
Dependent	The Insightful Advisor	The Sensitive Confidant	Pure Dependent	The Compliant Seeker	The Responsive Supporter
Avoidant		The Thoughtful Delayer	The Hesitant Conformist	Pure Avoider	The Unpredictable Escapist
Spontaneous		The Visionary Improviser	The Expressive Adherent	The Erratic Drifter	Pure Spontaneous

Think of it as a 5×5 matrix, with each of the five core styles forming both the rows and columns. Where they intersect, you get hybrid DMAs that capture the nuanced ways lawyers actually navigate complex choices. Some combinations are natural and common – like pairing rational analysis with intuitive insights, or seeking consensus while maintaining analytical rigor. Others emerge only under specific pressures or in particular contexts.

But here's what's really interesting – some combinations are psychologically impossible. Try finding someone who's genuinely both spontaneous and avoidant – someone who simultaneously wants to make immediate decisions and also delay everything indefinitely. Or look for a person who's both purely rational and completely impulsive. These opposing forces can't coexist comfortably in the same psychological space, which leaves some cells in our DMA matrix empty.

The analytical hybrids – when logic meets intuition

Let's start with some of the most common and successful DMA combinations. Take what is called the Logical Seer – someone who blends rational analysis with intuitive insight. These are the partners who start with meticulous data gathering and systematic evaluation, but then draw on their experience and pattern recognition to choose the optimal path. They're not abandoning logic for gut feelings – they're using both tools in sequence to make better decisions than either approach could achieve alone.

I know a corporate partner who perfectly embodies this DMA. She'll spend hours analyzing deal structures and financial projections, building detailed models and researching precedents. But when it comes to choosing between multiple viable options, she trusts her instinct about which approach will actually work in the real world. "The numbers can tell you what's possible," she says, "but experience tells you what's probable."

Then there's the Creative Architect – the reverse DMA combination that leads with intuition but verifies with logic. These are the lawyers who sense the right direction almost immediately, then work backward to build the rational case for their choice. They might walk into a negotiation with a strong feeling about the opposing party's real objectives, then carefully gather evidence to test and refine their initial hunch.

The collaborative analysts – mixing data with democracy

Other successful DMAs combine analytical thinking with collaborative approaches. The Insightful Advisor does thorough fact-finding and rigorous analysis, but seeks team confirmation before finalizing major decisions. They're not looking for the group to override their analysis – they want collective support to validate their data-driven conclusions.

I've watched these types excel in complex litigation management, where they'll research case law exhaustively and build comprehensive strategies, but then test their thinking with the trial team before committing resources. They understand that even the best individual analysis can miss something, and that team buy-in is crucial for successful execution.

The Methodical Diplomat works the opposite way – they start by gathering extensive input from colleagues, but then filter all that feedback through careful logical evaluation. They're not just averaging everyone's opinions – they're using collaborative input as raw material for systematic decision making.

The intuitive collaborators – when gut feelings meet group dynamics

Some of the most interesting DMAs emerge when intuitive decision making combines with collaborative tendencies. The Sensitive Confidant relies on pattern recognition and emotional intelligence to read situations, but seeks peer validation before acting on their insights. They might sense that a client relationship is deteriorating or that a deal is heading toward problems, but they want team confirmation before taking action.

These lawyers often excel at client management and internal politics because they can read unspoken dynamics, but they're humble enough to test their perceptions with trusted colleagues before making major moves based on hunches alone.

The Empathic Ally works in reverse – they start by building consensus and gathering team support, then use their intuitive abilities to finalize decisions based on the collective input. They're particularly effective in situations requiring both group alignment and nuanced judgment about timing, approach, or implementation.

The cautious combinations – when hesitation meets other styles

Some DMAs emerge when natural caution gets combined with other decision making approaches, often creating internal tension that can be both a strength and a weakness. The Thoughtful Delayer has strong intuitive abilities and can often sense the right path, but hesitates to act because they're constantly aware of complexity and risk.

I know a litigation partner who fits this DMA pattern perfectly. He can read judges and juries better than almost anyone, often predicting case outcomes with uncanny accuracy. But he agonizes over strategic decisions because his pattern recognition also makes him acutely aware of everything that could go wrong. His instincts are usually correct, but his caution prevents him from acting on them decisively.

The Compliant Seeker seeks group support and consensus but also wants to avoid taking responsibility for difficult choices. They'll participate extensively in collaborative decision-making processes, but when it comes time for someone to actually make the call, they find ways to defer or deflect. This can be frustrating for colleagues who are looking for leadership, but it can also prevent groups from rushing into poorly considered decisions.

The dynamic impulsive – when speed meets other styles

On the opposite end of the spectrum, some DMAs combine spontaneous decision making with other approaches, creating dynamic but sometimes unpredictable patterns. The Visionary Improviser fuses intuitive perception with impulsiveness, acting swiftly on pattern recognition and adapting confidently as circumstances change. These are often the partners who spot emerging opportunities before anyone else and move quickly to capitalize on them.

The Expressive Adherent is particularly interesting – they have a strong need for team approval and collaborative input, but when pressed for time, they'll make spontaneous decisions and then seek retroactive validation from colleagues. They might commit the firm to a new client relationship or strategic direction on the spot, then spend considerable energy afterward building consensus around their choice.

The conflicted archetypes – when opposing forces collide

Perhaps the most psychologically complex DMAs emerge when opposing tendencies somehow coexist in the same person. The Unpredictable Escapist combines avoidant and spontaneous styles in ways that can be bewildering to colleagues. They'll delay decisions for as long as possible, but when finally forced to act, they make impulsive choices without the careful deliberation you'd expect from someone who's been thinking about the issue for weeks.

I've seen this pattern in partners facing major career decisions – they'll agonize for months about whether to leave the firm or change practice areas, gathering information and seeking advice but never committing to any direction. Then suddenly, they'll announce they're leaving next month to join a start-up, having made the final decision based on a single conversation or opportunity that emerged unexpectedly.

The Erratic Drifter presents perhaps the most paradoxical pattern in partnership dynamics. These partners are dominated by avoidance – they dodge decisions, postpone discussions, and find endless reasons why "now isn't the right time". For weeks or months, they seem to drift without direction while the partnership waits for clarity.

Then, without warning, they suddenly make a dramatic spontaneous decision – and because they've been observing quietly for so long, their unexpected move often carries surprising wisdom. The partnership, having adapted to their prolonged silence, is caught off-guard when the Erratic Drifter abruptly announces a direction that cuts through weeks of circular debate.

Here's what makes this archetype both valuable and challenging – their extended period of avoidance isn't always procrastination. Sometimes they're processing, observing, waiting for the right moment. When they finally act, they often sweep the entire partnership along because their decision feels overdue and decisive. "They've been thinking about this for months – they must have figured something out" becomes the prevailing logic, and the accumulated momentum can galvanize the firm into action.

At their best, Erratic Drifters can break partnership deadlocks precisely because they operate outside normal deliberative processes. Their sudden interventions can redirect firms away from paths that everyone knew weren't working but no one had the courage to abandon. At their worst, their unpredictability undermines strategic planning – the partnership can't count on their engagement during deliberation, yet must somehow accommodate their sporadic but decisive interventions that might contradict months of careful consensus-building.

Why this DMA complexity matters

Understanding these more nuanced DMAs isn't just an academic exercise – it has real practical implications for how partnerships function and how individual lawyers can be most effective. When you recognize that your colleague isn't simply "the consensus seeker" but rather "the methodical diplomat who uses group input to inform systematic analysis", you can work with them more effectively.

It also helps explain why the same person might seem like a completely different decision maker in different contexts. The partner who drives you crazy with endless analysis in routine matters might be exactly the right person to make rapid strategic decisions during a crisis. The colleague who seems indecisive in group settings might be decisive and effective when working independently with clients.

Finding your own DMA

Most lawyers have a sense of their dominant decision-making style, but understanding your complete Decision-Making Archetype – including your secondary and situational approaches – requires more reflection. You might discover that your backup style emerges only under specific pressures, or that you've developed hybrid approaches that serve you well in particular contexts but create confusion in others.

The key insight is that there's no "best" DMA, just as there was no best individual style. Each combination brings unique strengths and faces particular challenges. The most effective lawyers and partnerships are those that understand these nuanced patterns and know how to deploy different approaches when circumstances require them.

What matters isn't fitting perfectly into any category, but understanding your own decision-making patterns well enough to use them strategically – and recognizing the patterns in others well enough to work with them effectively rather than against them. Once you accept that decision making is complex and contextual, you can stop trying to force yourself and others into simple boxes and start leveraging the full spectrum of the 16 DMAs available to tackle whatever challenges your practice throws at you.

The Logical Seer – the holy grail of partnership leadership

Now we get to dive into the really fascinating stuff – actual portraits of these DMAs in action. We're starting with what might be the most coveted DMA in law firm management – the Logical Seer. This is the partner that search committees dream about when they're looking for managing partners, the combination that clients love, and the approach that other lawyers secretly wish they could master.

The Logical Seer represents that elusive sweet spot where rigorous analysis meets seasoned intuition. These aren't the partners who get stuck in analysis paralysis, and they're not the ones making reckless gut decisions either. They've figured out how to use both tools – systematic thinking and pattern recognition – in a seamless dance that often produces remarkably effective results.

How the magic actually works

What makes the Logical Seer archetype so powerful is the sequence – they start with the data, do the analysis, build the models, and research the precedents. But then – and this is the crucial part – they step back and ask themselves what their experience and instincts are telling them about what all that information really means.

They're not abandoning logic for hunches, and they're not letting emotions override evidence. They're using analytical rigor to establish the facts and boundaries of a decision, then drawing on years of pattern recognition to choose the optimal path forward. It's like having both a microscope and a telescope – detailed examination of the specifics combined with a broader view of how everything fits together.

The remote work revolution – when it all clicks

Let me give you a perfect example of this archetype in action. Picture a managing partner at a mid-sized firm facing one of the most contentious post-pandemic issues – office versus remote work. The younger lawyers are demanding flexibility, the senior partners want everyone back in the office, and the firm's compromise solution is making nobody happy.

Most managing partners would handle this either by imposing a top-down decision based on their personal preferences, or by endlessly polling the partnership until they find some version of consensus. But the Logical Seer takes a completely different approach.

First comes the analytical phase – three months of granular data collection. They measure productivity across 15 different metrics, comparing remote work performance to office performance. They study retention patterns and discover that competitors are already poaching key talent with full-remote offers. They survey clients and find that 70 percent are comfortable with virtual meetings while 30 percent insist on face-to-face interaction.

What emerges is fascinating and counterintuitive – technical efficiency has actually increased by 18 percent with remote work, but creativity and complex decision-making speed has dropped 12 percent. The data paints a nuanced picture that simple "pro-remote" or "anti-remote" positions can't capture.

But here's where their intuitive insight becomes crucial. Looking at all these numbers, the managing partner realizes something that isn't showing up in the metrics: "It's not about hours or productivity scores. We're losing the magic of collective brainstorming. The best ideas don't spark in Zoom calls – they happen at the coffee machine, in hallway conversations, in those unplanned moments when people's minds collide."

The solution they develop is brilliant in its sophistication – instead of calendar mandates or blanket policies, they create "energy-based planning". They identify eight different types of legal work – including routine tasks that are perfect for home, creative work that benefits from in-person collaboration, strategic planning that requires the full team, and crisis management that demands everyone in the office immediately.

Result? Retention hits 98 percent, productivity surges by 23 percent, client satisfaction climbs by 31 percent, and five competing firms start to copy their model. That's what happens when you combine rigorous analysis with seasoned judgment about how people and organizations actually work.

When the formula fails – the AI disaster

But the Logical Seer archetype isn't foolproof, and its failures are often as instructive as its successes. The same managing partner who nails the remote work decision makes a costly mistake with artificial intelligence adoption.

After attending a legal tech conference, the partnership is excited about AI platforms promising to revolutionize document review. The rational analysis looks compelling – they pilot-test three platforms on 200 contracts, see impressive results, calculate an ROI with payback in 14 months and 180 hours saved monthly.

But the managing partner's intuition is sending warning signals: "This feels too good to be true. Something's off about these promises. Clients pay us for speed, but will they really accept sacrificing the quality that comes from human judgment? And what happens to our junior associates' development if they're not doing document review anymore?"

Here's where even experienced Logical Seers can stumble – they ignore their internal unease, succumb to FOMO, and sign a €45,000 annual contract despite their gut telling them something is wrong.

Six months later, the AI excels on standard documents but completely fails on 60 percent of the firm's non-standard deals – exactly the high-value, complex work that distinguishes them from competitors. Clients start to complain about "robotization" and the loss of personalized service. The firm ends up reverting to manual review, having wasted both money and time.

The lesson? Even flawless data can be misleading if it doesn't account for the subtle complexities of how your specific business actually operates.

The evolution of wisdom

What's particularly fascinating about the Logical Seer archetype is how it evolves over a career. Early-career Logical Seers (under 35) tend to be heavy on the analysis side but light on intuitive development. They'll spend weeks building elaborate financial models for partner hiring decisions but struggle to read the cultural and political dynamics that might make those decisions succeed or fail.

Mid-career Logical Seers (35-50) hit their sweet spot. They've developed enough experience to have reliable pattern recognition, but they're still close enough to current market realities to keep their analysis sharp. They can balance quantitative assessments with insights about team dynamics, using financial analysis alongside cultural considerations.

Late-career Logical Seers (over 50) face a different challenge. Their market intuition and people-reading skills are often incredibly refined – they can forecast industry trends with minimal data and anticipate interpersonal issues before they become problems. But they risk over-relying on experience and dismissing new evidence that doesn't fit their established patterns.

Crisis response – the pressure test

How a Logical Seer responds to stress reveals both the strengths and vulnerabilities of this archetype. Under moderate pressure – like losing a major client – they often thrive, combining precise analysis with creative insight to generate solutions that others miss.

But high stress can be their undoing. When facing firm financial difficulties, they can become paralyzed by excessive data collection, endlessly analyzing scenarios because the fear of making a wrong decision overshadows their normally reliable intuitive judgment.

During the COVID crisis, the Logical Seer spends two months analyzing firm survival scenarios, building detailed models comparing salary cuts versus layoffs. The data points toward cuts, but intuition whispers "people over money". While they agonize over the decision, their top talent starts to flee to competitors who act more decisively. By the time they finally choose to protect jobs over profits, it is too late to prevent the exodus.

Under extreme stress, Logical Seers can flip to one extreme or the other – either fixating obsessively on numerical data while ignoring intuitive warnings, or making desperate intuitive leaps that bypass their normally careful analytical process entirely.

The dream team and the nightmare scenarios

The Logical Seer's effectiveness often depends on who they're working with. Their dream collaborators are DMAs like the Empathic Ally, who can sense team sentiment and help communicate data-driven decisions in ways that people will actually accept and support. The Methodical Diplomat is another natural partner, using their consensus-building skills to secure buy-in for the Logical Seer's analytically-grounded strategies.

Productive partnerships can develop with the Insightful Advisor, who complements internal analysis with external perspectives, and even the Instinctive Impulsive, whose rapid response capabilities can offset the Logical Seer's tendency toward extended deliberation.

But some combinations create real friction. The Hesitant Conformist's endless need for discussion and consensus can drive a Logical Seer to distraction, especially when they've already done thorough analysis and developed clear recommendations. The Cautious Procrastinator's delays can be equally frustrating when the Logical Seer has invested significant effort in reaching well-reasoned conclusions.

The truly toxic pairing is with the Erratic Drifter, whose unpredictable decision making completely disrupts the Logical Seer's structured approach to problem-solving. When someone keeps changing direction without apparent logic, it undermines the entire foundation of careful analysis and seasoned judgment that the Logical Seer relies on.

Why this matters

The Logical Seer represents what many lawyers aspire to become – the synthesis of rigorous thinking and experienced wisdom that produces consistently effective decisions. But understanding this archetype isn't just about emulation – it's about recognizing when this approach is optimal and when other DMAs might be more appropriate.

Not every decision benefits from the Logical Seer's comprehensive analysis-plus-intuition method. Sometimes you need the Instinctive Impulsive's rapid response, or the Methodical Diplomat's consensus-building skills, or even the Cautious Procrastinator's risk-averse deliberation.

The real insight is that even this seemingly ideal archetype has specific strengths, particular vulnerabilities, and optimal contexts for deployment. Understanding your own DMA – and those of your colleagues – isn't about finding the "best" approach, but about knowing when to leverage which cognitive toolkit for maximum effectiveness.

The Instinctive Impulsive – lightning in a bottle

If the Logical Seer represents the thoughtful synthesis of analysis and wisdom, the Instinctive Impulsive is their polar opposite – and sometimes their perfect complement. This is the partner who makes decisions at the speed of thought, who acts on hunches before others have even identified the problem, and who either creates brilliant breakthroughs or spectacular disasters with roughly equal frequency.

The Instinctive Impulsive DMA combines spontaneous decision making with intuitive insight, creating a cognitive profile that thrives on rapid pattern recognition and immediate action. These are the lawyers who spot opportunities while everyone else is still forming committees to study whether opportunities might exist. They're energizing to work with and occasionally terrifying, because you never quite know whether their next lightning-fast decision will save the firm or require extensive damage control.

The speed of instinct

What makes the Instinctive Impulsive fascinating is how they process information. While other DMAs gather data, seek input, or deliberate on options, the Instinctive Impulsive is already three steps ahead, making connections that others miss and acting on insights that haven't yet crystallized into conscious thought.

This isn't recklessness or lack of consideration – it's a different kind of intelligence altogether. Their brains are constantly processing environmental cues, relationship dynamics, market signals, and opportunity patterns at a subconscious level. When they make what appears to be a "sudden" decision, they're often acting on a sophisticated analysis that happened too quickly for others to follow.

The challenge, of course, is that this rapid-fire cognitive processing doesn't always translate into optimal outcomes. Sometimes the pattern recognition is brilliant, sometimes it's based on incomplete information, and sometimes the speed of decision making doesn't allow for the kind of risk assessment that would prevent expensive mistakes.

The COVID pivot – when fast beats perfect

Let me show you an Instinctive Impulsive in their element. Same scenario as before – a law firm dealing with post-pandemic work arrangements – but handled by a completely different DMA approach.

Where the Logical Seer spent three months analyzing productivity metrics and client preferences, the Instinctive Impulsive managing partner makes a series of rapid decisions based on reading the room and sensing market dynamics. Within two weeks of the initial conflict between younger and senior lawyers, they have already implemented a solution.

Their process looks nothing like systematic analysis. Instead, they spend a few days having informal conversations with key people, observing energy levels during video calls versus in-person meetings, noticing which competitors are gaining traction with talent recruitment, and sensing the underlying anxiety that is driving both sides of the office-versus-remote debate.

"The data will tell us what happened," they tell their partnership, "but our gut tells us what's happening now and what's about to happen next. People aren't arguing about productivity – they're arguing about identity and control. We need to give everyone agency over their own work environment while maintaining the collaboration that makes us special."

Their solution is equally rapid – a "results-based autonomy" system where lawyers commit to specific outcomes for each quarter but have complete freedom to determine how and where they achieve these results. No mandated office days, no productivity tracking, no complex categorization of work types – just clear expectations and total flexibility in execution.

Implementation occurs in one week. Results? Within a month, voluntary office attendance actually increases because people feel they are choosing collaboration rather than having it imposed. Client relationships strengthen because lawyers are working when and where they feel most effective. Recruitment becomes dramatically easier because the firm can offer something that feels both professional and genuinely flexible.

The speed of this solution allows them to capture advantages that slower-moving competitors miss entirely. By the time other firms finish their analysis and form implementation committees, the Instinctive Impulsive's firm has already solved the problem and moved on to the next challenge.

When speed kills – the technology disaster

The same rapid decision making that created the remote work solution can lead to spectacular failures when pattern recognition goes wrong. Take the same managing partner's approach to legal technology adoption.

After attending a legal tech conference, they become convinced that artificial intelligence will transform document review within 18 months. Instead of pilot programs or careful vendor evaluation, they make a series of rapid decisions, signing contracts with two different AI platforms, hiring a technology consultant, committing to training programs for all associates, and promising clients that the firm would be "AI-native" by the end of the year.

The decision-making process takes about 72 hours from initial interest to full commitment. Their reasoning is pure Instinctive Impulsive logic: "Every successful firm will be using AI within two years. We can either lead this transition or scramble to catch up later. The risk of moving too slowly is greater than the risk of moving too fast."

What they miss – because their rapid processing focuses on opportunity rather than implementation complexity – is that their firm's client base consists largely of highly specialized, non-standard transactions that require exactly the kind of nuanced judgment that AI can't replicate. The platforms they choose work beautifully for routine document review but fail completely on the complex, relationship-dependent work that represents 70 percent of their revenue.

Six months later, they are dealing with client complaints about "depersonalized" service, associate frustration with technology that makes their jobs harder rather than easier, and a significant financial loss from technology investments that aren't generating the promised returns. The rapid decision that had seemed so strategically sound turns into an expensive lesson about the importance of matching solutions to actual business needs.

The evolution of lightning

What's particularly interesting about the Instinctive Impulsive DMA is how it changes over time. Early-career Instinctive Impulsives (under 35) tend to be all impulse and limited pattern recognition. They make frequent rapid decisions based on enthusiasm and optimism rather than genuine insight, leading to wildly inconsistent outcomes. They're the associates who volunteer for every new initiative, propose bold strategic changes, and sometimes create brilliant innovations alongside spectacular failures.

Mid-career Instinctive Impulsives (35-50) hit their stride as their pattern recognition becomes more sophisticated. They've experienced enough different situations to develop reliable intuition about market dynamics, client needs, and organizational behavior. They still make rapid decisions, but those decisions are increasingly based on genuine insight rather than just optimism and energy. They also develop the confidence to quickly correct course when their initial choices prove suboptimal, without becoming attached to being "right" about their original decisions.

Late-career Instinctive Impulsives (over 50) can be extraordinarily effective because their decades of experience have created almost supernatural pattern recognition abilities. They can anticipate market trends, personnel problems, and strategic opportunities well before others even recognize that decisions need to be made. The risk at this stage is overconfidence – becoming so certain of their intuitive insights that they dismiss input from colleagues or fail to account for how markets and organizations have evolved since their experience base was formed.

Crisis response – the double-edged sword

How an Instinctive Impulsive responds to stress reveals both the power and the peril of this DMA. Under moderate pressure – like an economic downturn or competitive threat – they often excel by identifying unconventional solutions that more cautious colleagues would never consider. Their ability to act quickly can capture opportunities that emerge during periods of uncertainty and change.

But high stress can trigger a cascade of rapid decisions that create more problems than they solve. Facing severe financial difficulties, an Instinctive Impulsive might implement cost cuts, launch new practice areas, restructure client relationships, upgrade technology systems, and reorganize staffing – all within a matter of weeks. Each individual decision might seem reasonable, but the cumulative effect can be operational chaos that makes the original problems worse.

During a cyberattack on the firm's IT systems, the Instinctive Impulsive makes five major decisions in a single day – switching to a new technology provider, purchasing backup servers, hiring external security consultants, implementing new data protocols, and reverting to an older backup system. The result is system conflicts that prolong the outage and create additional security vulnerabilities. Sometimes the cure becomes worse than the disease when rapid-fire decision making doesn't account for how multiple changes interact with each other.

Under extreme stress, Instinctive Impulsive can either freeze completely – overwhelmed by conflicting intuitive signals that their rapid-processing brain can't reconcile – or take desperate risks that bypass even their normally sophisticated pattern recognition abilities.

Dream teams and nightmare scenarios

The Instinctive Impulsive's effectiveness depends heavily on who they're working with. Their ideal collaborators are DMAs that can provide the analytical rigor and implementation support that complement rapid decision making. The Insightful Advisor is perfect for this – they can quickly validate spontaneous ideas with expert analysis, helping distinguish genuine opportunities from enthusiasm-driven impulses.

The Empathic Ally makes another excellent partner because they can sense how the team is responding to rapid changes and help facilitate acceptance of new directions. When an Instinctive Impulsive pivots strategy or implements new approaches, the Empathic Ally can read the organizational dynamics and smooth the transition process.

Productive partnerships can develop with the Logical Seer, whose analytical capabilities can add rigor to intuitive insights, and the Methodical Diplomat, whose consensus-building skills can help secure support for innovative strategies among more conservative colleagues.

But some combinations create real friction. The Cautious Procrastinator's constant hesitation can drive an Instinctive Impulsive to distraction, especially when they're sensing time-sensitive opportunities that require immediate action. The Hesitant Conformist's need for extensive consultation before any decision can feel like organizational paralysis to someone who thrives on rapid response.

The truly toxic combination is pairing two Instinctive Impulsives together without other DMAs to provide balance. When both leaders are making rapid decisions based on different pattern recognition and intuitive insights, the result can be conflicting directives that create operational instability and confusion throughout the organization.

The power and the peril

The Instinctive Impulsive represents one of the most dynamic and potentially valuable DMAs in legal practice. Their ability to spot opportunities, adapt quickly to changing circumstances, and act decisively when others are still deliberating can provide tremendous competitive advantages. They're often the partners who drive innovation, capture emerging market opportunities, and navigate crises with remarkable agility.

But this same archetype can be a source of significant organizational stress and occasional disaster when their rapid decision making outpaces their judgment or when their pattern recognition fails to account for important variables. Understanding how to work with Instinctive Impulsives – and when to deploy their capabilities versus when to constrain their impulses – is crucial for any partnership that includes this DMA.

The key insight is that the Instinctive Impulsive's lightning-fast cognitive processing is both their greatest strength and their primary vulnerability. When their pattern recognition is accurate and their timing is right, they can achieve results that more deliberate approaches would never reach. When their rapid analysis misses crucial factors or when speed becomes more important than accuracy, the results can be expensive and disruptive.

Like every DMA, the Instinctive Impulsive isn't inherently good or bad – they have a particular cognitive toolkit that's extraordinarily effective in some contexts and potentially problematic in others. The art lies in recognizing when their approach is optimal and creating systems that harness their insights while providing the analytical rigor and implementation support that complement their natural rapid-fire decision-making style.

The Hesitant Conformist – the art of productive procrastination

Finally, we come to perhaps the most misunderstood DMA in legal partnerships – the Hesitant Conformist. This is the partner that other lawyers love to complain about – the one who turns every decision into a consultation marathon, who seems allergic to taking definitive positions, and who can find a reason to delay virtually any choice until "we have more information" or "everyone's comfortable with the direction".

But here's what's fascinating about the Hesitant Conformist – sometimes their approach produces better outcomes than more decisive DMAs, and sometimes it leads to disaster. The difference often comes down to luck, timing, and whether the situation actually benefits from extended deliberation or demands immediate action.

The Hesitant Conformist combines dependent decision making with avoidant tendencies, creating a cognitive profile that prioritizes consensus-building and risk avoidance above speed or individual judgment. These are the partners who genuinely believe that better decisions emerge from extensive consultation and that most problems will either resolve themselves or become clearer if you just wait long enough.

When hesitation hits the jackpot

Let me show you the Hesitant Conformist at their most successful – and why that success can be misleading. Picture a firm facing a classic partnership dilemma – a major client hasn't paid their bills for three months (€85,000 owed) but keeps ordering new work. The CFO is demanding they halt all services immediately, but the partners are split between cutting off the relationship and continuing to serve the client.

A more decisive DMA might make a quick call based on firm policy or financial projections. But the Hesitant Conformist managing partner launches into full consultation mode – polling all partners, consulting with account managers, seeking input from the accounting department, and even bringing in three external crisis management experts. This process takes over a month, during which the firm continues working for the non-paying client.

Throughout this consultation period, the managing partner keeps finding reasons to delay a final decision: "We need more information about their financial situation. Maybe this is just a temporary cash flow problem. What if they pay everything next month and become even more loyal because we stuck with them? I don't want to make an irreversible decision based on incomplete information."

So, they don't decide – they just wait, hoping the situation will resolve itself.

And, remarkably, it does. Two months later, the client pays the full outstanding amount plus interest and commissions three major new projects. The partnership hails their managing partner as a hero who "avoided panic and saved a strategic client relationship through patience and wisdom".

But here's the uncomfortable truth – this was pure luck. The managing partner's approach succeeded not because of superior decision making, but because they happened to guess right about an unpredictable outcome. In eight out of ten similar situations, continuing to work for non-paying clients leads to bigger losses and damaged firm credibility.

When avoidance becomes destruction

The same Hesitant Conformist who gets lucky with a client payment situation can create a much more serious problem when faced with a toxic partner issue. A senior partner is chronically missing deadlines, treating junior staff rudely, and actively sabotaging firm initiatives. Four talented lawyers leave the firm explicitly "because of him" within a single year.

Again, the Hesitant Conformist launches into extensive consultation mode – month-long one-on-one meetings with all partners, focus groups with team members, consultations with HR experts. The feedback is unanimous – this partner is creating serious problems that are damaging the firm's culture and bottom line.

But even with clear consensus about the problem, the managing partner finds reasons to avoid decisive action: "But he brings in €300,000 in revenue annually. What if he leaves and joins a competitor? What if he sues us for wrongful termination? Maybe we can fix this with coaching or training programs."

Instead of making the difficult decision to remove the toxic partner, they spend a year trying "soft touches" – conversations, training sessions, mediation attempts. All these efforts prove futile because they don't address the fundamental issue – this partner's behavior is incompatible with a healthy workplace culture.

The result is catastrophic. Over two years, eight key staff members leave the firm, including two lawyers on track for partnership. The replacement and training costs exceed €180,000, and the firm develops a reputation in the legal market as having a "toxic workplace". Meanwhile, the problem partner remains, continuing to create the same issues that triggered the exodus in the first place.

The paradox of non-decisions

What this case illustrates is a crucial insight about the Hesitant Conformist DMA – refusing to decide is itself a decision, and often the worst possible one. By avoiding the difficult choice to remove the toxic partner, the managing partner effectively chooses to sacrifice firm culture, staff retention, and market reputation in favor of short-term revenue and conflict avoidance.

This is the central paradox of the Hesitant Conformist archetype. Their extensive consultation processes often surface valuable information and build genuine consensus around important decisions. But their avoidance of difficult choices can allow problems to metastasize until they become much more expensive and damaging than the original issue.

The evolution of diplomatic delay

The Hesitant Conformist DMA evolves significantly over a career, and understanding these changes helps explain when this approach is most and least effective. Early-career Hesitant Conformists (under 35) tend to exhibit anxiety about any decision that might cause conflict or displeasure. They'll spend excessive time seeking input on even minor operational choices, essentially becoming conduits for other people's opinions without adding synthesis or leadership.

At this stage, their consultation processes often lack focus and direction. They're gathering input not because they have a clear framework for decision making, but because they're uncomfortable with the responsibility of making choices that others might disagree with.

Mid-career Hesitant Conformists (35-50) often develop more sophisticated judgment about when their approach is valuable versus when it's counterproductive. They learn to differentiate between decisions that genuinely benefit from consensus-building and those that require swift action. They can manage routine operational tasks independently while reserving strategic choices for collective input, and they often become effective mediators in partnership conflicts.

Late-career Hesitant Conformists (over 50) frequently evolve into respected advisors who are valued more for their perspective and relationship-building skills than for decisive action. The risk at this stage is that their aversion to conflict and change can prevent firms from making necessary structural adjustments, leading to organizational stagnation when adaptation is crucial for survival.

Crisis response – when delay becomes dangerous

How a Hesitant Conformist responds to pressure reveals both the potential value and the serious limitations of this DMA. Under moderate stress – like losing a significant client – they often engage in extensive analysis of what went wrong, consulting with multiple stakeholders to understand the failure. While this can provide valuable insights, it can also delay corrective action when rapid response is needed to prevent further client defections.

High stress situations can trigger analysis paralysis, where the Hesitant Conformist seeks input from numerous experts in search of risk-free options that simply don't exist. During financial crises, this tendency to over-consult can waste precious time when decisive action is needed to stabilize the firm.

Under extreme stress, Hesitant Conformists can either delegate decision-making entirely to others or make sudden, poorly-considered choices under pressure. During a mass staff exodus, the Hesitant Conformist spends three months conducting focus groups and consulting HR experts to analyze why people are leaving. While they gather data and seek input, five additional key staff members resign. Their delayed response to an obvious problem makes the crisis significantly worse.

Dream teams and disaster combinations

The Hesitant Conformist can be remarkably effective when paired with complementary DMAs that offset their natural hesitation. Their ideal partner is the Instinctive Impulsive, who can handle rapid decisions and crisis response while the Hesitant Conformist focuses on building consensus around longer-term strategic directions.

The Creative Architect makes another excellent collaborator because they can generate innovative ideas that the Hesitant Conformist can then refine through extensive collaborative processes. This combination often produces well-developed, broadly-supported initiatives that might never emerge from either archetype working alone.

Productive partnerships can develop with the Empathic Ally, who shares the Hesitant Conformist's focus on stakeholder satisfaction but can occasionally drive action when consensus-building becomes counterproductive. The Logical Seer can also complement the Hesitant Conformist by providing analytical rigor that helps move consultation processes toward actual decisions.

But some combinations create organizational paralysis. Pairing a Hesitant Conformist with a Cautious Procrastinator can result in endless delays where every decision gets postponed indefinitely. The Insightful Advisor's reliance on external input can combine with the Hesitant Conformist's consultation tendencies to create cycles of information-gathering that never reach conclusions.

The most toxic combination is two Hesitant Conformists working together, which can result in extensive deliberation without any execution. Decision-making processes become ends in themselves rather than means to organizational progress.

The hidden value of productive hesitation

Despite their obvious limitations, Hesitant Conformists serve important functions in legal partnerships. They prevent rush decisions that might ignore important stakeholder concerns or overlook significant risks. Their extensive consultation processes often surface insights and build buy-in that more decisive approaches might miss.

In situations where relationship management and consensus-building are more important than speed, the Hesitant Conformist can be exactly the right DMA for the challenge. They excel at navigating complex political dynamics, mediating conflicts between strong personalities, and ensuring that major strategic decisions have broad organizational support.

The lessons of three archetypes

Looking at the Logical Seer, Instinctive Impulsive, and Hesitant Conformist together reveals the fundamental insight about DMAs – there's no universally "best" approach to making choices. Each DMA brings distinct strengths and faces particular challenges, and their effectiveness depends entirely on the context, timing, and complementary capabilities available.

The Logical Seer's integration of analysis and intuition can drive highly effective decisions, but risks paralysis under extreme pressure. The Instinctive Impulsive's rapid action can capture opportunities that others miss, but requires validation and support to avoid costly errors. The Hesitant Conformist's collaborative approach can build consensus and prevent rash decisions, but may create losses when decisive action is essential.

What matters isn't finding the perfect DMA, but understanding how different cognitive approaches can work together to tackle the full spectrum of challenges that legal partnerships face. The most successful firms aren't those with uniform decision-making styles, but those that have learned to deploy different DMAs strategically based on the situation and stakes involved.

A partnership might include a Logical Seer working alongside a Hesitant Conformist, a Creative Architect collaborating with a Cautious Procrastinator, or an Instinctive Impulsive balanced by a Methodical Diplomat. Each combination creates different organizational dynamics and capabilities, and understanding these patterns is crucial for effective leadership and collaboration.

The key insight is that challenges arise not from cognitive diversity itself, but from failing to understand how different DMAs operate or from trying to force incompatible approaches to work together without proper support systems. When firms dismiss the Hesitant Conformist as "indecisive" or the Instinctive Impulsive as "reckless", they're missing opportunities to leverage the unique value that each archetype brings to the partnership's collective decision-making capability.

See Appendix 5 for more information on the 16 archetypes.

References

1 These findings are based on the author's own survey of 237 lawyers from law firms across the CEE region, conducted in 2023-2024. The study explored decision-making styles, stress levels, and factors influencing decision-making within firms of various sizes. The battery of four standardized questionnaires (GDMSI, PSS, FNE, and NTB) was used for this research.

Chapter 6:
When Synergy + Conflict = Firm identity

Team synergy – when 1+1=5

What happens when bearers of different decision-making archetypes (see chapter 5) converge in a single boardroom? That's where the real drama of partnership dynamics unfolds.

In a law firm, one partner spots opportunities where others see obstacles. Another can pinpoint the flaws in any brilliant idea within half an hour. Alone, the first is a dreamer, the second a nitpicker. Together, they're a force capable of reshaping the market.

This is the alchemy of teamwork, where different decision-making archetypes don't just coexist but create something entirely new. The strengths of one transform the weaknesses of another into advantages.

When differences become a superpower

The Visionary Improviser sees strategy five years ahead but can get bogged down in implementation details. The Instinctive Impulsive senses what needs to be done now but may miss how it fits into the bigger picture. Pair them, and the architect gains a catalyst for their plans, while the improviser finds direction for their energy.

The Logical Seer can map out every risk in a complex deal but might overlook the simple human reasons behind a client's hesitation. The Empathic Ally intuitively reads the client's mood but may miss legal pitfalls. Together, they craft solutions that are both secure and client-friendly.

The Methodical Diplomat excels at securing agreement from all stakeholders, but the process can drag on. The Insightful Advisor quickly identifies key players and their motives. As a duo, they achieve consensus swiftly and effectively.

The magic of partnership lies in everyone doing what they do best, producing results that surpass what any could achieve alone.

Multiplier archetypes

Some archetypes have a remarkable ability to amplify others without overshadowing their individuality. These aren't traditional leaders – they don't command, but they create conditions where other archetypes can shine.

The Insightful Advisor is a master of asking the right questions. They don't impose their views but help others articulate their own. When the Visionary Improviser gets carried away with an ambitious plan, the advisor asks, "What do our key clients think about this?" When the Cautious Procrastinator hesitates over a new direction, they probe, "What happens if we do nothing?" These questions don't halt progress – they channel energy constructively.

The Empathic Ally fosters psychological safety, allowing other archetypes to be themselves. The Instinctive Impulsive can pitch a bold idea without fear of judgment. The Hesitant Conformist can voice doubts without being labelled a complainer. The Logical Seer can dive into details, knowing someone is minding the team's morale.

The Methodical Diplomat turns the chaos of differing opinions into a structured process. They don't force uniformity but establish ground rules that let diverse thinkers collaborate productively.

The resonance effect

In top-performing teams, something remarkable happens – they make decisions faster and more accurately than any individual could alone. It's akin to resonance in physics, where small, well-directed efforts create outsized impact.

The Instinctive Impulsive sparks an idea. The Logical Seer instantly identifies the data needed to validate it. The Insightful Advisor pinpoints who to consult. The Visionary Improviser envisions how it aligns with the firm's strategy. In half an hour, the team moves from a vague hunch to a clear action plan.

Each member contributes their piece, synchronized with the others. No one duplicates efforts or slows the process. This is true teamwork – not everyone doing the same thing, but each doing what they do best.

Perfect duos

Some archetype combinations work so seamlessly that they form enduring partnerships. These pairs don't compete – they complement each other so naturally that role allocation often happens instinctively.

- *Creative Architect + Insightful Advisor:* The architect paints the big picture through intuitive vision; the advisor validates it through rigorous analysis. The architect spots strategic opportunities – the advisor identifies implementation obstacles and builds team buy-in.

The architect crafts the vision – the advisor turns it into a plan that can be executed and supported across the partnership.

- *Methodical Diplomat + Logical Seer:* The diplomat builds consensus through structured processes – the seer ensures decisions are grounded in solid analysis. The diplomat understands what the partnership will support – the seer calculates what will actually work. The diplomat creates alignment – the seer provides the analytical foundation that makes alignment possible.
- *Logical Seer + Visionary Improviser:* The seer analyzes data and spots patterns – the improviser translates those insights into immediate action. The seer identifies what's strategically sound – the improviser senses the right moment to move. The seer guards against analytical blindness – the improviser prevents analysis paralysis.
- *Empathic Ally + Insightful Advisor:* The ally reads the room and senses resistance – the advisor provides rational frameworks to address concerns. The ally understands why people hesitate – the advisor identifies what data or consultation would build confidence. The ally builds emotional buy-in – the advisor creates intellectual justification.

Why three is better than two

Duos excel at tackling specific tasks, but for complex, firm-wide decisions, a trio of archetypes often proves optimal. The third member acts as a catalyst, preventing the pair from getting trapped in their own logic.

- *Innovation Trio: Creative Architect + Sensitive Confidant + Instinctive Impulsive.* The architect generates the concept; the impulsive finds ways to test it immediately; the confidant intuitively senses how the team will respond. The architect paints the vision; the impulsive creates momentum; the confidant prevents resistance from derailing progress. The result – bold innovations that move fast without breaking team cohesion.
- *Execution Trio: Logical Seer + Methodical Diplomat + Empathic Ally.* The seer plans with analytical rigor; the diplomat organizes the process and builds consensus; the ally ensures the team doesn't buckle under pressure. The seer guards against oversights; the diplomat keeps everyone aligned; the ally reads morale and prevents burnout. The result – complex projects delivered on time without breaking the team.
- *Adaptation Trio: Visionary Improviser + Insightful Advisor + Empathic Ally.* The improviser spots shifts in the market and senses when change

is needed; the advisor analyzes what the changes mean and validates the direction; the ally helps the team embrace new approaches. The improviser provides speed; the advisor provides validation; the ally provides acceptance. The result – a firm that adapts swiftly to new conditions without losing its people.

See Appendix 6 for more.

Universal connectors

In team alchemy, some archetypes pair well with nearly anyone. They don't dominate or suppress – they amplify the best qualities of others.

- The Logical Seer ensures decision quality in any team composition. They don't impose their logic but ensure critical factors aren't overlooked. They slow down risky decisions and accelerate those that are clearly sound.
- The Empathic Ally is indispensable in any team at risk of human conflict. They help archetypes understand each other, not just logically but emotionally. Without them, even the smartest decisions can fail due to resistance.
- The Insightful Advisor is perhaps the most versatile partner. Analytical enough to connect with rational types, yet not so rigid as to intimidate the cautious. Attentive to people, but not lost in emotions. They can speed up the overly slow or temper the overly hasty.

Why it works

Team alchemy works because different archetypes see distinct facets of the same situation. When these perspectives combine, they create a multidimensional view unattainable by any single archetype.

The Visionary Improviser sees opportunities. The Logical Seer sees risks. The Insightful Advisor sees people's reactions. The Methodical Diplomat sees processes. The Empathic Ally sees emotions. The Instinctive Impulsive sees moments for action.

No decision can be fully effective if it considers only one of these aspects. But when they come together, the result is a solution that works in the real world – complex, unpredictable, and filled with both opportunities and risks.

Team alchemy isn't just a sum of talents. It's a fundamentally new quality that emerges only when diverse ways of thinking complement, rather than compete with, one another.

When styles collide – the anatomy of partnership conflicts

Recall the last heated debate at a partner meeting. Was it about opening a new office? Setting bonus levels? Crafting a new growth strategy?

Now, shift your focus from *what* was discussed to *how*. Did someone demand more data? Did another push for a quick decision? Did someone want to poll the entire team? Did another suggest tabling the issue "until better times"?

What if the real conflict wasn't about the decision's substance but its preparation? What if partners agreed on the core issue but clashed fiercely over the approach? Until they recognize this distinction, they'll be battling shadows of their own assumptions about how decisions "should" be made.

The language of decision preparation

Each decision-making style speaks its own language, not just during the choice itself but in the preparation phase. What one partner sees as thoroughness, another sees as stalling. What one views as swift action, another considers superficial.

Rational: "Give me the data"

For the rational partner, decisions start with information – not ideas or gut feelings, but hard facts.

How they prepare decisions:

- Gathers extensive data from all available sources.
- Builds models and scenarios for potential outcomes.
- Analyzes risks and calculates consequences.
- Prepares detailed justifications for every step.

What frustrates others:

- "Enough with your spreadsheets – when are we deciding?" (*Spontaneous*)
- "We get it already; why dig deeper?" (*Dependent*)
- "While you're crunching numbers, competitors are acting." (*Intuitive*)

Intuitive: "I feel this is right"

The intuitive partner decides quickly, drawing on a lifetime of professional experience that "fires" at the right moment.

How they prepare decisions:

- Relies on precedents and past analogies.
- Spots patterns in seemingly unrelated events.
- Tests decisions against an internal "gut check".
- Formulates a vision and overarching logic.

What frustrates others:

- "What's your confidence based on?" (*Rational*)
- "What if you're wrong? Who's accountable?" (*Avoidant*)
- "We need to consult everyone first." (*Dependent*)

Dependent: "What does the team think?"
For the dependent partner, a good decision isn't just correct – it's embraced. Much of their preparation focuses on gauging opinions and building consensus.

How they prepare decisions:

- Conducts preliminary consultations with key stakeholders.
- Assesses who's for, against, or undecided.
- Seeks options that satisfy the majority.
- Lays the groundwork for consensus before formal discussions.

What frustrates others:

- "How long must we coordinate? Let's decide!" (*Spontaneous*)
- "Truth isn't decided by a vote." (*Intuitive*)
- "We're spending more time discussing than working." (*Rational*)

Avoidant: "What if...?"
The avoidant partner prepares by exploring every possible alternative, aiming to ensure not just a good choice but the best one possible.

How they prepare decisions:

- Generates a wide range of alternatives.
- Studies other firms' and industries' experiences.
- Evaluates long-term consequences of each option.
- Allows time for decisions to "mature."

What frustrates others:

- "We could debate this forever." (*Spontaneous*)
- "Analysis paralysis – let's act!" (*Intuitive*)
- "We have enough data to decide." (*Rational*)

Spontaneous: "Time is money"
The spontaneous partner prepares in real time. Their strength lies in grasping the core issue quickly and acting before opportunities slip away.

How they prepare decisions:

- Focuses on key factors, ignoring minor details.
- Makes decisions during discussions.
- Relies on common sense and team experience.
- Adjusts course as implementation unfolds.

What frustrates others:

- "We need more time to analyze." (*Rational*)
- "What about the team's input?" (*Dependent*)
- "This is a serious decision; we can't rush." (*Avoidant*)

A dispute about form masquerading as substance
Imagine a partner meeting discussing whether to open a new office. Everyone agrees it's necessary, but...

- *Rational:* "Before deciding, we need to analyze the market. I have a 50-page report – let's go through it point by point."
- *Spontaneous:* "We've been discussing this for three months! Competitors are already there while we're still analyzing."
- *Dependent:* "Not all partners are on board. Let's hold another meeting to hear everyone out."
- *Avoidant:* "Have we considered a franchise instead of our own office?"
- *Intuitive:* "All your analysis doesn't change the fact that this is strategically the right move."

Each is speaking truth. Each is defending a valid value. But they're not arguing about *whether* to open the office – they're clashing over *how* to approach the decision.

Protocol conflicts

The most painful conflicts arise when styles don't just differ but clash at the level of fundamental protocols:

- Speed vs quality:
  - *Spontaneous:* "While we're crafting the perfect solution, we're missing opportunities."
  - *Rational:* "Hasty decisions cost more in the long run."
- Expertise vs consensus:
  - *Intuitive:* "The decision should come from whoever understands the issue best."
  - *Dependent:* "The decision needs buy-in from everyone who'll execute it."
- Detail vs principles:
  - *Rational:* "The devil's in the details – we need to calculate everything."
  - *Avoidant:* "Let's define the direction first; we'll refine the details later."
- Action vs reflection:
  - *Spontaneous:* "Let's start and adjust as we go."
  - *Avoidant:* "Measure seven times, cut once."

The hidden cost of stylistic conflicts

When partners fail to distinguish between substantive and stylistic conflicts, a dangerous conflation occurs:

- The *Rational* perceives "decide faster" as a call for unprofessionalism.
- The *Spontaneous* sees "more analysis" as sabotage or procrastination.
- The *Dependent* interprets "expert-driven decisions" as dismissing team input.
- The *Intuitive* views "consensus" as diluting responsibility.
- The *Avoidant* takes "let's start" as recklessness.

As a result, they attack not the wrong position but the wrong person. A professional disagreement turns personal.

Escalation of misunderstanding – from miscommunication to personal conflict

Stylistic conflicts are dangerous because they escalate quickly. What begins as a professional disagreement morphs into personal animosity.

- Stage 1: Miscommunication
  - *Rational:* "We need more data."
  - *Spontaneous* hears: "You're slowing us down."
  - *Spontaneous:* "We need to decide faster."
  - *Rational* hears: "You're suggesting sloppy work."
- Stage 2: Irritation
  - "Not his spreadsheets again!" vs "She's rushing without thinking!" Each starts interpreting the other's behavior through a negative lens.
- Stage 3: Attributing motives
  - *Rational* thinks: "He just doesn't want to work seriously."
  - *Spontaneous* thinks: "She's deliberately overcomplicating to seem important."
- Stage 4: Personal conflict
  - "I can't work with them." Decisions are no longer based on substance but on personal dynamics.

Maturity – separating process from substance
Mature partnerships learn to distinguish two levels of conflict:

- *What* we're debating – substantive disagreements about the issue itself.
- *How* we're debating – procedural disagreements about how to prepare and make decisions.

The first type is inevitable and productive – it drives better solutions. The second often parasitizes the first, creating the illusion of fundamental disagreement where none exists.

The ability to say, "We agree on the substance but see the process differently" marks the start of true partnership. Here, styles don't fight – they complement. Form serves substance, not supplants it.

Recognizing stylistic conflicts in real time
The challenge isn't just understanding that stylistic conflicts exist – it's catching them before they poison partnerships. Here's how to recognize when you're fighting about process rather than substance.

You're likely in a stylistic conflict when the debate keeps circling without progress. Partners keep making the same points in different words, because they're not actually disagreeing about the decision – they're disagreeing about how to reach it. The frustration feels personal. If you find yourself thinking, "Why is she being so difficult?" rather than, "Why does she think this won't work?", you've shifted from substance to style.

The word "should" appears frequently. "We should analyze this properly." "We should decide quickly." "We should consult everyone." These aren't statements about what's right for this specific decision – they're statements about what decision making "should" look like in general.

Different partners are solving different problems. The rational partner is solving "How do we ensure this decision is analytically sound?" The spontaneous partner is solving "How do we capture this opportunity before it disappears?" They're both right – and both missing each other's point entirely. People start questioning motives rather than logic. "You just want to delay this." "You're trying to railroad everyone." "You don't trust the team." Once you're attributing intent, you've left substance behind.

In the middle of a heated partnership discussion, ask yourself, "If we agreed on my preferred process, would everyone agree on the decision?" If the answer is yes, you're fighting about style, not substance. "Can I articulate what decision my colleague actually wants, separate from how they want to reach it?" If you can't, you're probably not listening to their position – you're reacting to their process. "Am I more frustrated by what they're proposing or how they're proposing it?" If it's the latter, style is dominating the conversation.

Once you recognize a stylistic conflict, you can interrupt it. Name it explicitly: "I think we actually agree on opening the office. We're debating whether to analyze first or move quickly. That's a different question." Separate the discussions: "Let's first confirm – do we all believe this office is strategically necessary? Good. Now, separately – what process will give us confidence to proceed?" Acknowledge the valid concern behind each style: "You're right that we need solid analysis. And you're right that timing matters. How do we honor both?" Test for substance: "If I agreed to your timeline, would you support the decision? If I agreed to do the analysis, would you support opening the office?" This reveals whether process or outcome is the real sticking point.

Stylistic maturity in partnerships

Mature partnerships evolve through stages in handling stylistic differences:

- *Stage 1: Denial* – "Everyone should decide rationally."
- *Stage 2: Irritation* – "Why does s/he always complicate everything?"
- *Stage 3: Acceptance* – "Her/his approach is different, but it works."

- *Stage 4: Utilization* – "Her/his style is perfect for this task."
- *Stage 5: Synergy* – "Together, we see what neither sees alone."

The difference between junior and senior partnerships isn't that senior partners agree more – it's that they fight about the right things. They've learned to recognize when they're debating substance versus style, and they treat these as separate conversations requiring different resolutions.

A mature partnership can have a vigorous debate about whether to expand internationally (substance), then calmly discuss whether to make that decision through detailed financial modeling or rapid market testing (style). They understand these are different questions requiring different approaches.

An immature partnership conflates them, turning every strategic debate into a meta-argument about whose decision-making philosophy is superior. The substance gets lost in the style war.

Ultimately, the path to a decision matters less than the outcome. What matters is that the result satisfies everyone, that partners maintain respect along the way, and that they learn to leverage differences as a competitive advantage.

See Appendix 7 for more information.

How decision-making styles shape a firm's identity

Step into the office of any law firm, and within half an hour, you'll sense how decisions are made. Not because someone explains the procedures – you'll feel it.

In one firm, you're greeted with a 20-slide presentation and a detailed work plan. In another, they dive straight into business, discussing first steps within an hour. In a third, they introduce you to the entire team and solicit your opinion on every detail.

These differences aren't random or tied to individual lawyers' quirks. They reflect the corporate culture, shaped by the dominant decision-making styles of the firm's partners. How leaders approach decisions defines how the entire organization operates.

Five types of corporate culture

A law firm's corporate culture isn't the mission statement on the wall or the values printed in a brochure. It's the unwritten rules about how decisions are made, what's prioritized, and how risks and changes are handled.

When a particular decision-making style dominates a partnership, it permeates the entire organization. Employees adopt similar thinking patterns, clients expect a certain approach, and the firm's reputation aligns with that style.

1. Rational culture: everything through analysis and data

In firms dominated by rational decision-making styles, a culture of facts and evidence prevails. Decisions based on "gut feelings" are rare – every choice must be backed by analysis.

How it looks in practice:

- Proposals come with calculations and comparison charts.
- Partner meetings resemble academic conferences – data-heavy, low on emotion.
- Processes are highly formalized and documented.
- Employees learn to justify every decision with numbers.

What clients see: Thoroughness, professionalism, predictability. These firms attract clients who value meticulous analysis and detailed work, such as banks, large corporations, and government entities.

Advantages:

- High-quality analysis with minimal errors.
- Predictable results and timelines.
- Transparent processes and decisions.
- Strong client trust in professionalism.

Pitfalls:

- Slowness in fast-changing situations.
- Missed opportunities requiring quick decisions.
- Over-bureaucratization of processes.
- Difficulty attracting creative talent.

2. Intuitive culture: betting on experience and instinct

Firms with a dominant intuitive culture rely on accumulated experience and professional instinct. Analysis matters less than grasping the essence of an issue and spotting unconventional solutions.

How it looks in practice:

- Decisions often draw on past experiences and analogies.
- Partners trust their professional gut.
- Fewer formal procedures, more flexibility.
- Emphasis on the expertise and reputation of key individuals.

What clients see: Expertise, deep business understanding, and the ability to find creative solutions. These firms attract clients facing complex, non-standard issues that demand innovative approaches.

Advantages:

- Quick grasp of a problem's core.
- Creative solutions to complex issues.
- High adaptability to change.
- Strong expert reputation.

Pitfalls:

- Subjective assessments and decisions.
- Challenges in transferring knowledge and experience.
- Dependence on key experts.
- Unpredictability for clients.

3. Collegial culture: decisions through discussion and consensus

In firms with a collegial culture, major decisions are made collectively, with maximum consideration of all stakeholders' opinions. Teamwork is valued, and decisions aim for broad support.

How it looks in practice:

- Frequent meetings and discussions.
- A drive for consensus in decision making.
- Open communication across all levels.
- Attention to every employee's input.

What clients see: Team cohesion, attention to detail, and a willingness to listen and incorporate their perspective. These firms attract clients who want to be involved in the process and feel like partners, not just service recipients.

Advantages:

- High employee engagement.
- Decisions with broad support.
- Low internal conflict.
- Consideration of human factors in decisions.

Pitfalls:

- Slow decision making.
- Diffused responsibility.
- Challenges in crisis situations.
- Risk of compromising quality for consensus.

4. Cautious culture: thoroughness and risk minimization

Firms with a cautious culture take a measured approach to any change. They think multiple times before acting, meticulously analyzing risks and consequences.

How it looks in practice:

- Extensive preparation for any decision.
- Multiple rounds of checks and approvals.
- Conservative approach to innovation.
- Focus on stability and reliability.

What clients see: Dependability, thoroughness, and risk minimization. These firms attract clients for whom errors are critical, such as financial institutions and corporations in regulated industries.

Advantages:

- Minimal errors and miscalculations.
- High reliability and stability.
- Trust from conservative clients.
- Resilience in crises.

Pitfalls:

- Missed opportunities due to excessive caution.
- Slow adaptation to market changes.
- Difficulty attracting ambitious talent.
- Risk of losing competitiveness.

5. Dynamic culture: speed and readiness for experimentation

Firms with a dynamic culture prioritize quick decisions and openness to change. They're unafraid to experiment, believing it's better to act fast and adjust than to miss opportunities.

How it looks in practice:

- Rapid decision making.
- Willingness to experiment and adapt.
- Minimal bureaucracy and formalities.
- Focus on results over process.

What clients see: Speed, flexibility, and readiness for unconventional solutions. These firms attract dynamic clients like startups, tech companies, and businesses in fast-evolving sectors.

Advantages:

- Quick response to market changes.
- High employee motivation.
- Ability to capture new niches.
- Appeal to ambitious talent.

Pitfalls:

- Risk of hasty decisions and errors.
- Instability and unpredictability.
- High workload for employees.
- Challenges with long-term planning.

What the outside world sees

Corporate culture isn't just an internal matter. It shapes the firm's external image for potential employees, defines its competitive advantages, and acts as a natural filter during hiring – candidates intuitively sense whether a firm's atmosphere suits them.

- *Rational culture:* Attracts people who thrive on structure, analysis, and predictability. They want clear evaluation criteria and transparent rules.
- *Intuitive culture:* Draws those who value expertise and creativity. They're motivated by solving complex problems and honing professional mastery.

- *Collegial culture:* Appeals to team players who prioritize collaboration and mutual support.
- *Cautious culture:* Attracts those who value stability and dislike risks. They prefer evolutionary progress over revolutionary change.
- *Dynamic culture:* Pulls in ambitious individuals who seek rapid growth and embrace challenges. They thrive in an atmosphere of constant change and opportunity.

Blind spots of each culture type

When one decision-making style dominates a firm, it creates advantages – predictability, consistency, and a clear identity – but also significant risks.

1. *Rational culture:* Its main blind spot is underestimating the human factor and intuitive decisions. These firms may miss opportunities that can't be calculated in advance and struggle to motivate creative employees.
2. *Intuitive culture:* Its blind spot is a lack of systematic analysis. Relying on experience and instinct, these firms may overlook critical details or fail to notice situational changes.
3. *Collegial culture:* Its primary issue is slowness and diffused responsibility. In fast-changing situations, the drive for consensus can become a fatal flaw.
4. *Cautious culture:* Its blind spot is missed opportunities for growth and development. Excessive caution can lead to stagnation and loss of competitiveness.
5. *Dynamic culture:* Its main danger is hasty decisions and underestimated risks. Constant rushing can lead to accumulating problems and employee burnout.

The echo chamber effect

When all partners think alike, an echo chamber forms – the firm stops noticing signals that don't align with its dominant thinking style.

- A *rational firm* may ignore intuitive hunches signaling problems not yet reflected in data.
- An *intuitive firm* may miss critical details requiring systematic analysis.
- A *collegial firm* may overlook the need for swift decisions.
- A *cautious firm* may miss growth opportunities.
- A *dynamic firm* may fail to see accumulating risks.

Developmental constraints

Mono-style cultures create limitations for a firm's growth. They perform well in stable conditions but struggle when circumstances change.

- *Rational culture:* Effective in predictable industries but may falter in innovative fields.
- *Intuitive culture:* Excels at complex tasks but may struggle with routine processes.
- *Collegial culture:* Builds cohesive teams but can be inefficient in competitive settings.
- *Cautious culture:* Ensures stability but may hinder growth.
- *Dynamic culture:* Enables rapid development but can create challenges with employee retention.

Building a balanced culture

The most successful firms don't rely on a single decision-making style but deliberately cultivate a balanced culture adaptable to various situations.

Productive style combinations:

1. *Rational + Intuitive:* A powerful mix for strategic decisions. Rational analysis ensures quality; intuitive insights add creativity and speed.
2. *Collegial + Dynamic:* A strong pairing for growing firms. Collegiality fosters team cohesion; dynamism ensures readiness for change.
3. *Cautious + Rational:* A reliable combination for working with major clients. Caution minimizes risks; rationality ensures analytical rigor.
4. *Intuitive + Dynamic:* Ideal for innovative projects. Intuition spots opportunities; dynamism enables rapid execution.

The arrival of a partner with a new decision-making style can fundamentally transform a firm's culture. This is both an opportunity and a risk.

The opportunity lies in the new style compensating for the existing culture's weaknesses, adding missing competencies, and opening new growth avenues. The risk is that the new style may clash with the established culture, create team tension, or disrupt established processes.

Managing cultural change

Deliberately reshaping corporate culture is a complex process that requires understanding how decision-making styles influence behavior. Key features of successful cultural change include:

1. *Gradual change.* Abrupt cultural shifts rarely succeed. Introducing new styles gradually allows the organization to adapt.

2. *Explanation*. Employees need to understand why changes are necessary and how new approaches will benefit the firm. Without this, change is perceived as a threat.
3. *Support*. Individuals with dominant styles need support to adapt to new approaches. Training, mentoring, and gradually expanding responsibilities ease the transition.
4. *Patience*. Cultural change is slow. Leaders must be prepared for delayed results and stay committed despite early challenges.

Corporate culture is a living organism, shaped by people and shaping them in return. Understanding how decision-making styles form culture enables deliberate management of this process, creating an environment that maximizes each style's strengths and mitigates its weaknesses.

See Appendix 8 for more information.

Part III: Deconstructing the Concept of "Consensus": How to Achieve Genuine Buy-In, Avoiding Firm Paralysis

Chapter 7:
The mechanics of partner buy-in

The cultural code of "consensus"

"Consensus" is the magic word in partnership circles. It sounds democratic, fair, and reassuring – the promise that every voice matters. It's also a convenient shield against individual blame and a subtle way to spread risk around the room. When partners invoke "the need for consensus" they're appealing to high-minded governance principles while secretly hoping that if things go south, the whole group takes the hit, not just one person.

The problem is that lawyers typically confuse consensus with "unanimity". Everyone nodding, everyone smiling, zero resistance. That's the expensive mistake that paralyzes partnerships.

True consensus isn't about harmony – it's about structure. It's a framework where decisions work for the group even when nobody's thrilled about them. Political scientists make the distinction clear – unanimity requires 100 percent approval; consensus needs only no deal-breaking objections and a commitment to move forward. This isn't just academic hair-splitting. In partnerships where every rainmaker wields veto power – and has the client relationships to back it up – ignoring proper consensus tools creates predictable problems – the loudest voice wins, decisions drag on forever, or quiet resistance kills implementation.

Culture as crystallized consensus

Firm culture isn't some mystical force – it's crystallized consensus. Every "that's how we do things here" can be traced back to a decision. Every "we don't do that around here" stems from some agreement, spoken or unspoken.

Consider two mid-sized firms with identical practices. At Firm A, partner meetings are gladiatorial combat – brutal honesty, clashing ideas, raised voices. The unwritten rule? Conflict produces better outcomes. Better to kill a bad idea in the conference room than watch it implode at the client's office. Firm B operates on polished professionalism – criticism comes wrapped in diplomatic language, disputes get resolved in sidebar conversations, and consensus emerges through careful one-on-one discussions. The implicit understanding? Harmony matters more than brutal honesty. Open conflict threatens the firm's reputation more than any benefit from vigorous debate.

Both approaches work. Both involve trade-offs. The key point – neither culture happened by accident. They're the product of repeated partner decisions about what feels safe, efficient, or profitable.

Two-tier consensus system

Partnership consensus runs on two parallel tracks – and how they interact shapes the firm's cultural DNA.

Explicit consensus is what gets documented and discussed openly. You'll find it in partnership agreements, strategic plans, and meeting minutes. This is the official story – exceptional client service, collaborative decision making, developing junior talent. Implicit consensus is the shadow system everyone understands but rarely discusses openly. Who actually brings in the major clients. Whose opinion really drives the big decisions. Which subjects never make it onto the formal agenda. This unspoken understanding often determines how the firm actually operates.

Cultural patterns crystallize where the two tracks meet. Unspoken deals become daily routines; formal agreements transform into rituals and mission statements. Partners may fully understand the gap between public rhetoric and private reality, and that very gap can become another unwritten rule: just how honest we're willing to be.

The evolution of consensus

Consensus isn't a monument built when the partnership was founded. It's a living system, tested daily and quietly adjusted to fit new realities.

Picture this: a partner starts taking work from a client long "owned" by a colleague. No formal rule is broken – the client reached out directly. But the implicit understanding that "we don't poach each other's clients" just fractured. The firm reaches a cultural crossroads.

Three options emerge:

1. Make it official – turn the breach into explicit policy.
2. Let it slide quietly – allow the unspoken rules to shift without acknowledgment.
3. Leave it unresolved – neither enforce the old norm nor endorse the new one. That gray area becomes fertile ground for future conflicts.

This constant recalibration explains how cultures drift. Not because someone schedules a "culture change" retreat, but because the underlying consensus about partner behavior has shifted.

Decision-making architecture

The consensus that's taken hold inevitably shapes how decisions get made. It answers the core questions: Who gets input? How much discussion is "enough"? What ultimately drives the final call?

In egalitarian firms, consensus means every partner weighs in on major decisions. The process takes longer, but buy-in runs deep. In firms with clear hierarchies, the circle shrinks to senior voices – faster outcomes, but sidelined partners may harbor resentment.

Timing reflects consensus philosophy too. Some firms live by "good enough today beats perfect tomorrow" – speed is everything. Others follow "measure twice, cut once" – they fear hasty moves more than missed opportunities.

What counts as proof varies just as widely. One partnership demands spreadsheets and ROI models. Another relies on intuition and experience. A third looks to the market: "What are our competitors doing? What do the consultants recommend?"

Bifurcation points

The real drama happens when established consensus collides with new reality. These fork-in-the-road moments determine whether the firm adapts or stagnates.

A classic example is scaling from five partners to 15. The founding agreement was simple: "One team, one table". With a handful of voices, it delivered transparency, ownership, and swift alignment.

Add ten more seats and the model breaks down. Meetings become endless – everyone demands airtime. Compromises satisfy no one. Accountability evaporates – when everyone owns it, no one does. The close-knit culture that once fueled growth now strangles it.

The firm faces a stark choice – rewrite the decision-making consensus or accept creeping paralysis. And rewriting isn't a procedural adjustment – it's a gut-level rethink of how partners work together, one that challenges identities and core values.

This is consensus at its most paradoxical – it provides stability yet can block essential change. Firms that master the careful evolution of their consensus gain a real advantage. Those that don't risk locking into dysfunctional patterns – or outright collapse.

See Appendix 9 for more details.

The partner hierarchy

Behind the noble banner of "partner equality" lies a sophisticated pecking order – unwritten, unspoken, yet crystal-clear to every insider.

Lawyers – obsessed with precise language – build governance on half-truths and nuance. The louder a firm proclaims equality, the more elaborate the shadow hierarchy becomes. Open rank would shatter the partnership myth, so power wraps itself in dignity-preserving rituals. The result – a multi-level power structure where everyone knows their place but naming it aloud breaks the rules.

Climbing the ladder – three rungs of influence

The hierarchy isn't a caste system, it's a career escalator. Each step unlocks privileges or imposes constraints, with its own unwritten rules.

1. *Salaried partners* are partners-in-waiting – crowned with the title but not the economics. Think crown prince: inside the royal circle, yet the throne remains out of reach. They've crossed from senior associate to business co-owner in name only. In consensus-building, they're valued consultants. Their input is sought and heard, but the final decision happens elsewhere. They can shape debate but never block it. Psychologically, this is the toughest position. They shoulder partner-level duties and represent the firm externally, but remain employees when it comes to money – bound by consensus they only nominally helped create.
2. *Semi-equity partners* occupy a unique niche. Practice leaders or regional heads, they earn a slice of their unit's profits but not the firm-wide distribution. Their authority is territorial and functional – kings in their domain, vassals at headquarters. On practice or office matters, they drive consensus and expect firm-wide support. On global decisions, they become influential advisors – important voices, not decision-makers. This split role creates a distinct management mindset. The model works well in global firms – a local managing partner might take 15 percent of office revenue yet stay silent on worldwide strategy. Local sovereign, corporate vassal – different consensus rules apply in each realm.

3. *Equity partners* are full players in firm-wide consensus. On paper, votes are equal; in practice, influence flows through multiple filters. A subtle ranking system operates beneath the surface. *Founding partners* carry mythical weight. They invoke "original intent" and core values; their dissent signals a drift from founding principles, not just another opinion. *Rainmakers* wield de facto veto power on anything touching their client relationships. Consensus without them on such issues is unthinkable – ignoring them risks seven-figure departures.

"We talked it over and I decided" – enlightened monarchy in democratic clothing

Among the partnership's governance tricks sits the "We consulted, I decided" protocol. It's an elegant social arrangement that combines sole authority with collegial ideals – without ever breaking protocol.

Picture a stage production where every actor knows the script, yet the audience remains convinced by the performance. The senior partner plays the enlightened monarch who deeply values his advisors' counsel. Junior partners serve as wise consultants whose insights help the leader craft balanced decisions. Everyone derives satisfaction from their role, even though the outcome was predetermined.

The process begins with a democratic opening. The senior frames the issue in true Socratic fashion, invites input from every stakeholder, and creates an atmosphere of intellectual equality. He asks probing questions, seeks clarification, shows genuine curiosity – in short, behaves like the perfect discussion moderator.

Junior partners seize the opportunity to showcase their expertise, demonstrate analytical skills, and feel like influential advisors. Their views receive careful attention, their arguments get serious consideration, their expertise gains recognition. Psychologically, it's an extremely comfortable position – a sense of involvement in major decisions without the burden of final accountability.

But the curtain falls the moment the senior delivers the ritual phrase: "Thank you all for this valuable discussion. Having considered the points raised, I've decided..." or "Based on our conversation, the best course is...". The democratic facade vanishes instantly, revealing the process's monarchical core.

Remarkably, every participant leaves satisfied with the performance:

- The senior gains richer input plus moral legitimacy for the decision.

- Others feel heard and valued, even if their suggestions were ignored.
- External observers witness textbook collaboration.

Everyone benefits – except, perhaps, the quality of the decisions themselves. But that's just a minor detail.

Partnership initiation – the art of professional hazing

Law firms have developed perhaps the most sophisticated professional initiation system in the world – so refined that participants sometimes interpret it as a mark of special trust and recognition. This is a process designed for university graduates, operating not through crude intimidation but through subtle psychological mechanisms.

Honorary service serves as the first initiation tool. Newcomers get invited to "represent the firm's interests" in professional associations, charitable organizations, or public committees. The phrasing is always impeccable: "We want you to be the face of our firm at this important event". Who could refuse such an honor?

In practice, this means the new partner spends evenings at bar association ethics meetings, weekends at charity events, and vacations at young-lawyer conferences – instead of generating revenue or developing expertise. Declining risks being labeled selfish, someone who fails to appreciate the value of "networking" and "corporate citizenship".

Information rationing is the second mechanism for maintaining hierarchy. New partners gain gradual access to "adult" conversations, but the flow stays tightly controlled. They receive operational details and tactical thinking about practice growth, yet the real intelligence stays locked up – plans for lateral hires, nuances of senior partner dynamics, the firm's real financial health. The rationale sounds reasonable: "First get comfortable with current responsibilities, then we'll bring you into long-term planning". Result: new partners enter firm-wide discussions missing half the context.

Ritual assignments form the third element of initiation. Periodically, newcomers get assigned to defend unpopular decisions or losing positions. This might mean justifying compensation cuts to the team, defending fee increases to unhappy clients, or representing the firm in public disputes with regulators.

The goal isn't humiliation – it's testing willingness to take hits for the group. Success proves the essential partner trait – putting firm interests above personal comfort. It also teaches them not to get too independent – next time, the newcomer will think twice before challenging senior decisions.

Emotional conditioning is the fourth, most delicate, integration tool. New partners must demonstrate "professional maturity" – the ability to distance themselves from former friendships with lower-level colleagues. Yesterday's allies become subordinates; informal relationships turn strictly professional.

This stings most when the new partner must decide on firing or disciplining former peers. Inability to "be tough when necessary" gets interpreted as immaturity and unreadiness for partner responsibilities. Sacrificing personal relationships for "the business" becomes the price of admission to the inner circle.

The telling detail – this "maturing" is expected the morning after appointment. And everyone sincerely believes in its educational value. Seniors recall their own "initiation" as character-building and professional development. Newcomers view the trials as a necessary rite of passage. Outsiders see a mentorship and knowledge-transfer system.

The economic formula – transforming inequality into fairness

The real masterpiece of partner hierarchy is its economic justification. Lawyers – masters at identifying flaws in others' arguments – have built a defense system that withstands even the sharpest internal scrutiny.

The Doctrine of Sacred Risk anchors partner ideology. Equity partners put skin in the game – personal liability, loan guarantees, homes on the line. The logic is ironclad – greater risk earns greater control. It hits hardest during crises, when seniors could genuinely lose substantial assets over a bad decision. In calm periods, though, risks remain largely theoretical. Professional insurance covers most losses; diversified client portfolios cushion individual failures. Yet the psychology persists – even hypothetical ruin grants moral authority for privilege.

The Mystique of Client Relationships forms the second pillar. In professional services, clients often follow people, not institutions. A senior who rescued a client two decades ago knows the business, the personalities, the family dynamics. This personalization creates objective power imbalance. A rainmaker may lack the largest equity stake or formal veto power, but on matters affecting "their" clients, their voice carries outsized influence. The mystique cuts both ways. The same bond that empowers also constrains. The partner becomes hostage to client preferences – unable to support firm-optimal decisions if the client objects. Management judgment can deteriorate under client-pleasing pressure.

The Cult of Accumulated Wisdom is the third foundation. Legal expertise compounds over decades, unlike technology where knowledge becomes obsolete quickly. A senior doesn't just know more statutes – they understand how the system really operates. In high-pressure moments – high stakes, tight deadlines – their intuition, refined through countless transactions, often outperforms spreadsheet analysis. A junior may be technically sharper, yet the veteran senses which approach "will work" and which will fail. The cult's downside breeds presumption of senior infallibility, stifling innovation. "We tried that in '98 – didn't work." Such responses kill experiments, even when circumstances have changed completely.

The system's deepest secret isn't the existence of economic rationale – it's genuine. The problem – natural, rational inequality hides behind democratic theater. Instead of acknowledging that votes carry different weight, firms stage exhausting equality performances that exhaust everyone and convince no one.

A cleaner solution: openly structure influence with clear boundaries.

- Client decisions ➡ those who own the relationships.
- Strategy decisions ➡ those bearing the greatest risks.
- Operational decisions ➡ those doing the execution.

But that honesty requires abandoning the equality myth – and experience shows that's harder than maintaining the elegant, exhausting democratic facade.

(We haven't even addressed professional management relationships, which would further complicate consensus.)

The game of agreement

Partnership agreements rarely exceed 50 pages, but the real social contract of the partnership consists of hundreds of unwritten rules that exist solely in the collective understanding of the participants. These rules are no less binding than the legal formulations – and sometimes even more restrictive.

The paradox of partner consensus is that the most crucial agreements never make it to paper. Moreover, discussing them openly is considered poor form – a violation of the unspoken code of professional etiquette. As a result, a two-tier communication system emerges, where what is said and what is actually meant can differ dramatically.

The language of subtext – what partners say vs what they mean

In the partner vocabulary, every phrase carries at least two meanings – a surface one intended for the record and a deeper one understood by insiders. This system of coded language allows partners to address sensitive issues without violating the rules of professional courtesy.

When partners say, "We are all equal in this partnership," they mean, "We acknowledge formal equality while fully understanding the reality of unequal influence". In practice, this means agreement to maintain polite fiction, where differences in decision-making power get masked by collaborative discussion procedures.

The phrase, "It's important to hear everyone's perspective" in practice means, "Everyone will get a chance to speak, but the decision has already been made". This is a legitimation ritual, where the discussion process matters more than the substance of the debate. Junior partners understand the rules and dutifully perform their advisory role.

"The decision serves the firm's best interests" functions as a universal formula that shuts down any questions about motives and criteria. Under "the firm's interests" can hide anything – from objective economic necessity to the personal preferences of an influential partner. The elegance of this phrasing is that questioning "the firm's interests" is simply inappropriate.

Particularly sophisticated is the construction "I think we all agree that...". Formally, it invites discussion; in reality, it forces agreement. Objecting to a position that "everyone agrees" with automatically casts the dissenter as someone who undermines partnership unity.

"We need to show flexibility" typically means "We need to accept what you don't like". This is a euphemism for forced compromise, when one side must abandon principles for the "good of the partnership". Notably, flexibility is always required from the weaker party.

When "teamwork" gets discussed, what's really meant is the need to support a decision that someone may oppose. Teamwork gets measured not by the quality of collaboration but by willingness to suppress personal doubts in the name of visible unity.

Legitimizing unwritten rules

Consensus has a remarkable ability to transform temporary arrangements into sacred traditions. What begins as a practical solution gradually solidifies into an unshakeable norm of partnership life.

The mechanism is simple – if a practice encounters no active resistance, it gets silently accepted as appropriate. Lack of objection becomes consent; consent becomes endorsement; endorsement becomes established practice. Within a few years, no one remembers how or why the tradition started.

Consider the allocation of prestigious clients. It may have originated from personal relationships or chance circumstances. But unchallenged, it quietly evolves into a "historical right" to that client base. Any redistribution attempt now feels like an attack on the established order.

Influence hierarchies form the same way. When one partner's suggestions succeed more frequently, a presumption of expertise develops. Colleagues begin supporting those initiatives by default, further reinforcing authority. The cycle continues – influence generates more influence.

Access to information legitimizes itself most clearly. Partners routinely included in strategic discussions automatically become the "inner circle". Excluding others requires no justification – it's simply "how we've always operated".

Remarkably, participants often remain unaware of the legitimization process. They genuinely believe current practices emerged naturally and reflect objective necessity. Historical origins disappear, leaving only a sense of correctness and inevitability.

The tyranny of silence

The strongest constraints in a partnership arise not from explicit prohibitions but from topics considered undiscussable. These silences establish invisible boundaries of acceptable behavior – crossing them invites not formal sanctions but social isolation.

Financial transparency offers a classic example. In most partnerships, direct questions about colleagues' compensation, profit-distribution mechanisms, or financial-decision criteria are forbidden. Such information is "confidential" – curiosity signals poor judgment.

The result is predictable – partners develop strategies based on rumors and speculation. They lack clarity about the firm's true condition or decision-making logic yet maintain the pretense of full understanding. Ignorance becomes institutional culture.

Conflicts of interest create another silent zone. Partners may maintain personal client relationships, outside income sources, or competing obligations, yet raising the subject remains taboo. Everyone is presumed to act solely for the firm – questioning that assumption feels inappropriate.

Colleague performance joins the forbidden topics. Even when certain partners clearly underperform, open discussion gets labeled unprofessional. Instead of honest conversation come subtle hints, private complaints, and passive-aggressive behavior.

Strategic vision proves especially damaging when left unspoken. Partners may hold fundamentally different views of the firm's future, yet no one dares acknowledge the gaps. Critical decisions thus proceed under assumed agreement – each believing others share their perspective.

The tyranny of silence is dangerous precisely because it creates an illusion of harmony while underlying tensions build. Partners maintain professional courtesy while resentment grows. An eruption becomes inevitable – only the catalyst remains uncertain.

Quantifying partner harmony

Behind all the hierarchy dynamics lie hard numbers that signal trouble when the system begins to break down.

A veteran British consultant with four decades of experience once observed that partnership stability fractures when compensation gaps reach certain multiples. Through extensive trial and error, he established a 2-2.5× threshold. Exceed that ratio consistently, and destructive dynamics emerge.

The principle applies within each tier. If the highest-paid equity partner earns a million annually, the lowest should receive at least 400k. The same multiplier works across levels – if the bottom equity partner draws 400k, semi-equity partners should earn between 160k and 400k.

The second benchmark (30-50 percent) measures individual satisfaction. A partner remains content when at least 30 percent of their originated work flows to their personal compensation. Over time, that percentage typically grows toward 50 percent. Partners consistently below this threshold rarely stay long – competitors attract them with better revenue-sharing arrangements.

These numbers aren't absolute rules, but they serve as reliable warning indicators. Exceeding them doesn't guarantee immediate collapse, yet demands careful monitoring of partner morale. Experience demonstrates that ignoring these ratios ultimately costs talent and creates internal conflicts.

Chapter 8:
What true consensus actually means

From Cicero to partner meetings

The word "consensus" echoes through law firms with reverence. "We need consensus", "Let's build consensus", "We operate by consensus" – these phrases surface in every meeting. Yet most who use them have only a vague understanding of what consensus actually means.

The ancients who created the term were far more precise. In classical usage, *consensu* meant not mere agreement but informed, deliberate accord based on shared understanding. Cicero spoke of *consensus civium* – citizen harmony achieved not through persuasion or pressure but through common vision for the republic's welfare. Elegant concept, isn't it? Unfortunately, it bears about as much resemblance to modern partnerships as Latin does to text messaging.

Practicing partners rarely consult academic works on group dynamics – they're too busy managing client crises. But here's the paradox – those very studies explain why partner meetings so often produce nothing, why intelligent people make poor decisions, and why "unanimous" choices routinely fail.

Consensus theory isn't abstract philosophy – it's an instruction manual for human behavior. Political scientists and social psychologists have spent decades studying how groups reach collective decisions, the obstacles that trap them, and the methods to avoid those problems. Their discoveries apply remarkably well to daily operations in law firms.

Law firms exist in an unusual position between democracy and oligarchy, where traditional consensus models take unexpected forms. Frameworks designed for large societies or political systems operate differently in the close-knit environment of partnership – sometimes intensified, sometimes distorted beyond recognition.

Mansbridge – unitary vs adversarial models in partnership

Jane Mansbridge[1] distinguishes between two democratic processes – unitary, based on shared interests, and adversarial, which acknowledges conflicting ones. In law firms, these models don't simply coexist – they disguise themselves as each other.

Formally, partnerships adopt the unitary model. All partners supposedly unite around the firm's success; personal objectives align with corporate ones; disagreements are merely technical details. This story creates a comfortable illusion of fellowship, where conflicts are misunderstandings resolved through goodwill.

Reality tends toward the adversarial model. Partners maintain genuinely competing interests: junior partners want rapid compensation increases, senior partners value stability; specialists push for depth, generalists seek breadth; long-term players support strategic investments, those planning exits favor immediate returns.

The contradiction of partner consensus? It requires recognizing adversarial realities while presenting them in unitary language. Partners must understand the inevitability of conflict yet pretend it doesn't exist. This performance exhausts participants and creates cynicism, but the alternative – openly acknowledging conflicts – seems even more damaging.

Habermas – ideal communication conditions in partnership

Jürgen Habermas[2] described an ideal communication situation where participants have equal opportunities to speak and be heard, remain free from coercion, and genuinely seek mutual understanding. Law firms appear close to this ideal – small groups of educated professionals sharing interests and cultural background.

In practice, Habermas' conditions fail systematically, though subtly. Equal speaking opportunities exist formally, but time and attention distribute unevenly. Influential partners speak longer, face fewer interruptions, and receive more careful attention.

Freedom from coercion remains relative. No direct pressure exists, yet a network of implicit consequences operates – exclusion from informal discussions, "oversights" in assignment distribution. Partners quickly recognize the boundaries and modify behavior accordingly.

The pursuit of genuine understanding proves the weakest element. Partners often treat discussion not as truth-seeking but as position-building. They simulate openness to opposing views while seeking ways to neutralize or absorb them.

The result? Conversations that resemble rational dialogue yet function as performance of persuasion. Partners act the role of solution-seekers while actually negotiating for influence and resources.

Marcuse – repressive tolerance in partnership

Herbert Marcuse[3] warned of "repressive tolerance" – a system that projects pluralism and openness while neutralizing genuine critique. Law firms demonstrate this mechanism with remarkable clarity.

Formally, partnerships embody tolerance – every opinion gets heard, every partner has input, diverse perspectives receive welcome. "We're open to all ideas" appears in mission statements. The limitation – this openness operates within sharp, unspoken boundaries.

The system absorbs potential opposition, transforming critics into "constructive advisors". A partner cannot challenge the partnership's fundamental structure – that would undermine their own position. They can, however, suggest "improvements" within the existing framework. Critique becomes acceptable because it never addresses core issues.

Radical proposals receive particularly revealing treatment. They aren't rejected directly – that would violate tolerance. Instead, they get "discussed", "analyzed", "refined" until only a harmless remnant survives. The process remains democratic; the outcome stays predictable.

Marcuse described "one-dimensional thinking" – the system's capacity to absorb all alternatives into its logic. The same operates in firms – every proposal gets evaluated by "what's good for the firm", a phrase that can mask anything from objective business requirements to influential partners' personal preferences.

An illusion of open dialogue emerges while discussion parameters remain tightly controlled. Partners may debate specifics but not principles; tactics but not objectives; resource allocation but not power structures. Tolerance becomes a mechanism of control, not intellectual freedom.

Remarkably, participants often remain unaware of the constraints. They genuinely believe in their openness and democratic process. The system functions best when people least recognize its limitations. Self-censorship proves more effective than external pressure.

Sunstein – false consensus and social pressure

Cass Sunstein[4] identified groupthink risks in close-knit teams, where social dynamics can suppress critical analysis. Law firms provide ideal conditions – closed circles with deep interdependence and strong incentives to maintain harmony.

Social pressure in partnerships proves particularly subtle because it operates through positive reinforcement, not punishment. Partners aren't compelled to agree – they're rewarded for "constructiveness", "team spirit", and "flexibility". Eventually, a culture develops where dissent feels like an ethical violation, not independent judgment.

Information cascades develop quickly. When several influential partners support an idea, others begin questioning their own assessment. The logic: "If these experienced, intelligent people agree, perhaps I'm overlooking something." Critical mass of agreement forms well before critical mass of understanding.

Reputational cascades prove even more powerful. A partner convinced a decision is mistaken may still support it to avoid being labeled disruptive. The group ends up adopting choices that most members privately oppose.

Janis – groupthink among partners

Irving Janis[5] described groupthink – the pursuit of unanimity that prevents realistic evaluation of alternatives. Law firms display every classic characteristic, though in sophisticated forms.

Illusion of unanimity gets carefully cultivated. Partners avoid expressing doubt openly, preferring private conversations over public discussion. Each assumes they alone have reservations, while many colleagues harbor similar concerns.

Self-censorship operates through a complex network of social signals. Partners quickly identify which topics feel "inappropriate" and modify their behavior accordingly. They don't openly misrepresent facts but omit critical aspects of problems.

Illusion of invulnerability characterizes successful firms. Previous successes create a belief the firm can weather any challenge. This generates overconfidence in decisions and underestimation of risks.

Stereotyping outsiders – competitors, clients, regulators – strengthens internal unity. The external environment appears less capable and more predictable than reality justifies.

Ten distortions of partner consensus

Theoretical models explain underlying mechanisms, but practice exceeds any framework. Years of observing law firms reveal recurring distortions of consensus – patterns that simulate agreement while actually undermining it.

1. *False consensus.* When "everyone agrees" only because no one wants to speak first. It appears polished, but lacks substance. Typical scenario:

the managing partner presents a vision, pauses, and asks, "Any objections?". Silence. "Excellent, consider it decided." The contradiction: sometimes this works – if the decision is genuinely sound and partners simply avoid debating the obvious. Problems arise when half the room has serious doubts, each assuming they're the only skeptic. That consensus collapses at the first real challenge.

2. *Polite consensus*. When a partner remains silent not from agreement but from exhaustion, overload, or "not wanting to create problems". In small doses, this serves as social lubrication that keeps the group functioning without endless disputes. Experienced partners learn to distinguish when silence serves efficiency and when discussion is crucial. The risk: the mechanism breaks down easily – especially at the end of lengthy meetings or on complex issues late on Friday, when minds are already focused on weekend plans.
3. *Coerced consensus*. When "agreement" results from authority pressure, not reasoning. On the one hand, it enables rapid decisions amid uncertainty – senior judgment often outweighs prolonged debate. On the other, no one gets explicitly forced, yet everyone understands that dissent has consequences. The senior emphasizes not the proposal's merits but team loyalty. Experienced partners package doubts as "clarifying questions", preserving dignity while maintaining influence.
4. *Consensus pause*. Temporary agreement to postpone conflict, not resolve it. Sometimes this represents wise strategy – cool emotions, gather information, wait for a better moment. Skilled managing partners use time as a dispute resolution tool. The problem: pauses easily become decision avoidance. In some firms, the "deferred" list grows for years, becoming a cemetery of unresolved issues that eventually explode.
5. *Consensus as cover*. When a "unified position" serves as camouflage for hidden agendas. Cynical yet occasionally effective for advancing unpopular but necessary moves. An influential partner secures support privately, builds coalitions, then orchestrates an "open" discussion. If the decision is correct, the approach saves months of unproductive debate. The danger: it becomes corrupting – starting with justified cases, it evolves into manipulation for personal benefit.
6. *Performative democracy*. When the decision is already made but everyone gets invited to speak "for show". This isn't always dishonest – leaders sometimes genuinely hope for new arguments that might

change their perspective. Occasionally it works – even ceremonial consultations uncover overlooked considerations. More often, partners perform advisory roles whose contributions no one values. Experienced partners recognize these "consultations" by compressed schedules and superficial responses to substantive points.

7. *No-consensus as culture*. When no one agrees with anyone, yet the partnership pretends to function. Sounds disastrous, but some firms succeed this way – diverse opinions spark innovation, internal competition drives growth. The limitation: it exhausts participants and works only with strong financial bonds. When external conditions deteriorate, accumulated tensions explode.
8. *Consensus through abdication*. When all silently agree to avoid taking responsibility. It offers advantages – reduced conflict, faster decisions, shared blame for failures. In stable periods, it can continue for years. Ideal for eliminating initiative while minimizing risks. The danger: decisions get made, but no one feels ownership or advocates for implementation.
9. *Emotional consensus*. When "agreement" gets secured through emotional pressure – "Disagree and you're against the team". Effective for unity during crises – sometimes the firm genuinely must unite against external threats. Appeals to team spirit can be sincere and appropriate. Yet emotional coercion easily becomes a critical thinking inhibitor. Dissent gets framed as betraying shared values; defending against such accusations becomes nearly impossible.
10. *Symbolic consensus*. When everyone supposedly agrees, yet no one plans to act. It creates an illusion of progress with no results, but sometimes that's precisely what's needed – the discussion process matters more than the outcome. Partners express concerns, feel included in governance, release frustration. Meeting records overflow with resolutions and plans; everyone appreciates the process. The problem: six months later, nothing has changed, and time and energy got wasted.

These ten patterns can function as obstacles or tools in decision making and partner coordination. Most partnerships genuinely pursue authentic consensus but lack technical expertise. Few have studied how to distinguish genuine agreement from imitation, structure discussions, or manage group dynamics. Consequently, intelligent people fall into the same patterns repeatedly, confused to why their "unanimous" decisions fail.

The encouraging news? Consensus represents a learnable competency. It has its own methodology, stages, and techniques. The first step toward mastery is understanding what actually occurs when a group attempts to reach common ground.

Four phases of consensus life

Consensus in law firms follows natural patterns – it emerges, develops, deteriorates, and either dissolves or regenerates (see Table 8.1 on the next page). The cycle is as predictable as the seasons and equally inevitable. Understanding these phases allows partners to assess their firm's current state and anticipate future challenges.

Each phase has its own dynamics, opportunities, and risks. What succeeds during formation can prove destructive during decline. Strategies that work in stability fail during crisis. Partnership management wisdom lies in recognizing transition indicators and adapting leadership to the current phase.

Phase 1: Formation (honeymoon period)

This is the period of optimism, when everything seems achievable and disagreements feel like minor misunderstandings. Partners express enthusiasm for the joint venture, willingly sacrifice personal interests for the collective good, and genuinely believe their partnership is unique – unlike all others.

Psychology of the Formation phase

During the initial period, partners attribute their best qualities and intentions to colleagues. Each thinks, "Finally, I've found people who share my values and understand my objectives". Differences in approach get viewed as valuable additions, not threats. "John has a different client-management style, but it only enhances our practice."

Conflicts at this stage are uncommon and quickly resolved. Partners prefer to accommodate rather than insist. The environment emphasizes mutual support and willingness to compromise. "Let's not debate minor issues – we have more important priorities."

Characteristic indicators

Decisions get made easily and quickly. Extended discussions are rare – partners either agree immediately or one readily concedes. Meetings occur in a collegial atmosphere, often concluding earlier than scheduled.

Table 8.1: Four phases of consensus life

Phase	Characteristics	Opportunities	Risks / Warning Signs
Phase 1 Formation (Honeymoon)	High energy, shared vision, informal agreements, optimism, partners finish each other's sentences	Build strong foundation, establish trust, dream big, create shared identity	Avoiding hard conversations, ignoring differences, unrealistic expectations
PHASE 2 Institutionalization (Framework)	Written procedures, formal meetings, committees formed, precedents matter, decisions documented	Create scalable systems, establish clear authority, build institutional memory	Excessive bureaucracy, inflexibility, "no procedure for that" paralysis
PHASE 3 Erosion (Contradictions)	Procedure fatigue, sidebar conversations, slow decisions, sloppy execution, real choices happen informally	Surface hidden tensions early, address root causes before crisis	Denial, blame games, procedure band-aids, partners stop pulling together
PHASE 4 Crisis or Renewal	Breaking point: splits, exits, takeover or honest reset, outside help, rebuilding from scratch	Rebuild stronger consensus, realign on values, clear out dysfunction	Partnership dissolution, bitter splits, or half-hearted renewal that fails

Formal procedures remain minimal. Partners depend on mutual trust and shared principles rather than detailed regulations. "Why do we need complex rules? We're reasonable people – we'll always reach agreement."

Financial transparency reaches maximum levels. Partners freely share information about revenues, expenses, and client relationships. No one suspects colleagues of hiding important information or manipulating data.

Risks of the Formation phase

The primary danger of this phase is the assumption that current harmony will continue indefinitely. Partners don't prepare for inevitable conflicts and don't establish mechanisms for resolution. "Why anticipate problems? Everything works well for us."

The lack of formal procedures can create problems later. Decisions get made based on personal relationships and immediate circumstances, establishing precedents that become difficult to modify subsequently.

Excessive optimism creates unrealistic expectations. Partners accept too many commitments, overestimate their capabilities, underestimate risks. When reality doesn't match expectations, the disappointment proves painful.

Phase 2: Institutionalization (establishing operating framework)

The honeymoon ends when partners realize that clear rules are necessary for effective operations. This doesn't mean relationships have deteriorated – experience simply reveals the need for more structure.

Catalysts for transition

The first serious conflict that can't be resolved "amicably" triggers consideration of procedures. It might be a dispute over dividing a major fee or disagreement about admitting a new partner. Everyone recognizes that rules are necessary so such situations don't harm relationships subsequently.

Firm growth makes informal arrangements unworkable. With three partners, any issue can be addressed over lunch. With ten – meetings, agendas, and decision records become essential.

External factors contribute as well. Client requirements, regulators, and banks compel internal processes to formalize. "We need to demonstrate to auditors how we make risk decisions."

Characteristic indicators

Written procedures and policies emerge. The partnership agreement expands, acquiring appendices and supplements. Committees and working groups form with clearly defined authority.

Decisions require more discussion time. Partners learn to present positions, analyze alternatives, and consider long-term consequences. Meetings become longer and more formal.

Precedents acquire importance. "Last year we handled it this way, so we must maintain consistency now." Partners begin referencing past decisions as sources of legitimacy.

Benefits and risks

Institutionalization provides stability and predictability. Partners understand what to expect from each other, how decisions get made, and who handles what responsibilities. This reduces stress and conflict levels.

However, there's a downside. Rules can become objectives in themselves, with procedures mattering more than results. Bureaucracy emerges, decisions slow down, initiative gets constrained by formalities.

A particular danger is system inflexibility. Rules designed for past problems can prevent adaptation to future challenges. "We can't do that – there's no established procedure for it."

Phase 3: Erosion (building contradictions)

The most dangerous phase, because it sneaks up on you. On the surface, everything looks fine – the firm runs smoothly, clients are happy, the numbers work. But underneath, problems are piling up that will eventually blow.

How erosion happens:

- *Procedure fatigue.* What once felt like smart organization now feels like red tape. Partners start cutting corners, making decisions on the fly, dropping bombshells on colleagues without warning.
- *Interests start to split.* During the honeymoon, everyone seemed to want the same things. Now it turns out partners have different visions for where the firm should go, different priorities, goals that don't line up.
- *Uneven growth breeds tension.* Some partners are hitting their stride – building expertise, bringing in money. Others are stuck. The high performers feel taken for granted. The stragglers feel left behind.

Warning signs:

- *More sidebar conversations.* The real decisions happen in hallway chats, not official meetings. Formal discussions become theater – everyone just nods along with what's already been decided.
- *Everything takes forever.* Issues that used to get wrapped up in one meeting now drag on for months. The "parking lot" gets longer and longer.
- *Sloppy execution.* Partners say yes in meetings but drag their feet when it comes to actually doing anything. Or they find creative ways to ignore what they agreed to.

How partners react:

- *Denial.* "We're doing fine – just going through a rough patch." Nobody wants to admit the wheels are coming off, so they pretend everything's normal.
- *Blame games.* Instead of looking at what's really wrong, people hunt for someone to pin it on. "If it weren't for Bob's attitude problems, we'd be golden."
- *Procedure band-aids.* New committees, revised policies, extra rules. This almost never helps – the problem isn't the process, it's that people have stopped pulling in the same direction.

Phase 4: Crisis or renewal

Erosion can't go on forever. Eventually, all those built-up tensions have to go somewhere. The partnership hits a breaking point that either tears it apart or forces it to rebuild from scratch.

What triggers the crisis:

- *Outside shocks often light the fuse.* Losing a big client, economic meltdown, new regulations – anything that demands quick, decisive action. If the internal machinery is already broken, the firm can't respond when it matters most.
- *Internal fights reach the boiling point.* A dispute that would normally get handled through channels explodes into open warfare. People start talking about principles and values, not just money – and that's when compromise becomes almost impossible.
- *Generational clash adds fuel to the fire.* Younger partners want to shake things up; old-timers stick with what's worked before. Different ways

of working, different goals for the future – suddenly there's no middle ground.

How crisis plays out:

- *Breakup*. The most dramatic ending, but not as rare as you'd think. Partners realize they can't stand working together anymore and call it quits. Sometimes it's an amicable split with everyone getting their fair share. Sometimes it's a messy divorce with lawyers and lawsuits.
- *Takeover*. One partner or faction grabs control and basically turns the partnership into their personal kingdom. Everyone else either accepts being second-class citizens or heads for the exit.
- *Renewal*. The hardest path, but the only one that actually fixes things. Partners admit the current set-up is broken and agree to tear it down and build something better. This might mean new strategy, new structure, new ways of making decisions, new rules for splitting profits.

What renewal actually takes:

- *Facing facts honestly*. Everyone has to admit the system is broken and needs fixing. Trying to slap band-aids on the old ways just kicks the can down the road.
- *Real willingness to give ground*. Renewal means everybody sacrifices something for the greater good. People who won't bend usually walk away at this point.
- *Investing in new systems*. Just changing the rules on paper isn't enough – you need time and money to make new approaches actually work. Partners have to live with uncertainty while the new stuff gets figured out.
- *Outside help often makes the difference*. Consultants, mediators, coaches can see solutions that people inside the mess can't spot.

Signs it's actually working:

- *Partners get their energy back*. The exhaustion and cynicism fade away. People start caring again about shared projects.
- *Conversations get better*. Partners actually listen to each other, look for creative solutions, and stay open to changing their minds when they hear good arguments.
- *Decisions happen faster and stick better*. New procedures beat the old ones; fights get resolved quicker; people actually follow through.

- *The rebuilt partnership often ends up stronger than the original.* Having survived the crisis, partners know each other better, have realistic expectations, and build systems that can weather future storms.

Understanding how consensus evolves won't guarantee success, but it helps you avoid the classic traps. The key insight – each phase has something to teach. The honeymoon shows you how to dream big. Institutionalization teaches planning. Erosion forces you to be honest with yourself. Crisis demands tough choices. Partnerships that navigate all four phases deliberately give themselves the best shot at a long, productive run.

See Appendix 10 for more information.

The main trap of groupthink

Irving Janis[6] studied how smart, educated people in groups make spectacularly bad decisions. His research[7] on the Kennedy administration during the Bay of Pigs fiasco revealed a troubling pattern – the tighter the group, the more likely they are to collectively lose their minds. Law firms are perfect petri dishes for watching this happen in real time.

Groupthink isn't just some academic theory gathering dust in psychology journals. It's the daily reality of law firms, where pressure to fit in meets high stakes, and screwing up can be career-ending. What's worse, the legal profession creates perfect conditions for groupthink that Janis never even imagined.

How market forces make groupthink worse

The legal market punishes rebels and rewards conformists. This basic fact shapes how partners behave long before they realize what it's doing to their judgment.

Client pressure for unity

Big clients hate surprises and mixed messages from their legal team. They want a unified front – everyone singing from the same hymn sheet. A partner who contradicts colleagues in front of a client might as well pack their bags.

This creates massive incentives to present a united front. Partners learn fast – better to bite your tongue than look dysfunctional. Over time, putting on a show for clients becomes second nature – even when nobody's watching.

Long-term client relationships make this even worse. A firm that's served the same big client for decades starts thinking like they work for them, not with them. Partners stop asking tough questions, challenging assumptions, or suggesting uncomfortable alternatives. They turn into yes-men instead of advisors.

Competitive copying

The legal market is obsessed with keeping up with the Joneses. Firms constantly benchmark against competitors – how much they pay, who they hire, what practice areas they're in, what strategies they're pursuing. This creates a follow-the-leader mentality across the industry.

When the market leaders make a move, everyone else feels pressure to copy it. "If it works for them, it should work for us." Few bother asking whether what works for a white-shoe New York firm makes sense for a regional practice in Cleveland.

The result – an industry full of firms that look and act like carbon copies of each other. Differences disappear, innovation gets squashed, creative ideas seem too risky. Groupthink spreads from individual partnerships to the entire profession.

Regulatory fear

The legal profession lives under tight regulation, which creates even more pressure to play it safe. Step out of line and you could lose your license, so partners stick to tried-and-true approaches rather than experimenting.

This makes sense for day-to-day operations but kills strategic thinking. Partners fear not just breaking rules but doing anything that looks different from standard practice. "What will the bar association think?" becomes the phrase that murders innovation in its crib.

Regulators, without meaning to, become groupthink enablers. Their push for standardization and predictability crushes the diversity of approaches that keeps any profession healthy and evolving.

When partners fear standing out

Fear of standing out isn't just some personal quirk – it's baked into partnership culture. This culture builds up over years and gets passed down through countless unspoken rules and expectations.

Socialization of new partners

The road to partnership is a long vetting process that naturally filters out troublemakers. By the time lawyers make partner, they've already survived multiple rounds of selection that reward team players and weed out boat-rockers.

Young associates learn the unwritten rules fast – don't challenge seniors, don't air dirty laundry in public, don't push crazy ideas. Those who can't play by these rules either quit or get quietly shown the door.

By the time someone makes partner, they've internalized these norms so completely that they genuinely believe they're right and necessary. They don't feel oppressed – quite the opposite. They're proud to join an elite club of people who "get it".

Financial interdependence

The partnership model creates serious financial pressure to keep everyone happy. Each partner's paycheck depends not just on their own work but on how the whole firm does. Fighting with colleagues can literally cost you money.

This hits hardest in smaller firms, where every partner's contribution really matters. One stubborn holdout can torpedo important decisions, damage client relationships, or create PR disasters that hurt everyone's bottom line.

Partners figure out the math quickly – better to go along with a questionable decision than risk their financial security. Independent thinking becomes a luxury most can't afford.

Reputational risks of dissent

The legal world is surprisingly small, and reputation matters more than credentials. Get labeled as "difficult" or "not a team player" and the damage can follow you beyond your current firm.

Clients talk to each other about lawyers, judges remember who caused problems, and lawyers from other firms love to gossip. In this environment, having a reputation as someone who plays well with others can be worth more than being known as a brilliant maverick.

The worst label you can get is "can't work on a team". That can end a career, even if your legal skills are flawless. Partners would rather bite their tongues than risk that kind of professional death sentence.

Psychological self-protection

Constantly keeping your mouth shut when you disagree with something creates its own psychological defenses. Partners start convincing themselves that their doubts are probably wrong and the group is probably right.

When there's a gap between what you really think and what you say out loud, your mind resolves it by deciding the group must know something you don't. "If all these smart people agree, maybe I'm missing something." What starts as external pressure to conform becomes an internal need to avoid the discomfort of disagreement.

Eventually, the line between your real beliefs and group loyalty gets so blurred you can't tell the difference. Partners genuinely start believing in decisions they were originally against.

The cost of conformity in legal business

Groupthink in law firms carries a heavy price tag – for clients, partners, and everyone else. These costs usually stay buried until it's too late, which makes them especially dangerous.

Decline in legal service quality

When everyone thinks the same way, legal analysis gets lazy. Alternative interpretations never get explored, creative strategies get shot down, and potential risks fly under the radar.

Clients end up with cookie-cutter solutions to unique problems. The firm misses innovative approaches that could better serve client needs. In complex cases, this kind of tunnel vision can cost millions or lead to courtroom disasters.

Groupthink is especially toxic in cutting-edge legal areas where there's no clear precedent. That's exactly when you need diverse perspectives and willingness to try new approaches – but conformist culture kills both.

Strategic blunders

Partnerships that fall into groupthink make spectacularly bad strategic decisions. Classic mistakes – expanding into new markets without doing their homework, merging with firms that don't fit, buying technology their clients don't want.

These disasters could be avoided if different voices got heard during decision making. But the false consensus atmosphere shuts down critical thinking when it matters most.

When the mistakes become obvious, partners scratch their heads: "How did we miss this?" The answer is straightforward – they built a system designed to silence uncomfortable questions and ignore inconvenient possibilities.

Brain drain

Conformist culture drives away exactly the people who could help the firm most – independent thinkers, innovators, people willing to challenge the status quo.

Smart lawyers who won't trade intellectual honesty for group harmony either never make partner, jump to other firms, or go out on their own. The firm loses the very people who could drive future growth.

What's left is a homogeneous group of yes-men who can't generate breakthrough ideas or adapt when the market shifts.

Systemic damage to the profession

When groupthink becomes the norm at leading firms, the whole legal profession takes a hit. The quality of legal thinking deteriorates, new problem-solving approaches get strangled in the crib, and the gap between what society needs and what lawyers deliver keeps growing.

Clients start looking elsewhere – consulting firms, tech solutions, alternative service providers. Lawyers risk losing their monopoly in areas they've controlled for generations.

Fighting groupthink

Groupthink isn't some incurable disease – it's a manageable risk. There are proven ways to keep the benefits of working together while dodging the conformity trap.

Building in disagreement

The best way to fight groupthink is to make disagreement a formal part of how decisions get made. This means appointing a "devil's advocate" for every big decision, requiring teams to look at alternative scenarios, bringing in outside experts who see things differently.

The key is making sure the critic's role doesn't feel like punishment – it should be seen as an important job. A partner who consistently asks tough questions should get praise from colleagues, not dirty looks.

Some firms create special risk committees whose job is to poke holes in proposed strategies. These only work if their input actually changes decisions, not just gets filed away.

Diversity as a weapon

Firms need to actively build diversity – not just demographics, but different ways of thinking. That means bringing in partners with different educational backgrounds, work experience, cultural perspectives, and mental approaches.

Diversity isn't about checking boxes – it's about competitive advantage. Different viewpoints help you spot solutions others miss, see risks coming from around corners, and adapt when markets shift.

You have to create an environment where different opinions are treated as assets, not threats. That means changing culture at the deepest level.

Smarter decision processes

Well-designed procedures can counteract group bias. Anonymous voting on controversial issues, mandatory cooling-off periods between discussion and decision, facilitation techniques that get everyone to speak up.

Methods that force partners to spell out their assumptions and examine what-if scenarios work well. For example, the "pre-mortem" – figuring out what could go wrong before you make the decision.

Keep reviewing and improving how decisions get made, based on what you've learned and how things have changed.

Outside eyes

Regular contact with outsiders helps break the groupthink bubble. Consultants, academics, people from other industries – even clients willing to give you straight talk.

These outside advisors need real influence, not just ceremonial roles. Their opinions should actually affect strategy development.

Hold regular "challenge sessions" where outsiders question your basic assumptions and strategies. These meetings can be uncomfortable, but they're necessary to stay intellectually honest.

Psychological safety

Most importantly, create an atmosphere where partners feel safe expressing unpopular opinions. This requires leadership from the top – managing partners have to personally model openness to criticism and willingness to change their minds.

Psychological safety gets built through thousands of small moments. Every time a leader thanks someone for criticism instead of getting defensive, every time a minority view gets heard over majority pressure, every time someone admits a mistake – it reinforces a culture where truth beats harmony.

Fighting groupthink isn't a one-shot deal – it's ongoing work. It takes vigilance, discipline, and willingness to trade comfort for effectiveness. But the alternative – a slow slide into mediocrity – is much worse than the temporary pain of conflicting ideas.

The best partnerships get it – their main advantage isn't thinking alike but thinking well. And you think well not by shutting down disagreement but by using it constructively.

Consensus in crisis

Start with the hard truth. Consensus isn't harmony – it's decision architecture.

In partnerships, we love to say, "We reached agreement". Too often, we've simply kicked the can down the road – or avoided the conversation entirely. That habit turns deadly when crisis hits and there's no time left for endless back-and-forth.

Watching firms navigate crises reveals four patterns that completely rewrite how consensus has to work when everything's on fire.

What breaks first

Before rebuilding consensus, you need to understand what falls apart when the world goes sideways.

A crisis isn't a "rough patch" – it's a complete system failure that tears the firm apart, piece by piece.

Information flows collapse

First casualty – the quality and speed of information.

Partners used to monthly reports and quarterly reviews suddenly need data that goes stale in hours. Financial numbers require daily updates. Client moods shift minute by minute. Competitive landscapes change overnight.

But the firm's systems weren't built for this speed. Reports fall behind. Analytics become useless. Forecasts turn into wild guesses.

Partners end up making decisions based on rumors, gut feelings, and wishful thinking – exactly when accuracy matters most.

Emotional meltdown

Crisis doesn't just mess with logic – it breaks people.

Veteran partners, used to controlling outcomes, suddenly feel helpless. Experts who spent decades building their reputations watch their strategies blow up.

Fear, anxiety, and anger become constant companions. Long-term thinking disappears. People get short-tempered. Trust evaporates.

One panicked partner can poison the whole room. Fear spreads faster than facts, setting off chain reactions of terrible decisions.

Roles fall apart

In normal times, everyone knows their job – rainmakers bring in business, operators run things, strategists plan ahead. The system works because everyone plays their part.

Crisis destroys specialization. Business developers find their networks worthless. Operations people see their procedures crumble. Strategists watch their plans become irrelevant in days.

Total chaos follows. Everyone tries to do everything. Nobody owns anything. Partners step on each other's toes, duplicate work, create confusion – exactly when coordination means survival.

Decision systems seize up

The final nail in the coffin – consensus systems designed for calm waters sink in the storm.

Monthly committees can't handle daily crises. Week-long approval processes block life-saving moves. Collegiality – once a strength – becomes a death sentence.

Partners argue about how to make decisions instead of actually making them. They debate process while competitors steal clients. They chase unanimity on issues that demand immediate action.

Financial panic

Crisis shrinks every timeline. Partners who used to think in years now scramble week to week. Long-term investments? Can't afford them. Short-term cash flow? Life or death.

Pressure exposes every hidden crack between partners. Profit-sharing discussions that used to end in handshakes now turn into survival fights. Each partner starts running the numbers: What am I putting in? What am I getting out? The shared future vanishes.

Insight #1: Consensus as a living system

Consensus isn't some fixed set of rules – it's a living system that needs constant tweaking, especially when the world changes around you.

Most partners treat consensus like a one-time deal that holds until someone rocks the boat. "We already agreed on how things work," they say whenever fights break out. You hear this at every firm. But crisis quickly shows why this thinking is broken.

Consensus has an expiration date

Agreements made under one set of circumstances can become useless – or downright harmful – when things shift. Profit-sharing deals that worked great during boom times turn into war zones when money gets tight. Decision processes that hummed along in calm periods can completely paralyze a firm when chaos hits.

The smartest partnerships get this – consensus needs constant fine-tuning to match what's actually happening. Far from showing weakness, this approach shows you've got a living, breathing governance system.

How you decide beats what you decide

Trying to nail down consensus with detailed rules and procedures is pointless. Nobody can predict every curveball, anticipate every crisis, or make every decision ahead of time.

Instead, build consensus architecture – flexible principles and tools that let you adapt quickly when circumstances change. Focus on how you'll make decisions rather than what those decisions will be. Care more about the decision-making process than the content of any individual choice.

Context is everything

Every consensus exists in a specific situation. When the situation changes, the consensus needs a fresh look. This isn't breaking faith – it's natural evolution.

Recent crises prove the point. Firms that stuck to outdated agreements either froze up or made terrible decisions. Those that quickly adapted their processes to new realities didn't just survive – they came out ahead.

Insight #2: The fragility of good intentions

Good intentions fade fast. They work in the short run – but without solid structures backing them up, they won't survive.

Crises have this amazing ability to bring people together. "We're all in this together." "We need to stick together." "The firm comes first." These feelings genuinely motivate people. But only for a while.

The honeymoon phase

In the early days of a crisis, partnerships experience a dramatic shift. Differences in rank, pay, and clout suddenly matter less than the shared threat. Partners who spent months fighting over tiny details suddenly agree on major decisions.

Agreements happen fast and without argument. Personal agendas get shelved for the common good. A spirit of teamwork and mutual support takes over the firm. Many partners later remember these moments as the best times they ever had working together.

But this unity runs on emotion, not solid ground. It feeds on crisis adrenaline, shared fear, and strong leadership. Once the immediate pressure lets up, that emotional fuel runs out.

Burnout is inevitable

Good intentions can't sustain themselves forever. People get tired of constant stress, personal sacrifice, and repeated appeals to put the firm first. What felt natural and right during the crisis starts feeling like a burden once things calm down.

Partners start keeping score of what they've given up and what they've lost. Those hit hardest by the crisis want payback. Those who came through relatively unscathed wonder why they should subsidize everyone else's problems. Solidarity turns into resentment.

Without proper systems to ensure fairness and give-and-take, good intentions become a source of conflict. Partners feel used and lied to, poisoning trust for years.

You need real systems

Lasting consensus requires more than emotional agreement – it needs rational systems to back it up. Clear ways to make decisions, fair principles for sharing risks and rewards, reliable methods for resolving disputes.

These systems have to be built ahead of time, during peaceful periods when thoughtful discussion and real compromise are possible. In a crisis, there's no time to build new systems – only to use what's already in place.

Insight #3: The unity trap

The harder we push for everyone to get along, the more we kill off the disagreements we actually need.

Crises trigger a natural urge to circle the wagons. Leaders call for an end to bickering and tell everyone to rally against the common enemy. Partners agree to put their differences aside for the firm's survival. On the surface, this looks smart – even noble. In reality, it's poison.

Criticism becomes treason

In a crisis, any pushback against the chosen path gets painted as sabotage. A partner who asks tough questions about strategy risks getting branded a troublemaker. Someone who questions the crisis leader's judgment might get tagged as disloyal.

This cuts especially deep in partnerships, where work relationships and personal friendships blur together. Challenging a strategy can feel like a personal attack. Questioning decisions can look like a vote of no confidence in your colleagues.

Keeping your mouth shut feels safer than speaking up. Partners bottle up critical thoughts, hold back different ideas, and don't flag obvious risks. The firm marches confidently toward disaster, with everyone nodding along.

Killing the diversity you need most

Here's the killer irony – crises are exactly when we need different viewpoints and approaches most.

The stakes are sky-high, time is running out, and mistakes cost everything – which is precisely why we need multiple angles, alternative scenarios, and serious challenges to our thinking.

Uniform thinking in a crisis isn't strength, it's weakness. It strips away flexibility, creativity, and the ability to course-correct. When everyone thinks alike, nobody spots the blind spots, sees problems coming, or builds backup plans.

Business graveyards are full of companies that failed not because of outside forces but because of inside groupthink. They marched forward in perfect formation – straight off a cliff – each one reinforcing everyone else's mistakes.

Protecting the right to disagree

Smart leaders know they have to protect space for legitimate disagreement, even when the pressure's on. They deliberately create ways for alternative views to surface, encourage tough questions, and defend people's right to challenge.

This takes real wisdom and serious self-discipline. The gut reaction in a crisis is to grab control and shut down dissent. Leaders need genuine conviction to fight that urge and stay open to criticism when every minute counts.

Yet this openness often determines who survives and who doesn't. Critical voices help dodge catastrophic blunders, uncover unexpected solutions, and adapt when circumstances shift.

Insight #4: The leadership balancing act

Crisis leadership is all about balance. Staying calm is crucial – but so is making room for tough conversations.

Leading a partnership through crisis means juggling competing demands. Partners want decisive leadership and collaborative input, quick decisions and thorough vetting, hope and honesty – all at the same time.

The reassurance trap

Partners in crisis need emotional anchoring. They want to hear that the situation is under control, that there's a plan, and that the firm will emerge stronger. Reassuring messages keep morale up and prevent panic.

But too much reassurance breeds false comfort. If leaders paint too rosy a picture, partners might downplay the threat and push back against necessary but painful steps. "Why slash budgets if things aren't that bad?"

The flip side – constant doom and gloom – can freeze decision making or trigger desperate moves. The trick is mixing hard truth with steady confidence.

The participation puzzle

Partnership DNA expects collaborative decision making. Even in crisis, partners expect their voices to be heard and their input to matter. Leaders who ignore this lose credibility and face quiet resistance.

But collaboration eats time – and time is exactly what crisis strips away. Every hour of discussion can cost clients, cash flow, or reputation. Leaders have to know when to cut off debate without trashing the partnership culture.

Smart crisis leaders master what can be called "rapid facilitation" – the ability to quickly spot key disagreements, zero in on critical issues, and get enough buy-in to move forward without waiting for everyone to agree.

Symbolic vs practical leadership

Crisis leaders have to be both steady presence and hands-on problem-solver. Partners need to trust the leader's ability to steer through rough waters, but they also expect concrete actions and visible results.

Symbolic leadership means communication, projecting control, and showing confidence and resolve. Practical leadership means digging into data, making hard choices, coordinating execution, and tracking progress.

Getting this balance right is everything. Leaders who focus only on the symbolic stuff look lightweight. Those who disappear into operational weeds lose the ability to rally and unite the team.

The only consensus that matters in a crisis

These dynamics point to a game-changing insight. In a crisis, you don't need consensus on every issue – just on one thing: who's going to run the show.

Revolutionary simplicity

This breaks completely from traditional partnership thinking, which tries to get agreement on every major decision. Under normal conditions, that works – there's time to hash things out, the stakes aren't life-or-death, and you can fix mistakes.

Crisis flips the script. Trying to reach consensus on every decision when time is running out and everything's on the line leads to disaster. While partners debate the fine points, competitors steal their clients.

The breakthrough is shifting consensus from what to decide to who decides. Not the content of decisions, but who gets to make them.

Consensus on trust, not tactics

When partners agree to hand crisis management to a specific leader, they're not rubber-stamping every future decision. They're giving that person the authority to make calls on the firm's behalf during the emergency.

This is totally different. It's based not on agreement about specific moves, but on shared confidence in the leader's judgment and character. Partners might hate individual decisions, but they accept the leader's right to make them.

This frees up massive amounts of time and energy – both in desperately short supply during crisis. Instead of endless arguments about what to do, everyone focuses on giving the leader the information and resources needed to decide well.

Conditions for success

This approach only works if you've set up the right conditions:

- *Advance planning.* Crisis triggers, handoff procedures, oversight rules, and accountability – all defined ahead of time, when heads are cool. In a crisis, there's no time to invent new systems.
- *Deep trust.* Partners have to believe the leader will act for the firm, not use the crisis to grab power. This kind of trust can't be whipped up overnight – it builds over years.
- *Time limits.* Crisis powers need clear expiration dates, with extensions only by partner vote. Emergency measures can't become the new normal.
- *Post-crisis review.* Once the dust settles, honest assessment of what worked and what didn't. This isn't about pointing fingers – it's about learning.
- *Exit rights.* Partners who fundamentally disagree with the crisis leader's direction have to be able to leave on fair terms. This safety valve prevents toxic resentment from building up.

The main lesson

Crises teach partnership firms a vital lesson – decent decisions made fast beat perfect decisions made too late. The only way to get that speed is to agree beforehand on who will decide – and how – when there's no time for long discussions.

Harmony is a luxury only stable firms can afford. Working decision systems are essential for survival when everything's falling apart.

This thinking points to a new understanding of consensus – not as everyone thinking the same way, but as effective systems for running complex organizations in an uncertain world. These principles form the foundation of the TRUE Consensus approach.

TRUE consensus – a practical framework

After slogging through all the traps, contradictions, and twisted versions of partnership consensus, the obvious question hits you – what's the right way to do this? Is there actually a reliable method to tell real agreement from all its cheap imitations? Can we build decisions that won't crumble the moment they hit reality?

Years of watching law firm partnerships handle everything from routine meetings to life-or-death crises have revealed four key markers that separate lasting consensus from its various knockoffs. These markers form the backbone of a practical tool that helps partners build decisions tough enough to survive both time and pressure.

How do you know whether your partnership decision represents genuine consensus or just another fake agreement dressed up as unity? Put it through the TRUE framework – four crucial tests of sustainable agreement (see Table 8.2 on the next page).

The framework works as a diagnostic. If your decision passes all four tests, it's got a real shot at working. Fail even one? Better get back to the drawing board before it's too late.

T – TRUST: the safety to disagree

You can safely say "no" without fear of punishment or getting frozen out.

The first and most crucial marker of real consensus is the ability to disagree with it. Sounds backwards, maybe, but there it is – the safer it is to voice dissent, the more likely you are to reach genuine agreement.

What safe disagreement looks like

In a healthy partnership, any partner can say, "I don't buy this decision" or, "I need more time to think this through" or, "I'm seeing serious risks we haven't talked about" – without worrying about payback to their status, income, or relationships with colleagues.

The safety to disagree isn't some abstract ideal. It's a real atmosphere you can actually feel in the room. A partner should be able to openly voice doubts without getting accused of being difficult. They can ask for more information without facing charges of not trusting their colleagues. They're free to suggest alternatives without getting tagged as the troublemaker who kills momentum.

Even better, a partner has the right to sit out a vote without worrying about getting shut out of the "inner circle". They can change their position during discussion without losing face. This freedom to maneuver is absolutely essential to making good decisions.

How to test for trust

Think back to a recent big decision at your firm. Did anyone publicly voice serious doubts? If every decision sailed through "unanimously" without a single pushback – that's a red flag. Chances are, your system doesn't actually feel safe for expressing disagreement.

Table 8.2: The TRUE consensus framework

Element	What it means	Key test questions
T **TRUST** **The safety to disagree**	Partners can openly voice doubts, change their minds, or abstain without fear of punishment or being frozen out. Dissent is welcomed as a gift that improves decisions.	• Did anyone publicly voice serious doubts? • Were concerns heard with interest or talked down? • Can partners change positions without losing face?
R **RATIONALE** **Shared logic behind the decision**	Everyone understands *why* this specific decision was made, what alternatives were considered, and why they were rejected. The logic is transparent and explainable.	• Can each partner explain the decision to an outsider? • Do explanations vary wildly? • Are expected outcomes concrete and measurable?
U **UNITY** **A decision that brings people together**	The decision energizes people and creates momentum. It is not just a compromise that satisfies no one. People feel ownership, not resignation.	• Are people energized or exhausted? • Is this "good enough" or genuinely exciting? • Do people own it or just accept it?
E **ENGAGEMENT** **Amplified energy for implementation**	Partners are ready to actively make it happen, not just delegate to others. Implementation discussions are concrete and enthusiastic.	• Are people ready to personally invest time? • Do they see their role in making it work? • Is implementation talk concrete or vague?

Watch how the group reacts when someone raises concerns. Do they get heard with real interest, or are they immediately talked down? Are their questions treated as ways to improve the decision, or as roadblocks slowing things down?

Another telltale sign – does your firm have partners who regularly ask "uncomfortable" questions while staying respected by their colleagues? If not, dissent might be getting punished in sneakier ways than you realize.

Common trust violations

- *Emotional manipulation* masquerades as efficiency. "We're all beat from these discussions, let's just decide" sounds reasonable enough, but creates the feeling that more questions are selfish time-wasting. The partner wanting to dig deeper suddenly becomes the one holding everyone hostage.
- *Moral pressure* appeals to the partnership's noble values. "We need to show unity in front of clients." "Competitors can't see our divisions." "Staff will lose confidence in leadership." These arguments turn any disagreement into betrayal of the common good. Who wants to be the party-pooper?
- *Artificial deadlines* create fake time pressure. "We've only got thirty minutes because there's another meeting after." Boundaries like these prevent real exploration of doubts and force people to accept the first decent option.
- *Expert intimidation* shuts down doubt through appeals to competence. "Those who really understand this issue support the decision." Statements like these turn disagreement into admitting you're out of your depth. Nobody wants to publicly confess ignorance.

Building real trust

Trust can't be created through speeches or policies. It builds through countless small moments and reactions that pile up over months and years. When leaders thank people for criticism instead of getting defensive, they show that truth matters more than personal comfort. When "uncomfortable" questions get treated as gifts that make decisions better rather than obstacles to bulldoze, you create a culture where doubt is welcome.

Especially telling is how the group responds to partners who change their minds based on arguments. If flexibility gets recognized and rewarded, people won't fear rethinking their positions. If changing your mind looks like weakness or flip-flopping, people will stubbornly stick to wrong positions to save face.

Just as crucial is how you handle decisions made despite voiced concerns. If such decisions regularly get revisited and tweaked, people know their warnings weren't ignored – just put on hold pending more information. If doubts stay unaddressed even when decisions blow up, partners quickly learn the lesson – better to keep quiet than waste time on useless warnings.

R – RATIONALE: shared logic behind the decision

Everyone understands why this specific decision got made – the logic doesn't disappear into the fog of "because we all agreed".

Real consensus demands more than just going along with a decision – it requires understanding the thinking behind it. Everyone should be able to explain why this particular option won, what factors mattered, what alternatives got shot down, and why.

What shared logic looks like

Problem understanding needs to be consistent across the group. This doesn't mean everyone sees things identically, but the basic facts, root causes, and consequences of doing nothing should be interpreted similarly. If one partner views the situation as a crisis while another sees routine hassle, there's no foundation for shared thinking.

Evaluation criteria also need upfront agreement. What matters most here – speed or quality? Does short-term profit trump long-term reputation? Should we play it safe or swing for the fences? Without settling these questions, people will judge identical options against different yardsticks and reach opposite conclusions.

Analysis of alternatives assumes the main options got considered with honest assessment of their pros and cons. The selection logic should be clear and make sense to anyone looking at it. People must understand – and be able to explain – why other approaches got rejected. And the explanation shouldn't be, "We didn't have time to discuss it," but rather, "This better fits our agreed priorities". If the choice relied on gut feeling, personal preferences, or hidden factors, there's no shared logic.

Finally, *expected outcomes* need to be concrete enough that you can judge whether the decision worked after a set period. Vague goals like "improve the situation" or "increase efficiency" don't allow for real evaluation or learning from what happened.

How to test the logic

Simple test: ask each partner to explain the decision to someone who wasn't in the room. If the explanations vary wildly, there's no shared understanding.

Another approach: ask people to name the three main reasons this specific decision got made. Do these reasons line up across different people? Can they explain why alternatives got rejected?

Pay attention to the language used when describing decisions. If vague statements dominate ("It's the right thing," "This will be better," "Everyone agrees") while specific arguments are missing, chances are there's no real logic.

Common logic problems

The biggest trap is substituting authority for reasoning. Instead of analyzing arguments, the group relies on rank or experience: "The managing partner thinks this is right, and he knows these issues better than anyone". This might work in straightforward situations, but in complex cases even experts get it wrong, and their opinions need testing against logic.

Just as dangerous is circular reasoning, where the fact of reaching agreement gets used as proof the decision is correct. "We made this decision because everyone agreed" – sounds reasonable, but doesn't explain why this particular option beats the others.

Emotional arguments often dress themselves up as rational justifications. "This decision will boost team morale" or "Staff will be happy" – points like these appeal to feelings but don't explain the business logic behind the choice.

Incomplete analysis shows up when only one or two options get considered while other possibilities get ignored without explanation. The group might not even realize alternatives exist if the search for solutions was shallow.

Especially sneaky are hidden assumptions – when decisions rest on beliefs that seem so obvious to participants they don't need stating. Yet these unspoken premises often become the source of future problems.

Building quality logic

Quality logic doesn't just happen – it comes from a deliberate thinking process that roughly breaks into stages.

It starts with honest diagnosis of the situation. What exactly needs deciding? People need to dig down to the root problem rather than stopping at surface symptoms. Important too is understanding the cost of doing nothing – what happens if we leave things as they are?

Next stage: defining evaluation criteria. What principles will the group use to compare options? What constraints absolutely must be considered – time, money, reputation? These criteria must be spelled out, otherwise everyone will judge decisions against their own hidden priorities.

Then comes generating alternatives. Here it's crucial not to settle for the first options that come to mind, but to hunt for less obvious yet potentially better approaches. The more alternatives considered, the higher the chance of finding a truly optimal solution.

Comparative analysis demands honest evaluation of each alternative against agreed criteria. No room here for emotional preferences or hidden agendas – just facts and logic.

The final choice should rest on clear understanding of why this particular option best fits the situation and criteria. And crucially, it's essential to ensure all participants can explain this logic – only then can you speak of shared decision reasoning.

U – UNITY: a decision that brings people together

This decision brings people together – it doesn't just satisfy everyone "a little" or represent "the least bad option".

Real consensus creates a sense of shared mission, not just an absence of open rebellion. Partners should feel the decision reflects their common values and interests, rather than being the result of mutual horse-trading whittled down to whatever everyone can barely stomach.

What a unifying decision looks like

Genuine unity starts with shared purpose – everyone sees the decision as a path toward goals they all want. They understand that each person's success helps everyone else succeed, rather than coming at someone else's expense. This is fundamentally different from compromise, where each side gives up part of what they want for the collective result.

Just as important is alignment with values – the decision can't violate principles that matter to people. If partners value quality, the decision can't be based on cutting corners to save money. If the team prides itself on reputation, the chosen path should build it up, not put it at risk.

Closely tied to values is positive motivation. People support the decision not because there aren't better choices, but because they see real opportunities for growth. This kind of motivation creates willingness to invest time and energy in making it work, because people genuinely believe in where it's headed.

Especially crucial is collective ownership – everyone should feel like co-creators of the decision. Nobody feels like a victim of circumstances or a passive follower of someone else's orders. Each person understands their role in shared success and is ready to be held accountable for results.

However, unity is easily faked, and false agreement often poses as the real thing. Most commonly it's born from exhaustion with endless discussions, when people are ready to accept any decision just to end the debate. "Let's just decide something already" – a classic phrase that signals this kind of fake alignment.

Fear of conflict is another common source of false unity. People go along with a decision not because they like it, but because they're afraid of damaging relationships with colleagues. "Better to agree with a bad decision than have a fight" – logic like this might preserve peace short-term, but creates hidden resentment that erupts later.

Similar effects come from time pressure. "We don't have time to find a better option, we need to decide now" – statements like these force people to accept the first decent solution, even when they can see its problems. Choice becomes performance art.

Sometimes the illusion of unity stems from lack of alternatives. When it seems there are no other options, people accept the single proposal not from enthusiasm, but from having no choice. This kind of resignation easily gets mistaken for agreement.

Finally, mutual concessions down to the lowest common denominator often get packaged as consensus. "Everyone gives up something, but overall it's fair" – logic like this might sound reasonable, but actually produces a decision that truly satisfies nobody.

Real unity differs completely from all these knockoffs because a unifying decision actually energizes people. They see not constraints but new possibilities. Their interests aren't just accommodated – they're woven together so that one person's success boosts everyone else's.

How to test for unity

Pay attention to the energy in the room. The best gauge of real unity is how the discussion feels. When a group moves toward genuine consensus, people's enthusiasm builds as the conversation develops. They start riffing off each other's ideas, spotting new opportunities, suggesting ways to make the decision even better. A sense of creative momentum emerges where everyone's input makes the whole thing stronger.

False unity follows the opposite pattern. The group's energy slowly bleeds away, people get tired of talking and want to wrap things up. Agreement comes not on a wave of excitement but in a fog of collective burnout.

Another telltale sign – the mood when people discuss the decision after the meeting ends. If they share it with excitement and pride, unity is probably real. If their words carry doubts, regrets, or buried frustration, they've probably reached just a compromise that might not survive contact with reality.

Also worth watching – people's willingness to put extra resources into making the decision work. When people genuinely support the chosen path, they're ready to invest more time and effort than technically required. They look for ways to improve the outcome rather than just doing the bare minimum.

Obstacles to unity

Understanding what kills genuine unity helps avoid common traps. *Hidden agendas* destroy unity before it starts. When some people are pursuing goals they won't discuss openly, real alignment becomes impossible. The group might reach formal agreement, but it's brittle, built on incomplete information.

A similar problem is *unequal influence*, which creates decisions that reflect powerful people's interests at weaker people's expense. On the surface this might look like unity, especially if less influential partners don't dare openly object. But real coming-together doesn't happen – disguised arm-twisting does.

Time pressure also prevents the hunt for creative solutions that could work for everyone. When time is tight, groups tend to pick from ready-made options rather than building new, more sophisticated approaches.

Often the problem is simply *lack of creativity*. People might genuinely want to find a path that works for everyone but lack the skills or experience to discover such options. So they have to settle for compromises.

Finally, *focusing on problems rather than possibilities* channels energy in destructive directions. When discussion centers on what people want to avoid rather than what they want to achieve, finding an inspiring decision becomes nearly impossible. Fears unite people more weakly than dreams.

Creating unity

Real unity doesn't just happen – it requires deliberate effort and a particular approach to decision making. The key is shifting focus from hunting for compromises to hunting for synergy, where people's interests don't just get accommodated but actually strengthen each other.

Building unity starts with shared values and goals. Before diving into specific decisions, make sure everyone understands and buys into the basic principles guiding the team. When people are aligned on what really matters, finding paths that energize everyone becomes much easier.

Next step – invest time in understanding what each person actually needs. Surface-level knowledge of colleagues' positions won't allow for creative solutions. You need to understand not just what people want, but why it matters to them. Often different demands hide identical underlying needs, and uncovering these opens the door to elegant solutions.

Crucial is hunting for opportunities rather than constraints. Instead of asking, "How do we split up limited resources?" try asking, "How can we create more value for everyone?" This approach opens space for innovative solutions that previously seemed impossible.

This requires encouraging creativity and experimentation. Standard solutions rarely create genuine unity because they're based on past experience and established patterns. The group needs permission to explore unconventional options, even if they seem risky at first.

Just as important is creating a safe space for expressing doubts and alternative ideas. Unity achieved by squashing disagreement is fragile and short-lived. Real strength emerges when different viewpoints get openly discussed and woven into a more sophisticated decision.

Finally, constantly check the emotional response to the decision. Genuine unity always carries positive energy. If people agree with the decision rationally but remain emotionally flat, it's probably a compromise, not consensus.

E – ENGAGEMENT: amplified energy for implementation

After agreeing, partners don't disappear – they dive into implementation with renewed energy, not thoughts of, "I was against this from the start".

The fourth and final test of real consensus is people's readiness to actively make the decision work. Simply not fighting it isn't enough – you need positive energy, and genuine desire to contribute to success.

What engagement looks like

Real engagement always starts with taking initiative. Partners come up with implementation approaches without waiting for marching orders from above. They spot opportunities where others see only chores, and jump at the chance to lead.

Just as important is resource commitment – people willingly invest their time, knowledge, and connections in bringing the decision to life. This isn't grudging allocation of the bare minimum, but readiness to contribute more than the job description requires, because the project's success feels personally important.

Especially valuable is flexibility during implementation. When inevitable problems and roadblocks appear, truly engaged people hunt for solutions rather than using difficulties as excuses to ditch the original plan. They see obstacles as puzzles requiring creative approaches.

Genuine engagement also shows up in willingness to sell the decision – partners eagerly tell others about it, explain its logic, rally colleagues to participate. They become natural evangelists for the chosen course because they genuinely believe in its merit.

Finally, active feedback matters. People regularly share updates about implementation progress, suggest adjustments, report new opportunities. They don't just execute their piece of work in isolation but stay plugged into the collective effort.

Signs of forced participation

Forced participation, meanwhile, is easily spotted by its minimalism – people do exactly what's required, no more and no less. "They told me to prepare a report by Friday – here's the report" is the classic position of the reluctant executor.

Just as telling is going through the motions. People follow the letter of the decision while ignoring its spirit. They perform prescribed actions but don't question whether the desired result is actually happening.

Passivity shows up in constantly waiting for detailed instructions instead of showing initiative. "What should I do next?" is a frequent question from those participating under protest.

Often, forced participation turns into quiet sabotage – hunting for reasons why the decision can't be implemented. "We tried, but clients aren't ready for such changes" – explanations like this often mask unwillingness to put in real effort.

Especially characteristic is dodging responsibility. "I warned this wouldn't work" – declarations like this appear at the first sign of trouble and signal that internal buy-in never happened.

Real engagement vs going through the motions
Genuine engagement differs completely from all these patterns. It shows up as creative approach to implementation – people don't just follow instructions but look for better ways to achieve the goal. They're ready to exceed expectations, do more than the minimum, because they feel personally invested in the outcome.

Real engagement always involves active collaboration – people don't retreat into their own tasks but look for chances to work productively with colleagues. They see problems as shared challenges requiring team solutions.

The ultimate mark of engagement is feeling personal responsibility for collective success. "This is our decision, and I'm on the hook for making it work" – an attitude like this fundamentally changes execution quality.

How to measure engagement
The most reliable method – watch people's behavior in the first weeks after making the decision. Genuine engagement shows up quickly and clearly; it's hard to fake long-term.

Worth noting is speed of getting started. When people truly support a decision, they don't delay implementation but push to move from talk to action as quickly as possible. Stalling and hunting for reasons to postpone often signal internal resistance.

Just as revealing is execution quality – whether it's by-the-book or creative. Engaged people don't limit themselves to literal instruction-following but think about how to make results better.

A key indicator is initiative in solving problems that pop up. Obstacles are inevitable in any project, but reactions to them reveal a lot about internal motivation. Engaged people see difficulties as puzzles requiring solutions, not as excuses for failure.

Also important is willingness to bear extra costs in time, effort, or resources. When people genuinely support a cause, they're ready to invest more than the formally required minimum.

Finally, a telling detail is the excitement when discussing progress. If people enjoy sharing achieved milestones, discoveries and insights, this shows genuine absorption in the process.

Especially important is reaction to obstacles. If at the first difficulty people start recalling their initial doubts ("I said this wouldn't work"), it means agreement was surface-deep and the decision never became truly unifying.

Common obstacles to engagement

Even with genuine desire to create active participation, many factors can kill people's engagement. *Lack of real influence* over decision making is one of the biggest roadblocks. When people know their opinion gets heard out of courtesy but doesn't affect the final choice, their willingness to actively participate in implementation naturally tanks.

A serious barrier is *unclear personal payoff*. If people don't understand how their efforts will affect career, income, or professional development, expecting enthusiasm becomes unrealistic. Abstract promises of "this will benefit everyone" don't substitute for concrete understanding of what's in it for them.

Mismatch between tasks and skills also kills motivation. When people are required to do things they're neither good at nor interested in, they feel awkward and try to minimize participation. This hurts especially when the person knows there are colleagues who'd handle the task much better.

Unrealistic expectations quickly turn enthusiasm into disappointment. When goals are impossible to achieve due to insufficient time, resources, or authority, even the most motivated people start backing away to avoid getting tagged with predictable failure.

Especially toxic is *ignoring contributions and achievements*. When someone's efforts go unnoticed or get credited to others, persistent unwillingness to put in extra effort takes hold. "Why bother if nobody notices anyway?" – logic like this spreads quickly through a team.

No feedback about overall progress also reduces engagement. When people work in an information black hole, not understanding how their actions influence collective results, the sense that their contribution matters gets lost.

Creating real engagement

Genuine engagement requires deliberately creating the right conditions. The process starts at the decision-making stage, when it's crucial to ensure maximum participation from everyone involved in discussion and decision development. The more people influence plan formation, the stronger their subsequent commitment to implementation.

Critically important is clearly spelling out the personal value of participation for each individual. Explaining why the decision benefits the company overall isn't enough – you need to show how it will affect a specific person's career, skills, status, or financial position. This connection must be concrete and understandable, not abstract.

Hand out roles that play to people's strengths. When tasks align with people's skills and interests, execution quality improves naturally. It's worth spending time figuring out who's good at what and enjoys doing what, then using that knowledge during planning.

Also necessary is setting realistic expectations and timelines. Unrealistic plans not only reduce motivation but undermine trust in leadership. Better to allow more time and beat expectations than constantly explain why goals weren't met.

Special attention should go toward creating a recognition and feedback system. People should regularly get updates about how their work influences overall results, which achievements have been noticed, what's working especially well. Positive feedback sustains energy and motivation throughout the entire implementation process.

It's important to keep open dialogue going throughout implementation. When people can freely share doubts, suggestions, and observations, the decision stays alive and adapts to changing circumstances. This prevents buildup of hidden frustration and maintains the sense of collective responsibility.

Finally, it's worth planning shared victories along the way – moments when the team can collectively celebrate achieved progress. Events like these strengthen team spirit and remind people that their efforts are producing results.

Applying TRUE consensus

The framework works both when making decisions (to prevent problems) and when analyzing decisions already made (to diagnose what went wrong).

Preventative use

Before closing discussion on any important issue, run a quick check against the four criteria:

- *Trust:* Does anyone feel they can't openly voice their doubts?
- *Rationale:* Can each person explain the decision's logic to an outsider?
- *Unity:* Does the decision energize people, or are they agreeing out of exhaustion/resignation?
- *Engagement:* Are people ready to actively make it happen, or planning to dump it on others?

If even one criterion isn't met, keep talking.

Diagnostic use

If a decision is getting stuck in implementation, analyze it against TRUE criteria:

- Maybe people were afraid to share their doubts (Trust problem).
- Maybe people understand goals and methods differently (Rationale problem).
- Maybe the decision is a compromise that excites nobody (Unity problem).
- Maybe people formally agreed but internally aren't ready to put in real effort (Engagement problem).

Spotting the problem area helps focus efforts on fixing it.

TRUE consensus isn't a magic bullet for partnership governance problems, but it is a practical tool for improving collective decision quality. It helps tell genuine agreement from its many fakes and build decisions that can survive both time and chaos.

In a world where change keeps accelerating and the cost of mistakes keeps climbing, the ability to create real consensus becomes a crucial competitive edge. Partnerships that master this approach gain the power to make better decisions and execute them more effectively.

References

1 Mansbridge, Jane (1983). *Beyond Adversary Democracy*. Chicago: University of Chicago Press.

2 Habermas, Jürgen (1984). *The Theory of Communicative Action*. Vol. 1. Boston: Beacon Press.

3 Marcuse, Herbert (1965). "Repressive Tolerance." In *A Critique of Pure Tolerance*, edited by Robert Paul Wolff, Barrington Moore Jr., and Herbert Marcuse, 81–123. Boston: Beacon Press.

4 Sunstein, Cass R. (2006). *Infotopia: How Many Minds Produce Knowledge*. Oxford: Oxford University Press.

5 Janis, Irving L. (1972). *Victims of Groupthink: A Psychological Study of Foreign-Policy Decisions and Fiascoes*. Boston: Houghton Mifflin.

6, 7 Janis, Irving L. (1972). *Victims of Groupthink: A Psychological Study of Foreign-Policy Decisions and Fiascoes*. Boston: Houghton Mifflin.

Part IV: How Law Firms Choose Their Strategy

Chapter 9: The philosophy of partnership

The architectural decisions that determine everything – and whether you can change them

Every law firm takes shape through dozens of architectural decisions, whether you make them consciously or stumble into them by accident. Some partners agonize over every step, others trust their gut, still others simply copy successful competitors. However you make them, these decisions determine not just how you operate today but what growth becomes possible, what constraints you'll face, and how you'll handle the inevitable crises.

Here's what makes architectural choices treacherous – their consequences don't show up immediately. The decision to work with government or keep your distance from power may seem tactical – until political winds shift. The choice between exclusivity and volume looks like a positioning question – until you hit your growth ceiling or face pricing pressure. Betting on individual partner brands feels natural – right up until your star player decides to launch their own firm.

There are no universally correct answers – only answers that match your ambitions, resources, and understanding of the market. What matters is making these choices deliberately, grasping their long-term consequences.

The architectural framework – five layers of decision making

Think of your firm as a building. The foundation determines what you can build on top. Load-bearing walls define the basic structure. Interior partitions can be moved, but only within constraints set by those walls. The façade signals to the world what kind of building this is. And the mechanical systems – invisible but essential – keep everything running.

Law firms work the same way. Some decisions create the foundation – nearly impossible to change without rebuilding from scratch. Others sit higher up the stack, more flexible but still constrained by what lies beneath. Know which layer each decision belongs to and you'll know two critical things – how hard it'll be to change, and how much you'll break trying.

Meta-choices sit at the bottom – the partnership's core philosophy about what matters and why you're working together. Is this firm a vehicle for individual wealth creation or a collective enterprise building something larger than any single partner? Do partners see themselves as owners investing in a long-term asset, or as high-paid professionals extracting maximum current income? These aren't just cultural questions – they're architectural. They determine whether aggressive reinvestment makes sense, whether young partners will ever become true equity holders, whether the firm can survive the departure of a rainmaker.

Strategic positioning sits on top of that foundation. Who you serve, what you're known for, where you compete – these choices flow from your philosophical commitments but create their own constraints. A firm built around government relationships operates by different rules than one serving private entrepreneurs. Generalists play a different game than specialists. Elite boutiques can't suddenly pivot to volume – high-volume operators can't easily claim premium positioning. The market won't let them.

Your service model defines how you actually deliver on that positioning. Retainers versus projects. Standardized solutions versus bespoke advice. Partner-led versus team-based delivery. Fixed fees or hourly billing. Each choice creates operational requirements and economic logic. You can't run a high-volume standardized practice with a partner-heavy model – the economics don't work. You can't maintain premium positioning while delegating most work to junior associates – clients won't pay for it.

Your organizational model brings structure to service delivery. How you're organized internally, how decisions get made, how you develop talent, how you share (or don't share) financial rewards. All of this has to align with everything below it. If your positioning requires deep specialization but your compensation system rewards individual client origination above all else, you've created structural tension. If your service model demands sophisticated project management but your org chart is flat and consensus-driven, nothing will actually get managed.

Execution mechanics sit at the top – systems, processes, tools. This is where most firms focus their energy, because it feels tangible and controllable. A new CRM system. Revised billing procedures. Knowledge management initiative. These matter, but they succeed or fail based on alignment with the layers beneath. The fanciest project management software won't fix a service model that doesn't actually deliver what clients want. The most sophisticated knowledge database can't overcome a culture where sharing expertise threatens individual power.

Why architectural decisions are so hard to reverse

The deeper the layer, the harder to change – but not for the reasons partners typically think. It's not that changing partnership philosophy or strategic positioning is technically difficult. The problem is everything you've built on top of those decisions.

Consider a firm that started with a hunter philosophy – strong individual partners, decentralized decision making, each partner essentially running their own book. Over 15 years, it's attracted a certain type of partner – entrepreneurial, independent, protective of their client relationships. It's developed compensation systems that reward individual origination. Its brand in the market emphasizes partner expertise rather than firm capabilities. Clients have relationships with specific partners, not with the firm.

Now imagine this firm decides to pivot towards a farmer philosophy – collective approach, shared clients, coordinated strategy. What actually has to change?

First, compensation. The current system rewards individual hunters. You can't just announce "we're farmers now" while keeping the old formula – behavior follows incentives. But changing compensation means some partners will earn less. Which means they'll leave. Which means losing their clients and revenue. Which threatens the firm's financial stability. You might phase it in gradually. But then you're running two systems simultaneously, creating confusion and resentment.

Second, people. Your current partners joined precisely because they wanted to be hunters. They'll resist becoming farmers, or they'll leave for firms that still reward individual performance. You'll need to recruit different partners, but your reputation in the market is as a hunter firm. The farmers you want to attract don't see you as their natural home.

Third, clients. They chose your firm partly because they wanted access to specific partners. Tell them, "Actually, you'll now work with our team" and some will balk. Tell departing partners they can't take their clients and they'll challenge you legally, arguing those were always personal relationships.

Fourth, systems. Everything from how you structure engagements to how you manage knowledge to how you develop junior lawyers was built for the hunter model. Now you need to rebuild it all for farmers. While still running the business. While managing the transition. While bleeding revenue from partners who've left.

This is why architectural decisions matter so much. Not because they're technically hard to reverse, but because reversing them means unbuilding everything you've constructed on top of them, then rebuilding it all while the business keeps running. It's like trying to change a building's foundation while people are still living in it.

The illusion of gradual change

Faced with the difficulty of architectural change, most firms reach for the same solution – we'll do it gradually. We'll phase it in. We'll find a middle ground.

This rarely works as planned. Some architectural decisions don't have a middle ground. You either maintain confidential compensation or you don't. You either have lockstep partnership progression or you have discretionary points. The middle ground – "We'll share some information but not all" or "We'll have mostly lockstep but with some discretion" – often gives you the worst of both approaches.

Other changes can't be phased because they need critical mass to work. Moving from individual billing to team-based delivery doesn't help if only 30 percent of partners participate – you just create confusion about how the firm actually operates. Trying to build a collaborative culture while keeping individual-focused compensation in place doesn't produce gradual change, it produces cognitive dissonance.

But here's the real problem with gradual change – it prolongs internal conflict and uncertainty. During the transition, different partners hold incompatible mental models of what the firm is and where it's heading. Every decision becomes an argument about philosophy rather than pragmatics. "Should we hire this lateral partner?" turns into "Are we hunters or farmers?". "How should we structure this engagement?" becomes "Are we premium or volume?". Years can pass in this liminal state, with enormous energy spent on internal debates rather than serving clients or developing the business.

Which isn't to say architectural change is impossible. It just means acknowledging that you're essentially creating a new firm within the shell of the old one. Some partners will come along. Others won't. Some clients will stick. Others will follow departing partners. Revenue will probably drop before it recovers. This kind of change is possible – but only if you're honest about what it entails and whether you have the stomach for it.

How to make better architectural decisions

So how should you approach them, given how consequential they are and how hard they are to reverse?

- *Make them explicit.* Most architectural problems don't come from choosing wrong – they come from never choosing at all. Partnerships drift into positions through accumulated small decisions and unstated assumptions. Then they discover they've been operating under incompatible models all along. Better to force the conversation early, when you still have flexibility to choose consciously rather than discover later what you've inadvertently chosen by default.
- *Test for coherence across layers.* Each architectural decision should logically support the ones below it and enable the ones above it. If your meta-choice is to be investors building long-term value, but your service model is high-volume transactional work with wafer-thin margins, something's wrong. If your positioning is premium specialists but your compensation system rewards partner volume above expertise, you've created structural tension. Map out your decisions across all five layers and look for contradictions.
- *Recognize path dependence.* Where you've been constrains where you can go. A firm built around government relationships can't easily pivot to private equity. A generalist practice can't suddenly become sector specialists. A lockstep partnership can't quickly adopt eat-what-you-kill compensation. Not because these changes are impossible, but because pulling them off means acknowledging that you're essentially starting a different firm. Sometimes that's the right move – but it's a rebuild, not a renovation.
- *Accept that optimization has costs.* Every architectural choice optimizes for some outcomes while making others harder to achieve. Specialization delivers expertise but limits market size. High margins per client mean limiting client volume. Strong individual brands create exit risks. Distributed decision-making enables entrepreneurship but slows strategic pivots. Don't pretend you can have everything. Choose what matters most and accept the tradeoffs.
- *Build in flexibility at the edges.* You can't make core architecture flexible – trying to leads to incoherence. But you can design the organization to experiment at the margins. Create space for pilots and test cases that don't commit the whole firm. Allow individual partners or practice groups some autonomy to explore different approaches. When market conditions change, you'll have data about what works rather than just theoretical debates about strategic direction.

Here's what most partners miss – the hardest part of architectural thinking isn't making individual decisions, it's recognizing that you're making them at all. Most partners don't wake up thinking, "Today I'll make foundational choices that will constrain this firm for the next decade". They think they're just solving immediate problems – hiring this person, taking this case, setting this price, adjusting this compensation formula. But those tactical decisions, accumulated over time, become architecture. The question isn't whether you'll make architectural choices – you're making them right now, whether you realize it or not. The question is whether you'll make them consciously. See Table 9.1.

Table 9.1: The five layers of architectural decisions

Layer	What it defines	Key questions	Difficulty to change
Layer 1 Meta-Choices (Foundation)	Partnership philosophy – what matters and why you work together Core values and fundamental beliefs about fairness, success, time horizons	Hunters or farmers? Renters or investors? Transparent or confidential? Growth or balance? Serve firm or be served?	EXTREMELY HARD ⚠⚠⚠⚠⚠ Changing this means rebuilding everything above it
Layer 2 Strategic Positioning (Load-bearing walls)	Who you serve, what you are known for, where you compete Market identity and competitive stance	Exclusivity or volume? Local or global? State or business? Which clients, which matters?	VERY HARD ⚠⚠⚠⚠ Market reputation takes years to shift
Layer 3 Service Model (Internal structure)	How you deliver on positioning What you sell and how you produce it	Specialization or full-service? Formality or relationships? Innovation or tradition? Delivery model?	HARD ⚠⚠⚠ Requires operational overhaul and client re-education

continued on next page

Layer 4 Organizational Model (Interior layout)	Internal structure and governance How you organize, decide, compensate	Partnership or corporation? Personal brands or corporate brand? Individual or team rewards? Power distribution?	MODERATE ⚠⚠ Painful but feasible with commitment
Layer 5 Execution Mechanics (Systems and tools)	Day-to-day systems and processes Tools, procedures, workflows	CRM systems? Billing procedures? Knowledge management? Project management? Technology stack?	EASY ⚠ Tangible, controllable, reversible

Critical insights:

The foundation fallacy: Most firms focus 80 percent of energy on Layer 5 (systems and tools) because it feels tangible and controllable. But Layer 5 succeeds or fails based on alignment with Layers 1-4. The fanciest CRM cannot fix a service model that does not deliver what clients want.

The reversal cost: The deeper the layer, the harder to change – not because it is technically difficult, but because everything built on top must be unbuilt and rebuilt. Changing meta-choices means reconstructing the entire firm while it keeps operating.

The coherence requirement: Each layer must logically support the ones below it and enable the ones above it. Tension between layers (e.g., farmer philosophy + hunter compensation) creates structural dysfunction that no amount of process improvement can fix.

The unconscious architecture: You are making architectural decisions right now, whether you realize it or not. Every hiring choice, pricing decision, and compensation adjustment accumulates into architecture. The question is not whether you will make architectural choices – it is whether you will make them consciously.

Meta-choices – the philosophy of partnership

Partners are brilliant at building consensus – and equally brilliant at sidestepping the most important questions. They can spend hours debating operational process details while avoiding any conversation about why they're actually working together in the first place.

Meta-choices are precisely those unspoken agreements that define a partnership's character for decades ahead. This hidden consensus rarely gets articulated openly yet influences every decision. When partners argue about whether to take on a new project or how to divide profits, what they're really arguing about is their fundamental beliefs on fairness, time, success, and relationships.

Here's the paradox – the more important the question, the less it gets discussed. Partners might spend six months choosing a new CRM system but never openly agree whether short-term profit or long-term development matters more to them. They'll write detailed procedures for hiring staff while never discussing whether they're willing to sacrifice family time for firm growth.

These unspoken philosophical differences don't vanish just because nobody mentions them. Quite the opposite – they determine the real logic behind decision making, creating invisible fault lines through the partnership. Sooner or later these differences surface, and you discover partners have spent years working together without understanding each other's basic motivations.

Meta-choices demand honest conversation about what each partner considers success, fairness, a life well lived. Uncomfortable topics, because they touch not on business technique but on the meaning of shared existence. Which is precisely why you can't stay silent about them. The cost of misunderstanding runs too high.

Hunters or farmers?

This choice defines the partnership's core philosophy – do you build around strong individuals or collective team strength?

Hunters believe in the power of personality. Each partner is a separate profit center, an independent fighter who wins through personal mastery. They see internal competition between partners as the engine of development – let everyone strive to outperform the rest. Management here is decentralized. Each hunter makes autonomous decisions in their patch. The leader is the best hunter – whoever's shown outstanding personal results.

Profit comes first, and they measure success in money. Hunters see themselves as "street fighters" – self-reliant, tough, capable of surviving any conditions.

Farmers, by contrast, believe in collective wisdom and synergy. The team can achieve more than the sum of its parts. Collaboration between partners matters more than internal competition. Shared strategy and focus deliver greater advantages than flexibility and scattered efforts. They make decisions in coordinated fashion, often unanimously. The leader in a farmer model is a wise mentor who unites people around common values. Mission and values come first – profit matters, but you've got to achieve it through methods that align with shared principles. Farmers see themselves as "team players" – people for whom collective success trumps personal ambition.

In a period of profound transformation, when technology is reshaping the very concept of legal services and clients are becoming impossibly unpredictable, can you afford to make an unequivocal choice? One successful example is the portfolio approach – 70 percent of revenue from stable farmer clients, 30 percent from hunting projects. But this demands resolving cultural contradictions: "Is it fair that he earns from one deal what I make in a year of daily graft?"

Perhaps the question is no longer whether you're a hunter or farmer. Perhaps what matters is how quickly you can switch between these roles depending on circumstances.

Renters or investors?

This choice touches on partners' fundamental attitude towards the asset they're collectively creating. Do they see the firm as a cash cow to be milked for maximum profit, or as a garden requiring patient cultivation for future harvests?

Renters think in "here and now" terms. For them, the firm is a tool for maximizing current income. Why put money aside for tomorrow when you can spend it today? They prefer high current distributions over long-term investments. Spare funds appear – divvy them up among partners. They only make infrastructure investments when under pressure – the office gets refurbished when it no longer impresses clients.

Investors see the firm as an asset whose value can and should be grown. They're willing to constrain current consumption for future growth. They reinvest a significant chunk of profits back into the business. New offices, modern technology, staff training, developing new practices – all viewed not as expenses but as investments. They think years ahead and accept temporary profit reductions for strategic goals.

But each approach carries its price. The renter model limits the firm's potential value growth – partners receive high current income but don't accumulate capital. The investment model demands financial discipline and long-term thinking. Not everyone's prepared to wait years to see returns on their money.

Transparent or confidential?

Do all partners know how much each of them earns? This seemingly technical question actually touches on fundamental principles of fairness and trust.

Transparent firms practice complete openness. All partners know the exact income figures for each colleague. The logic is straightforward – if the distribution formula is fair, why hide anything? Transparency eliminates suspicion and speculation, and encourages healthy competition within the partnership.

Confidential firms keep partner income information private. Everyone knows only their own figure. Advocates of confidentiality argue this reduces conflict – when people don't know exact numbers, there's less occasion for envy. Confidentiality also allows more flexible formula adjustments without triggering heated debates.

Here too there's no universal solution. Transparency can provoke conflict and jealousy, especially if income disparities are substantial. Confidentiality creates fertile ground for suspicion and speculation – partners may overestimate colleagues' earnings and undervalue the fairness of their own compensation.

Aggressive growth or work–life balance?

This choice defines what partners are actually running a joint business for. Are they willing to sacrifice personal time and comfort for ambitious goals?

Partners who choose aggressive growth live in constant forward motion. For them, business isn't merely a way to earn money but a form of self-actualization. They accept high work intensity – they see overtime, business travel, and working weekends as the normal price of success. These firms constantly set ambitious targets – double revenue in three years, become leaders in a new practice, open offices in five cities. Each achievement becomes the platform for the next leap.

The alternative philosophy puts partners' quality of life front and center.

Business should provide decent income, but not at the expense of health, family, and personal interests. These firms consciously limit growth pace to preserve a comfortable work rhythm. Partners value predictability – stable income, clear responsibilities, the ability to plan personal life.

Once again, each choice demands sacrifices. Aggressive growth can lead to burnout and problems in personal life. High ambitions don't always materialize, and failures hurt. Work–life balance may constrain the firm's growth potential – while partners enjoy stability, competitors might overtake them.

Serve the firm or be served?

This is the most fundamental choice, the one that shapes all other decisions. What comes first – the firm's interests as an institution, or the interests of the specific partners who created it?

"Serve the firm" means institutional thinking. Partners are willing to subordinate personal interests to the firm's strategic goals. They're building an institution that should outlive its founders and become greater than the sum of the people comprising it. In these firms, strategy comes first. If it demands painful decisions – replacing partners, reorganizing practices, investments at the expense of current income – partners make these sacrifices. Partnership here is a variable. Effectiveness matters more than loyalty.

"Be served" puts partners' interests and comfort front and center. The firm exists to provide partners not just income but a pleasant working environment, like-minded colleagues, a predictable future. In these firms, strategy is secondary – it can be altered to preserve harmony in the partnership. Peace and partnership cohesion are sacrosanct. Better to develop more slowly but keep the team intact.

Each choice carries its price. The institutional approach can create internal tension and lead to losing talented people who aren't prepared to subordinate personal interests to abstract strategic goals. The partnership-first approach may constrain the firm's growth and adaptability. The need to constantly accommodate all partners' interests slows decision making and can lead to missed opportunities.

How it all hangs together

These five dichotomies aren't independent of each other. Certain combinations create internal logic; others breed contradictions.

Hunter-renters with a "be served" philosophy form a coherent system – maximize personal short-term income from existing assets. Farmer-investors with a "serve the firm" philosophy (the opposite yet equally logical cluster) build an institution for long-term prosperity.

Trying to mix incompatible elements creates internal conflict. You can't be a renter with a growth mindset – growth demands investment. It's difficult to combine transparency with a "be served" philosophy – openness can disturb partnership harmony.

Unlike operational decisions, meta-choices are virtually irreversible without a generational shift in ownership. They shape the firm's DNA, its cultural code, its value system. Trying to radically change partnership philosophy usually leads to splits. Some partners leave, rejecting the new values. Those remaining start building the firm afresh, on a different foundation.

Meta-choices therefore demand particularly careful consideration and complete consensus among founding partners. This is the foundation upon which the entire firm will be built.

Strategic positioning – who we are in the market and for whom

Strategic positioning answers the most fundamental business questions: who are our clients, what do we offer them, and why should they choose us? In legal services, these questions become particularly tangled because the work is simultaneously deeply personal and rigidly standardized, locally specific and globally unified.

Three dilemmas determine where you sit in the competitive landscape. Each looks strategic on paper, but in practice they shape your daily operational calls – whom to hire, which projects to take, how to structure processes, where to hunt for growth.

Exclusivity vs volume

A thousand dollars per hour or a dollar per thousand?

Elite boutiques focus exclusively on the most fascinating matters and heavyweight clients. Meanwhile, large international networks pride themselves on volume – hundreds of corporate clients served through standardized products each month.

Two worlds. Two approaches. Two completely different understandings of what legal business actually means.

Exclusivity versus volume isn't just about pricing. It's a philosophy about whom you exist for and what your ideal working week looks like. Do you want to be Bentley or Toyota? And no, you can't be "premium Toyota" – the market won't believe you.

Boutiques for the chosen few

Elite firms naturally become the last resort for the most complex matters – people turn to them when everyone else has thrown in the towel. Their clients are Fortune 500 companies, private individuals with labyrinthine asset structures, or states resolving territorial disputes in international arbitration.

Exclusivity begins with refusal. In a proper boutique, they say "no" more often than "yes". Not because they don't want the money, but because reputation matters more. When you're known as the best in a narrow niche, each failed case can cost you ten future clients. Tax boutiques have been known to turn down multimillion-pound mandates for reputational reasons – insufficient probability of success outweighing financial appeal.

Exclusivity demands unique expertise, but not in everything at once. You can't be elite across the board – the market won't buy it. You can be the best in international arbitration, in M&A deals involving major corporates, or in tax planning for energy companies. But you can't be the best at everything.

Elite firms invest in personal service at levels mass-market players simply can't match. Client rings on Sunday – partner answers. Client needs an opinion for tomorrow's board meeting – your entire team works through the night. The philosophy – clients should never think about cost, only results.

Elite pricing works on value-based principles. Cost isn't determined by hours spent but by what the result's worth to the client. If your work saved them a hundred million, a million for the advice looks more than reasonable.

The high cost of exclusivity

Exclusivity doesn't come cheap. The biggest constraint? Market size. Even the most attractive niche has a ceiling. You can become the absolute best in a narrow field, then discover there's barely any demand for it. Maritime law, for example, might throw up a dozen major disputes a year if you're lucky.

Elite firms are also sitting ducks when market cycles turn. If your niche hits a crisis, you're stuck. Specialize in development projects and watch what happens when property markets collapse – generalist firms pivot to insolvency and restructuring work, while narrow specialists just... wait for things to pick up again.

Finding experts in niche fields is exponentially harder than recruiting solid all-rounders. Want to grow one internally? That's years of investment. Your candidate can't just know corporate law – they need to understand a specific industry inside out, grasp its regulatory landscape, have genuine experience dealing with relevant authorities. You're fishing in a very small pool.

Then there's reputational risk. Elite firms can only handle clients within their sweet spot. Everything else goes unmet. Major clients frequently want to hand over all their legal work to one firm, but specialists can only take their bit – the rest gets farmed out to competitors.

The multiservice factory

On the other side of the barricades sit the volume players. Their philosophy is diametrically opposite – maximum number of clients, standardized processes, predictable quality, accessible pricing.

The volume player philosophy rests on McDonald's principles – clients should know exactly what they'll get, what they'll pay, and when they'll get it – regardless of which office they walk into.

Volume begins with standardization. There are template products for template situations. Registering a company, sorting employment contracts, handling tax inspections – you do it all through proven algorithms. The lawyer becomes not a creator but a quality executor of tested procedures.

Technology plays a starring role in the volume model. CRM systems track every client, automated processes eliminate human error, knowledge bases let any staff member quickly find solutions to standard problems. Volume firms often invest more in IT than tech start-ups – technology becomes their main competitive edge.

Volume pricing underpins the entire economics. Margin per client is modest, but sheer numbers more than compensate. Instead of one client at a hundred thousand euros, they have a thousand clients at a hundred euros each.

Recruitment at volume firms follows the same standardized approach. You don't need stars – you need solid executors. People who can quickly master procedures and follow them precisely. Training runs on industrial scale, career paths are transparent and predictable.

The price of volume

But the volume model demands its own sacrifices. The main casualty? Depth of expertise. It's hard to be the best at everything simultaneously. Partners at multiservice firms often admit, we've got good lawyers across all areas, but in any narrow field there's a specialist boutique that knows the subject better.

Multiservice firms also scatter resources across numerous directions.

Investment in developing each practice area ends up smaller than what specialized competitors can manage. It's difficult to explain to the market what exactly you're best at when you do everything.

Multiservice firms can't charge the same premium rates as narrow specialists. They're forced to compete on price, which erodes profitability. And managing a multiservice firm proves far more complex – different practices demand different approaches to management, motivation, and development.

Clients can also encounter a sense of impersonality. The system can become self-serving – processes function, but nobody asks "why?" Partners start hiding behind rules to avoid discussing difficult situations.

Cultural worlds

The differences between elite and volume firms show up in every detail of corporate life.

In an elite boutique, the working day is unpredictable. You might leave at three in the afternoon or work until dawn – it depends on client needs. Planning holidays is tricky – what if an interesting matter crops up? But when you're working, you're working on genuinely significant projects that the entire industry will discuss afterwards.

In a volume firm, life runs more predictably. Working hours are regulated, procedures documented, holidays planned in advance. Less drama, more stability. In a day you might help ten clients solve their problems – not as earth-shattering as what elite players handle, but important to the specific people involved.

Your attitude to mistakes differs fundamentally too. In an elite firm, any error can cost reputation, so you elevate perfectionism to an absolute principle. In a volume firm, what matters more is a systematic approach – mistakes happen, but you need to identify and fix them quickly, preventing recurrence.

Elite firms build around partner expertise – flat structure, minimal hierarchy. The main thing is not getting in the stars' way. Volume firms resemble well-oiled machines with clear hierarchy and documented procedures. Standardization reigns supreme.

The perils of the middle ground

Naturally the question arises: what if we try taking the best from both models? But the middle ground here is the most dangerous path.

Attempts to create "accessible exclusivity" usually end in failure. You get expensive but not elite. Clients are baffled – why pay such money when results are no better than what volume players deliver?

The reverse mistake – "premium volume". Standardized processes with pretensions to exclusivity. Clients quickly realize they're paying for marketing, not quality.

Practice shows – attempts to combine corporate practices using the elite model with volume service in other areas create reputational problems. Corporate clients doubt the expertise – how can you be an M&A expert while simultaneously doing volume work? And volume clients consider such firms unjustifiably expensive.

Here's the middle ground's problem – it demands compromises in everything, including hiring, pricing, and positioning. But markets don't like compromises. Markets want a clear answer to the question, "Who are you and why should I choose you specifically?"

The honest choice

Ultimately, the choice between exclusivity and volume is a lifestyle choice. Not just for the firm, but for everyone working in it.

If you enjoy working on unique projects, if you're willing to sacrifice predictability for the chance to handle genuinely fascinating work, if high responsibility motivates rather than frightens you – perhaps the elite model is your calling.

If you value systematic order, if you want to help large numbers of people, if stability matters more than exclusivity, if you believe in the power of well-organized processes – the volume model might be your natural home.

The main thing – be honest with yourself. Don't try building an elite firm if you're a process systems administrator at heart. And don't construct a service factory if you dream of stardom and uniqueness. The market will forgive many mistakes, but it won't forgive insincerity. And in current conditions, it'll ruthlessly punish any attempts to sit on two chairs at once.

Local vs global

The choice between deep roots and wide wings?

Leading regional firms often emphasize their main advantage as intimate knowledge of the local market – every key player, every enforcement peculiarity. This is their city, and here they're the best.

Partners at international firms live to a different rhythm – video conferences with Tokyo, flights to New York, European projects. For them, the world genuinely has become small.

Two worldviews, two lifestyles, two completely different understandings of success. Local versus global – the choice between deep roots and wide wings.

Local kings: home advantage

Local leaders possess what international players will never have – thorough knowledge of local context. They understand not just the letter of the law but how that law gets applied in practice. They know the peculiarities of local business culture, unwritten rules of the game, historical context behind decisions.

The advantage of years of regional history is hard to overstate. Local leaders often advised most major local companies back when they were being established. They know these businesses inside out, understand the logic behind their decisions – knowledge impossible to acquire flying in from the capital for a week.

Relationships in local markets build on principles global players often underestimate. Here, what matters isn't just professional reputation but personal too. Where the partner's children went to school, which sports club he belongs to, what charitable projects he supports – all this influences business decisions.

Local firms can afford more personalized service. Clients ring the partner directly, not a call center. Meetings happen not in faceless conference rooms but in cozy offices where walls display diplomas from the local university and photos from city events.

Pricing advantages are substantial too. Local firms don't bear costs of international infrastructure, don't pay licensing fees to global networks, don't maintain offices in other countries. These savings can translate into more competitive rates for clients.

Speed of reaction is another trump card. While international firms coordinate decisions with head office and study local specifics, local players are already acting. They don't need to explain to distant headquarters why everything works exactly this way in this jurisdiction.

The limits of being local

However, local leaders face serious constraints that become increasingly obvious in a globalized world.

Market size remains the fundamental limitation. Even as absolute leaders in their region, local firms are capped by the local economy's volume. The number of major deals is finite, the number of paying clients too. Regional leaders often admit, we've taken everything available in our market – further growth is only possible through expansion.

The math of leadership also works against local players. Each jurisdiction can support at most one or two genuine local leaders – simple market arithmetic. Everyone knows who's number one here. There's the leader, there's their main competitor for conflict situations, and that's it. Everyone else plays in a different league.

Unlike the international market, where a dozen major players can coexist, local leadership is a zero-sum game. Either you're the leader or you're not. There's no such thing as semi-leadership. This creates constant pressure – every day you need to reaffirm number one status.

The paradox of local leadership is that the more successful the firm, the less attractive its market becomes to other ambitious players. Why go where all the best clients are already taken? But this also means the number of seats "at the throne" is extremely limited.

Access to talent becomes problematic when the best law graduates head for capitals or international firms. Local players must settle for second-tier candidates or overpay to retain stars. Typical situation – your best corporate lawyer leaves for a Magic Circle firm at double the salary plus the opportunity to work on international projects.

Project complexity also constrains local firms. They rarely encounter genuinely complex, multi-jurisdictional deals. Their experience may prove insufficient when a local company decides to enter international markets or attract foreign investment.

And finally, there are reputational constraints. In international business's eyes, a local firm can be perceived as "provincial", regardless of actual expertise level. There are known cases of regional leaders not even being considered for major M&A deals solely because they're not from the capital.

International players – the world as playing field

Global firms operate at a fundamentally different scale. For them, national borders are administrative formalities rather than real business constraints.

Typical situation for international firms: client buys a company in Germany, financing comes from Singapore, structuring runs through the Netherlands, and listing is planned for London. And they can provide legal support across all these jurisdictions using their own offices.

Access to the largest projects is the global players' main advantage. Multibillion deals, restructuring of transnational corporations, international arbitrations – this world remains practically closed to local firms. At leading international firms, the minimum project threshold might be a million euros – anything below simply doesn't get considered.

Human resources also favor global players. They can attract the best talent from around the world, offer unique career opportunities, and provide access to the most prestigious projects. Harvard and Oxford graduates go to them – international firms can offer possibilities unavailable to local players.

Technological advantages are obvious. Global firms invest millions in IT infrastructure, knowledge management systems, and process automation. They can afford the most modern solutions and the best specialists to implement them.

Reputational advantages matter substantially too. An international firm's brand itself is a quality guarantee in major business's eyes. "Nobody gets fired for choosing McKinsey" – this principle works in legal services as well.

The price of globality

International players do however pay dearly for their advantages – and not just financially.

Loss of local flexibility becomes the main problem. Global standards don't always suit local specifics. Decisions must be coordinated with head office, which slows reaction to local changes. Managing partners of local offices often complain about months of coordination to hire a partner because they don't meet the firm's global standards.

High operating costs are the inevitable price of international infrastructure. Offices in prestigious districts, high salaries, expensive IT systems, marketing budgets – all this must be recouped through high rates.

Cultural distance can alienate local clients. International firms can seem detached and impersonal. You often hear criticism from local entrepreneurs – they fly in, do their work, and fly out again; they have no emotional connection to local business.

Dependence on global processes creates uncontrollable risks. Crisis in one part of the world can affect local practice. Strategic decisions from head office can radically alter the local situation. There are known cases of offices being closed not due to inefficiency but because the firm decided to exit the region.

And finally, ethical dilemmas. Global standards may conflict with local practices. What to do when head office demands compliance with standards that make the firm uncompetitive in the local market?

Hybrid strategies – searching for balance

Naturally the question arises, what if we try combining local expertise with global reach?

One popular approach is creating alliances and networks. Local firms join forces with counterparts from other countries for joint work on international projects. Formally remain independent, effectively gain access to the global market.

Selective international expansion is another variant. First become leaders at home, then open offices in two to three key jurisdictions. Slowly and cautiously, but systematically expand geographic coverage.

Specializing in export works too. Become experts on your jurisdiction for international clients. Don't try competing globally, but be the best local advisers for foreign business.

There's reverse movement as well – international firms create local practices with high degrees of autonomy. Global brand plus local flexibility.

Moment of truth

In the modern world, the choice between local and global becomes increasingly crucial. Business globalization means even local companies increasingly need international expertise. On the other hand, regulatory complexity makes local knowledge more valuable.

Regional leaders increasingly face a dilemma – previously you could simply be good local lawyers; now clients expect understanding of international context. Yet international players often don't grasp local specifics.

Perhaps the future belongs to those who can find balance between deep local roots and broad international perspective. For now, such balance remains the exception rather than the rule.

An honest conversation about ambition

Ultimately, the choice between local and global is a choice of life philosophy. What motivates you more – being the undisputed leader in your region or participating in the global game?

Are you willing to sacrifice the stability of local leadership for the uncertainty of international expansion? Or would you rather preserve the comfort of familiar territory, even if it caps your growth potential?

Do you want your children to be proud that you're the best lawyers in town? Or do you dream of your name being known in international business circles?

There are no right or wrong answers – only honesty with yourself and understanding the price of each choice. And willingness to bear responsibility for its consequences – whatever they turn out to be.

State vs business

Whom shall we serve? Influential firms working with power structures often emphasize, the authorities need reliable people. Meanwhile, independent practices hold a fundamentally different position – they categorically avoid working with state structures, considering it too risky.

Two approaches to one of legal business's most delicate questions – what relationship to build with power? Go where the big money and influence are, but also the big risks? Or keep your distance, preserving independence and flexibility while losing access to serious projects?

This choice determines not just your client base but the firm's entire way of life. And unlike other architectural decisions, it's particularly difficult to reverse if things go sideways.

Proximity to power – advantages of the insider position

Government contracts, state company boards, privatization deals, sovereign debt restructuring – a world where one transaction can bring in more than a small firm earns all year.

Firms specializing in government contracts often note the absence of client acquisition problems. When you're in the trusted circle, work flows naturally. Ministries know whom to approach. State companies receive recommendations from above. The system runs smoothly.

Pro-government firms gain access to insider information. They know about impending legislative changes long before public discussion. They understand the logic behind regulatory decisions from the inside. They can influence the wording of subordinate legislation while it's still being drafted.

The financial appeal of the government segment is obvious. State contracts run into millions. Privatization advisory can bring in more than an average boutique's annual revenue. Crucially, client creditworthiness is beyond question. The state might delay payments, but it won't go bankrupt.

Reputational bonuses matter substantially too – at least in certain circles. When a minister recommends your firm or you advise the country's largest state bank, it creates an aura of influence. "The government itself works with us" is a powerful marketing message for corporate clients.

Pro-government firms often get exclusive access to certain niches. Banking regulation, energy projects, infrastructure deals – many spheres are de facto controlled by the state. Without good relationships with regulators, working there is simply impossible.

The dark side of loyalty

However, proximity to power comes at a cost – and the price isn't always obvious from the start.

Loss of independence becomes inevitable. Firms closely tied to the state sector face constant constraints – they can't take on a case against their key client. Conflicts of interest become a constant companion. You can't represent opposition media if you advise the information ministry. You can't defend activists if your main client is a security department.

Reputational risks accumulate imperceptibly. In democratic countries, connection to power can turn toxic when political cycles shift. A firm that was influential under one government can find itself in disgrace under the next. There are known cases of firms losing half their private clients after a change of power – business didn't want association with the previous regime.

Ethical compromises creep up gradually. State clients don't always adhere to the same ethical standards as private companies. Sometimes you must turn a blind eye to questionable practices, sometimes you must actively support them. Partners at such firms often admit they understood it was wrong, but these were key clients.

Dependence on political cycles creates fundamental vulnerability. Government contracts can vanish overnight when priorities shift or budgets tighten. Privatization programs get frozen. Regulatory projects get postponed. A firm built on state orders finds itself in an extremely vulnerable position.

And finally, there are corruption risks. Even if the firm itself acts with absolute integrity, proximity to power automatically makes it subject to heightened scrutiny from anti-corruption bodies. Every transaction gets examined under a microscope. Every contract is checked for possible conflicts of interest.

Proud independence

Partners at independent firms often emphasize their position's main advantage – they sleep soundly, knowing they won't wake up reading about their clients in the crime pages, or won't have to explain to their children why they work with dodgy people.

Independent firms build business on private clients – corporations, banks, investment funds, family offices. Their clients choose lawyers not through recommendations from above but by professional reputation.

This model delivers maximum freedom of choice. You can represent any clients, take on any matters, without glancing over your shoulder at the political climate. Managing partners at leading independent firms note they've had clients on different sides of political divides, and nobody minded because everyone knew – they work exclusively within the legal framework.

Independence's reputational advantages matter especially for international business. Global corporations prefer working with firms unconnected to local political elites. This reduces compliance risks and simplifies internal approval procedures.

Independent firms are less vulnerable to political upheaval. A change of power doesn't affect their client base. Anti-corruption campaigns don't touch them. Geopolitical crises can even work in their favor – when ties to power become toxic, private business seeks independent advisers.

Ethical advantages are obvious too. There is no need to turn a blind eye to clients' questionable practices. You can choose matters based on legal merit, not political expediency. The principle "We only work with those we wouldn't be embarrassed to introduce to our children" is only affordable to independent players.

The price of independence

Independence doesn't come free either. Limited access to major projects becomes a reality. Many attractive deals are somehow connected to the state. Privatizations, major infrastructure projects, bank restructurings – without connections in power structures, getting in proves difficult.

Absence of insider information also constrains possibilities. Independent firms learn about impending changes from public sources, like everyone else. There's no opportunity to prepare in advance for new regulatory requirements or warn clients about coming changes.

In the private sector, competition runs higher – more players, wider choice. Clients are more demanding about price and quality. There's no "administrative resource" to ensure a flow of orders.

The need for active marketing also demands resources. If pro-government firms receive clients through recommendations, independents must actively promote their services. Invest in PR, participate in conferences, develop partners' personal brands.

And finally, political risks don't vanish. In authoritarian systems, independence can be interpreted as opposition. Representing unwelcome clients can lead to problems with regulators. As some partners joke bitterly, "Neutrality is also a political position".

The gray area – attempting to balance

Naturally the question arises: can't you work with the state while preserving independence? Theoretically, you can try. Practically, it demands exceptional management skill.

Some firms attempt creating "Chinese walls" between state and private practices. Different partners, different teams, different offices. But clients see the common brand, and reputational risks don't disappear.

Others choose a selective approach – work only with certain state structures or only on certain projects. Advise the Central Bank but don't work with security departments. Participate in privatization but don't handle political cases.

Temporary balancing is a third variant. In stable times, work with the state; during political turbulence, distance yourself. But such strategy demands extremely acute sensitivity to the political climate.

There's also a geographical solution – work with the state in some jurisdictions while preserving independence in others. But this is only possible for large international players.

The irreversibility of choice

Here's the thing about choosing between state and business – there's no going back. Once you've positioned yourself close to power, clawing your way back to genuine independence is brutally hard. The "government firm" label sticks like glue.

The reverse journey proves equally tricky. A firm that's spent years keeping its distance from power can't suddenly waltz in as the government's trusted adviser. You've got no connections, no reputation in the right circles, no insider grasp of how the bureaucratic machine actually works.

This choice demands serious thought. You're not just weighing up current pros and cons – you're deciding which world you want to inhabit for the next decade or more.

An honest conversation about values

Strip it all back, and the choice between state and business comes down to values. What drives you more – the ability to shape serious outcomes or maintaining your independence? Financial upside or sleeping easy at night? The security of being an insider or the freedom of a market player?

There are no right or wrong answers here. Just brutal honesty with yourself. This choice won't merely reshape your revenue – it'll define your firm's entire philosophy.

Critical point: don't kid yourself. You can't be slightly pregnant. You can't be "a bit pro-government" or "moderately independent". Markets, clients, and society work you out fast. They'll know whose side you're on and judge you accordingly.

In today's world – with transparency rising and ethical standards tightening – sitting on the fence costs more every day. Better to pick a side clearly and own the consequences than try playing both ends against the middle.

Service model – what and how we sell

If strategic positioning answers "who we are", the service model defines "what we do". Here you decide whether you're selling expertise or relationships, standards or creativity, innovation or reliability.

These three dichotomies directly shape client experience and internal processes. They determine how you structure teams, which competencies you develop, and how you measure success. Unlike strategic choices that can live in partners' heads, the service model shows up in every client interaction and needs to be crystal clear to all staff.

Specialization vs full-service

Know everything about something or something about everything?

Specialist boutiques often express their philosophy brutally simply – we're the best in our field, full stop. When asked what happens if clients need help in adjacent areas, the standard answer is, "We'll recommend the best specialists, but for our area, come only to us".

Managing partners at full-service firms follow the opposite logic – the client is an entrepreneur, not a bundle of legal problems. Today they need help with M&A, tomorrow an employment dispute, the day after tax optimization. Why force them to hunt down different specialists?

Specialization versus full-service – one of the most fundamental choices in legal business architecture. It's not simply a marketing positioning question. It's choosing how you perceive the world – through the lens of expertise or through the lens of client needs.

The power of expertise – advantages of narrow specialization

Specialist firms live by the principle, "Better first in a category than second in the world". They pick a narrow niche and become absolute experts in it.

Leading arbitration boutiques often limit themselves to international disputes only, investment cases only, projects above a certain threshold only. Sounds restrictive? Yet when a transnational corporation faces a problem in this area, alternatives don't even get considered.

Depth of expertise creates insurmountable barriers for competitors. When you know the subject better than anyone, clients will pay a premium for your knowledge. Some specialist firms have partners who remember every significant case in their field over the past decade – try finding that level of expertise elsewhere.

Specialization lets you create unique products. While full-service firms offer standard solutions, narrow specialists develop innovative approaches to complex problems. They don't just apply existing tools – they invent them.

Reputational advantages are obvious. When your name becomes synonymous with a particular area of law, you become the automatic choice for difficult matters. IP boutique partners often note, "In our niche there's no competition – there's us, and there's everyone else".

The economics of specialization also favor narrow players. High expertise allows premium pricing. Clients will pay extra for guaranteed results. And work efficiency rises through accumulated experience in a narrow field.

Specialist firms are easier to scale – but only within their niche. Processes get standardized, knowledge systematized, junior lawyers become experts faster in a limited area.

The price of narrow specialization

But specialization demands sacrifices, and the cost isn't always obvious from the start.

Market size remains a fundamental problem. Even the most attractive niche has a ceiling. Practice shows, firms can become the best in a narrow field, then discover demand for that expertise is vanishingly small. Competition law in a small jurisdiction, for instance, might produce only a handful of major merger clearances annually.

Dependence on market cycles becomes critical. If your niche hits a crisis, there are no alternatives. There are known cases of specialization in development projects becoming problematic when property markets collapsed –

full-service firms pivoted to insolvency and restructuring, while narrow specialists simply waited for market recovery.

Finding experts grows increasingly difficult. Finding an expert in a narrow field proves far harder than recruiting a solid generalist. Growing one internally demands years of investment. The candidate must not simply know corporate law but understand a specific industry, grasp regulatory requirements, have experience dealing with relevant authorities. Such people are few and far between.

Risk of obsolescence can prove fatal. Narrow specialization can suddenly become irrelevant due to legislative or market changes. Some partners recall bitterly how their expertise in foreign exchange regulation lost value overnight after currency controls were abolished.

And finally, client constraints. Specialist firms can only serve clients within their profile. Other needs go unmet. Major clients often want to hand all legal work to one firm, but specialists can only take their segment – the rest gets farmed out to competitors.

Universal soldiers – advantages of full service

Full-service firms build on the opposite philosophy – the client matters more than expertise. They aim to meet all their clients' legal needs under one roof.

The universal firm's mission: become clients' sole legal adviser. Clients needn't think about whom to approach with which question. They ring one place, and everything gets sorted.

Client-centricity is universal players' main advantage. They don't study an area of law – they study the client's business. Understand its strategy, know its problems, anticipate its needs. Such firms have partners who oversee all matters for major clients – from transactional deals to employment disputes – knowing the business better than many internal managers.

Risk diversification works as insurance. When one practice hits crisis, others compensate for losses. In 2008, many full-service firms noted that M&A dropped, but insolvency and restructuring surged, meaning overall revenue actually increased.

Synergy between practices creates additional value. Corporate lawyers bring in tax specialists for deal structuring. Employment teams work with corporate on reorganizations. Litigators receive matters from all other practices. At successful full-service firms, cross-selling can account for 40 percent of revenue.

Geographic scaling becomes simpler too. Full-service firms can open offices in new regions with complete service offerings without worrying whether sufficient demand exists for narrow specialization in that location.

Attracting talent gets easier. Young lawyers see greater development opportunities at full-service firms. They can try different practices, find their calling, and build a well-rounded career.

The price of being universal

The full-service model demands sacrifices too – sometimes painful ones.

Focus gets diluted through scattered resources across numerous directions. Investment in developing each practice ends up smaller than what specialist competitors can manage. Managing partners note, we can't send all our tax lawyers to an expensive specialist conference – narrow specialists don't have such problems.

Positioning becomes problematic. It's difficult to explain to the market what exactly you're best at when you do everything. Full-service firms get known as reliable and professional, but when a client needs the absolute best expert on a specific question, they head to specialists.

Economics also work against generalists. Full-service firms can't charge the same premium rates as narrow specialists. They're forced to compete on price, which erodes profitability.

And finally, management complexity. Running a full-service firm proves far harder than running a specialist one. Different practices demand different approaches to management, motivation, and development. Managing partners face the dilemma: how do you motivate star partners and middle-tier partner-managers equally?

Searching for the golden mean

Naturally the idea arises, what if we create several specialist practices under one roof?

The most common European approach is the "firm with several leading practices" model. It's a sort of golden mean between narrow specialization and full universality. The firm picks three or four areas where it aims to become a leader, and adds a basic set of supporting services.

The typical structure is three flagship practices (say, M&A, banking law, and energy), aiming for top-three market position in each, plus corporate law and employment for supporting the main areas and handling standalone projects.

This model proves especially popular among mid-sized European firms.

It lets them compete with specialist boutiques in key areas while offering clients a broader service range. Clients can arrive with a complex deal, knowing the firm will handle M&A, tax optimization, and employment issues – not at narrow specialist level, but competently enough.

The model's advantages are obvious – risk diversification greater than single-practice firms, but focus stronger than full-service firms. You can invest in developing key areas without scattering resources across a dozen weak practices. Positioning gets easier too: "We're the best at A, B, and C, and can handle the rest as well".

But drawbacks are substantial. Management complexity demands balancing investment between "star" and "supporting" practices. Risk of diluted positioning remains – clients may not grasp whether you're genuinely expert in chosen areas.

Some firms attempt building a "house of brands" – a collection of narrowly specialized practices with different positioning under a single legal structure but separate marketing. Disputes practice works as premium arbitration, IP as a tech boutique, corporate as universal service.

Temporal specialization is another variant. The firm concentrates on one area until achieving leadership, then systematically adds new practices. There are known cases of successful development from tax boutique to multi-practice firm – but only after bringing in recognized experts from the market. But all these approaches demand exceptional management discipline and a clear understanding of where one model ends and another begins.

Reversibility of choice

Unlike other architectural decisions, the choice between specialization and full-service is relatively reversible. Specialist firms can add new practices, whilst full-service firms can focus on their strongest areas.

Such transformations prove painful and time-consuming. You can't build a specialist reputation in a year. And abandoning weak practices means losing clients and staff.

Practice shows, firms that spent decades building full-service reputations can lose significant chunks of their client base when shifting to specialization. Markets don't believe in radical repositioning – clients won't buy that generalists can suddenly become best at one thing.

The modern market seems increasingly tilted towards specialization. Clients grow more demanding about expertise. Information transparency makes finding the best specialists in each field easy. But full-service firms find their niches too – especially among clients who value convenience and long-term relationships over narrow expertise.

An honest conversation about calling

Ultimately, the choice between specialization and full-service is a question of what excites you more – deep study of a subject or broad understanding of clients' businesses.

If you're ready to dedicate your life to studying one area of law, if becoming better and better at one thing fascinates you, if you dream of your name being synonymous with particular expertise – perhaps specialization is your path.

If you enjoy variety in tasks, if you want to understand clients' businesses in all their complexity, if you're happy being good at many things to better serve client needs – full-service might be your calling.

The main thing – don't try serving two masters simultaneously. Markets will quickly realize you can't clearly explain what exactly you're best at, and punish the ambiguity.

Formality vs relationships

Operations directors at large international firms often emphasize that they've got a procedure for everything. How to take on clients, how to draft documents, how to invoice, how to conduct interviews. Any staff member in any office knows what to do and in what sequence.

In contrast, partners at family practices follow a different philosophy – all their clients are personal acquaintances or friends of friends. They know everyone's birthdays, children's names, holiday plans. No CRM systems or procedures – everything runs on trust and personal relationships.

At first glance, this might seem like an administrative question – formalize processes or leave everything to people? But it's actually one of the most fundamental architectural choices – choosing your mechanics of trust. What will your firm's reliability rest on: system or people? Rules or context? Universality or personal precision?

The formal model – reproducibility over context

The formal model bets on reproducibility. Here every action gets described, every step documented. Partners don't say, "I have a feeling" – they cite approved policy. Manageability comes not through personality but through structure.

This delivers serious advantages during growth and geographic expansion. New staff adapt faster, new offices slot into a unified cycle, client experience stays stable regardless of team. Consultants note, at formal firms, onboarding a new lawyer takes a week – they get access to all databases, read the procedures, and from day one know how to work with clients.

Standardization becomes the system's foundation. Uniform document templates, standard approaches to solving problems, standardized client communication processes. Partners at international networks often emphasize that a client in Amsterdam gets exactly the same service quality as in Milan or Madrid, because the same standards operate everywhere.

Document workflow gets meticulously regulated. Every document passes through defined approval stages, every action gets logged in the system, every decision has written justification. IT directors at such firms note complete process transparency – at any moment you can reconstruct who did what and when on a specific matter.

Quality control is built into processes. Multi-level checks, peer review, automatic monitoring of deadlines and budgets. Managing partners assert that errors are virtually eliminated; the system won't let you send a document without necessary approvals or exceed budget without authorization.

Formalize hiring and staff development too. This involves clear candidate requirements, structured interviews, standardized training programs, and regular performance reviews against uniform criteria.

The advantages of predictability

The formal model delivers serious advantages for growing firms. Scalability is the main plus. Standardized processes make opening offices, hiring staff, and expanding easy. Result predictability means clients know what they'll get, when, and for how much. Resource efficiency runs higher through automation and optimization. Risks of errors and compliance breaches drop.

There are known cases of firms opening five offices in different countries within three years, implementing their procedures, standards, and culture everywhere.

The price of formalization – when the system becomes self-serving

Formality carries serious costs too, which don't surface immediately.

Newcomers struggle to integrate if they can't grasp context. Junior lawyers often note that they worked from instructions for six months but didn't understand the logic behind decisions – they knew what to do but not why.

Clients start encountering a sense of impersonality. The system can become self-serving – processes function, but nobody asks "why?" Partners start hiding behind rules to avoid discussing difficult situations: "That's what it says" becomes a substitute for thoughtful decisions.

Flexibility suffers particularly noticeably. Junior partners complain that a simple contract change requires sign-off from three management levels; by then the client's already sorted it another way. In unstable conditions, an overly rigid structure can't handle the need for rapid adaptation.

The relationship model – trust through culture

The relationship model works fundamentally differently. Here, trust gets created through culture, involvement, and team stability. Decisions happen faster – not because procedures are absent, but because mutual understanding exists.

In such firms they say, "This is how we do things" – and that "we" signifies an unformalized norm sustained by collective memory and personal engagement. Clients feel individual attention. Young lawyers receive support through mentorship. Consultants note that, in the relationship model, newcomers spend months absorbing the team's rhythm through conversation and observation – efficiency rests on loyalty, not rules.

Personalization is such firms' main value. Clients work with specific people, not a faceless organization. Partners emphasize that clients know them personally – mobile number, personality quirks, family situation. The lawyer becomes not merely a service provider but a trusted confidant.

Flexibility in decisions comes naturally to relationship-built firms – no rigid procedures preventing optimal solutions for specific situations. Each matter gets approached with fresh eyes, examining the situation's particulars, client interests, possible solution routes. No templates.

Trust becomes the foundation of all processes – between partners, between lawyers and clients, and within teams. Managing partners explain that a partner's word is a contract – there is no need for written confirmations and formal procedures. Everything rests on mutual trust and respect.

Client relationships build for the long-term. Partners share experiences – they've got clients they've worked with for two decades, weathered crises together, celebrated successes, navigated personal troubles. These aren't merely business relationships – they're friendships.

The advantages of being human

Depth of client understanding is the relationship model's main advantage. When connections build over years, the lawyer grasps not just current needs but long-term plans and decision-making peculiarities.

Client loyalty runs higher, adaptability to change improves – there are no rigid procedures preventing quick pivots. Creative approaches flourish and staff motivation grows from the sense of personal responsibility.

Partners note that their clients don't defect to competitors even when they're cheaper, because they've got relationships with them, not merely business contracts.

The price of informality

But the relationship model carries serious limitations.

Scalability remains the main problem. Personal relationships can't be replicated. Dependence on key figures becomes critical – their departure can prove catastrophic. This can result in unpredictability without standards, difficulty controlling quality, compliance risks – all inevitable companions of the relationship model.

It can be a painful experience at many firms – the founder may retire and take half the clients with him, as it turned out loyalty was to him personally, not the firm. Managing partners admit that sometimes they only learn of problems when they're already irreversible – no early warning system exists.

What actually holds your system together?

Here's what this choice is really about – how you maintain control amidst growth, generational change, crises, and uncertainty.

Architectural consequences manifest at all levels. In the formal model you hire against competency matrices, build KPIs, and make decisions through procedures. In the relationship model you select people by values, grow culture through mentorship, and hold knowledge in people's heads.

Size matters critically. Firms up to 25 lawyers naturally run on relationships. Above 50-100 lawyers, formalization becomes virtually inevitable. Partners recall that when there were ten of them, issues got sorted over coffee; now there are 80, and you can't function without procedures.

Cultural peculiarities play a role too. In Germany and Switzerland, clients value formality as professionalism. In Southern European cultures, personal relationships are favored.

Hybrid models – navigation rather than universal answer

Naturally the question arises: what if we create a system combining procedural reliability with human flexibility?

In practice, hybrids only work with clearly demarcated boundaries. Formality can underpin back-office, compliance, hiring, and document management, while relationships get preserved in client work, project communication, within the partner group.

Some managing partners explain their strategy: they've got clear procedures for routine operations – billing, document workflow, quality control – but in client work each partner acts at their own discretion. Formality in processes, humanity in relationships.

But without open conversation about priorities, the mixed model breeds conflicting logics. One partner demands, "Document everything in the system"; another acts by habit: "We've always sorted this on the fly". Teams don't understand which logic takes priority or what the decision-making mechanism is.

The illusion of control

The hybrid's main trap is the feeling it runs itself. The firm believes it's got both order and humanity. Closer inspection reveals that procedures get broken for exceptions, exceptions get perceived as system, and trust as a guarantee that everything will sort itself out.

Managing partners confess that they supposedly have regulations, but each partner does things their own way anyway. The result is that neither model gets developed to maturity. An illusion of control emerges, masking fragmentation.

Hybrids demand maturity – the ability to recognize that mixing models isn't compromise but a new quality altogether. Here what matters is a clear roadmap – where do we want reproducibility, and where are we willing to rely on context? Who's responsible for maintaining culture in relationship zones, and who administers formal zones?

Navigation is the ability to distinguish where we apply protocol and where we bring in human judgment. Where responsibility for deviation lies with the system, and where with the specific decision-maker. Answers to these questions determine not management style but the firm's architecture.

An honest choice about the mechanics of trust

Ask yourself honestly: what holds your system together? Which trust mechanism suits you specifically – not the best in a vacuum, but the one reflecting your team, your ambitions, and your decision-making style.

If you value predictability, efficiency, scalability, if you're ready to sacrifice some humanity for systematic reliability – the formal model is for you. If you believe legal services are fundamentally about human relationships, if you're willing to limit growth for a personal approach – the relationship model might be your choice.

The main thing – understand the price of each decision. In law firm architecture there are no neutral decisions. Only those you'll start paying for at some point. Or those on which you can build resilience.

And remember, in a world where technology increasingly standardizes processes, the human dimension of legal services can become one of your main competitive advantages. But only if it's consciously cultivated, not accidentally present.

Innovation vs tradition

Partners at tech-savvy firms proudly demonstrate fully automated AI-powered due diligence systems capable of analyzing thousands of documents. Their start-up clients are thrilled – what used to take weeks now gets done in days.

Meanwhile, representatives of traditional practices hold a different philosophy – their clients are conservative family corporations who want every document personally read by an experienced lawyer. They don't trust machines with their most important matters. And rightly so.

Innovation versus tradition isn't simply a question of whether to use new technology. It's a fundamental choice between two different philosophies of practicing law and serving clients.

Client dictate – he who pays calls the tune

The choice between innovation and tradition most often gets determined not by the firm's internal preferences but by client base demands.

Technology companies don't merely expect innovation – they demand it as a condition of collaboration. There are known cases of major IT corporations conducting regular process audits of their legal advisers. If a firm doesn't use the latest technology for workflow optimization, clients start doubting its competence.

Start-ups prove especially sensitive to lawyers' innovativeness. For them, what matters isn't just service quality but understanding their culture, their speed, their problem-solving approaches. Venture partners observe that young entrepreneurs want to work with lawyers who think as quickly and unconventionally as they do. The traditional "We've always done it this way" approach repels them.

Conversely, conservative clients may perceive excessive innovation as frivolity or unprofessionalism. Traditional partners explain that the chairman of a century-old family company's board doesn't want to hear about blockchain and smart contracts. What matters to him is having his affairs handled by an experienced old-school lawyer who understands the value of proven approaches.

Government structures, state companies, traditional industries – metallurgy, energy, chemicals – all gravitate towards conservative legal approaches. Partners clarify that energy companies operate in highly regulated environments; any experiments mean risks for them. They prefer solutions proven over decades.

Technology trailblazers – at the cutting edge

Firms choosing the innovation path live in constant renewal. They're first to implement new technology, experiment with approaches, and create products competitors don't yet have.

Managing partners at tech firms describe proprietary R&D departments studying AI applications in legal practice. They test machine learning for contract analysis, automate routine processes, and experiment with predictive analytics for litigation.

Technology investment at such firms can reach 15-20 percent of revenue. In-house IT teams, subscriptions to dozens of specialist services, constant staff training on new tools – all this demands substantial resources.

Recruitment at innovative firms runs differently too. They're hunting not just good lawyers but people with technical minds, ready for constant learning, open to experiments. HR directors explain that they hire lawyers with technical backgrounds – former programmers, data science specialists. What matters isn't just legal knowledge but understanding of technology.

Client service gets built differently as well. Online platforms for client communication, mobile apps for tracking matter progress, automated reporting systems – everything aimed at boosting convenience and transparency.

Partners demonstrate that clients can log into their portal anytime and see what stage their matter's at, how much time's been spent, what the next steps are. No calls asking, "What's happening with my contract?" – all the information is available 24/7.

The price of being first

Every innovation strategy carries risk, and in professional services, those risks are amplified. The most obvious one? Technology. Not every platform or process improvement delivers on its promise. Investment in the wrong solution can drain time, money, and credibility. One managing partner recalled spending half a year and a significant budget on implementing an AI platform – only to discover that it didn't suit the firm's needs. The system had to be dismantled and rebuilt from scratch.

But technology is rarely the hardest part. People tire faster than systems do. Constant adaptation exhausts teams, especially senior lawyers who have built their reputation on mastery and predictability. Several firms report that turnover among experienced associates has grown noticeably. The pattern is always the same – the more frequent the internal change, the lower the retention of those who value stability.

Reputation risks, however, can be existential. When innovation fails publicly, clients rarely forgive quickly. One automated contract review system missed a critical clause, leading to client losses and months of reputational repair. The cost of rebuilding trust outweighed the original investment in technology many times over.

Finally, regulatory constraints can quietly undermine the most progressive intentions. Not every jurisdiction is ready to embrace digital transformation in legal processes. Partners in several firms mentioned their attempt to introduce e-signatures firm-wide, only to be reminded that local legislation still requires traditional wet-ink signatures for specific categories of documents.

Guardians of tradition – the strength of proven experience

Traditional firms build their identity on what has already stood the test of time. Their philosophy is simple – why reinvent the wheel when the old one still runs smoothly?

Senior partners in such firms take pride in their archives of precedent – 40 years of carefully documented cases, strategies, and judgments. Whatever challenge arises today, there is almost always a prior example to consult. Experience itself becomes their most powerful competitive advantage.

Investment, accordingly, flows not into technology but into people.

Competitive salaries attract seasoned lawyers; resources go to training, secondments, and building institutional knowledge. As one partner put it, "Our technology is our lawyers".

These firms spend more on developing human capital than tech-driven competitors do on IT infrastructure. They sponsor LL.M. programs at leading universities, invite outside experts for internal seminars, and run mentoring schemes to ensure that wisdom is transferred, not lost.

Client service, too, is deeply personal. Long-term relationships are at the heart of the business model. Clients often stay with the same partners for 20 years or more. These partners know not only the current matters but also the company's history, culture, and leadership preferences. No CRM system can replicate that kind of understanding.

Their internal processes reflect the same philosophy of refinement over reinvention. Procedures are codified, quality control is layered, and every step is documented. Operational partners describe checklists for nearly every scenario – tested over decades and designed to ensure that nothing essential ever slips through the cracks.

The cost of conservatism

Tradition offers comfort – but also carries a quiet penalty. What has been perfected over decades can start to resist change. For many long-established firms, the very discipline that once defined their reliability has become a source of friction.

Speed is the first thing to suffer. Meticulous procedures and layered approvals, once designed to protect quality, now slow delivery to a pace some clients find intolerable. One senior partner admitted that while his firm is still aligning documents across departments, a tech-driven competitor already has a draft ready for review. In a market where responsiveness often outweighs reputation, this lag can be fatal.

Growth, too, is constrained by tradition. A service built on personal mastery is difficult to scale. Every partner has a distinctive rhythm, an idiosyncratic way of managing work. What ensures excellence on individual matters becomes an obstacle when the firm seeks collective expansion.

The generational gap deepens the challenge. Younger lawyers, fluent in digital tools and impatient with repetition, hesitate to join organizations that still pride themselves on manual precision. HR directors note that interviews now start with a simple question: "What systems do you use?" When the answer sounds like a museum catalogue, enthusiasm fades.

Even efficiency – the last refuge of conservative pride – begins to erode. Manual work absorbs more time and resources, pushing up cost per matter. CFOs acknowledge that their margins shrink each year, not because clients pay less, but because their methods refuse to evolve.

Conservatism, in this sense, is not a flaw but a tax – a hidden cost paid for the privilege of certainty.

The nature of law – different games, different rules

Law does not exist in a vacuum. The type of work a lawyer chooses inevitably shapes how they think, act, and even define professionalism. The nature of the practice itself pulls one towards certain methods – and away from others.

At one end of the spectrum lies the world of crypto and start-ups, where both the substance of law and the pace of change defy tradition. Every week brings new technologies, regulations, and risks. In this world, a lawyer who cannot navigate DeFi protocols or anticipate shifts in digital-asset policy becomes obsolete overnight. Clients here expect their advisers to understand the business as deeply as they do – sometimes even better.

At the opposite end are the oldest, most human corners of the profession – criminal defense and family law. When a lawyer meets a client accused of a serious crime, no algorithm can replace belief in innocence or the will to fight. When a widow seeks guidance on her husband's estate, a chatbot offering legal options misses the essence of the moment. What she needs is presence – someone who listens, interprets, and cares. In such contexts, technology is not merely irrelevant; it can be harmful.

Between these poles stretches the full landscape of legal practice. M&A lawyers, for instance, operate on the frontier where tradition meets transformation. The fundamentals of deal structuring remain unchanged, yet the tools have evolved dramatically. Virtual data rooms, digital signatures, and automated due-diligence platforms are no longer innovations – they are infrastructure.

The essential insight is that the nature of your practice defines the boundaries of your choice. Within those boundaries, freedom still exists – but it is not limitless. The game you choose determines the rules you must play by.

An honest choice of strategy

In the end, the decision between innovation and tradition comes down to honesty – about your clients, your practices, and your own capacity for change.

If your clients are tech companies, start-ups, or fintech players – if your field shifts as fast as the regulations that govern it – innovation is not a luxury but a condition of survival. The tools, the mindset, and even the speed of response must evolve with the market.

If, on the other hand, your clients operate in more stable sectors, if your strength lies in deep expertise and personal trust, a traditional model may serve you better. In such cases, continuity can be a strategic asset, not a liability.

What matters most? The integrity of the choice. Chasing innovation for its own sake leads to fatigue and confusion – clinging to tradition out of fear leads to stagnation. Every firm must locate its own equilibrium – between the pace of technology and the permanence of principle.

Even the most conservative practices cannot ignore technological progress entirely, just as the most innovative ones cannot afford to forget the ethical and qualitative foundations on which the profession stands. Progress without integrity is as hollow as tradition without courage.

Chapter 10:
Organizational model – how the firm is built from within

Think of your organizational model as your firm's skeleton – its internal architecture.
It determines how you make decisions, how power gets distributed, and how growth happens. These choices might look purely technical on paper, but they shape everything – your ability to adapt, attract talent, and scale.

Of all the strategic shifts you might attempt, organizational change is the hardest.

It hits partners where it hurts – their personal interests, the culture they're used to, how things have always been done. That's why you need to make these choices consciously right at the start, understanding that every structural decision opens certain doors and slams others shut.

A firm can reposition itself or redesign its service model without too much pain. Changing its organizational DNA? Almost nobody pulls that off.

Partnership vs corporation – brotherhood or hierarchy?

Managing partners of classical partnerships often take genuine pride in how collegial everything is.

Want to change the office coffee supplier? Call a partners' meeting.

Want to hire a new associate? Everyone gets a vote. Democracy in its purest form.

Leaders of corporate-style firms live by a completely different philosophy.

While partnerships are spending two months debating what color to paint the meeting room, corporations have closed three deals and hired five new lawyers. Efficiency, they'll tell you, means having someone who decides and others who get on with it.

Partnership versus corporation isn't about legal form. It's a choice between two fundamentally different philosophies of governance, power, and accountability.

The brotherhood of equals – the power of partnership

A classical partnership rests on one principle – equality.

All partners are co-owners of the business, all have a voice, and all share equal responsibility for what happens.

Founders of traditional partnerships like to say that there are no bosses and subordinates among partners – just different jobs. One handles marketing, another does the finances, another looks after HR. But when it comes to the big calls? You make them together.

Consensus becomes the foundation of how you run things.

Important matters get talked through until everyone's on board. The process can drag on for weeks or months, but once you've reached that decision, everyone owns it and executes without pushback.

Some partners recall spending half a year debating whether to open a new office – modelling, arguing, running scenarios. The final decision was unanimous, and the project ran like clockwork because everyone had been invested from day one.

Personal responsibility in a partnership is absolute.

Each partner's accountable not just for their own actions but for what their colleagues do. This responsibility is both moral and financial – if something goes wrong, partners are on the hook with all their personal assets.

As one managing partner puts it, "When you know that someone else's mistake could cost you your flat, you choose your partners very differently".

The selection process is meticulous – you're not hiring an employee; you're inviting someone into the family.

Motivation in a partnership stems from ownership.

Every partner knows that the better the firm performs, the bigger their share. There's no hired-hand mentality, no shrugging at outcomes. Partners work as if it's their own business – because it is.

The price of equality

Partnership democracy comes at a cost – sometimes a heavy one.

The very structure that protects fairness can suffocate agility.

Decision-making speed takes the first hit. When every step needs discussion and alignment, you lose momentum. Several partners recall losing clients simply because decisions took too long. One client, after waiting a month for the partners to agree on whether to take a new mandate, quietly moved to a competitor – where a single managing partner made the call within a day.

Managing peers is far harder than managing subordinates. Managing partners admit you can't just say, "Do this because I've decided". You have to persuade, explain, negotiate, compromise – and that burns through vast amounts of time and emotional energy.

The risk of paralysis is ever-present. When partners can't agree, the entire firm freezes.

Some partnerships tell war stories of two partners who didn't speak for six months after falling out over strategy. Every key decision got blocked until someone brought in a mediator to get them talking again.

Growth itself becomes constrained. The partnership model doesn't scale easily. The more partners you've got, the harder it is to maintain consensus. Managing partners note that with three partners, decisions took an hour; with seven, a week; with 12, it became completely unmanageable.

And finally, there are personal risks. Partners bear unlimited liability not only for their own mistakes but for those of their colleagues. There are painful stories in many firms – one partner's professional error led others to sell their country houses to cover the losses.

Partnership, for all its ideals, demands a kind of courage rarely acknowledged – the courage to share not just power, but consequence.

Corporate efficiency

The corporate model rests on opposite principles – clear hierarchy, defined functions, and limited liability.

Leaders of corporate law firms describe a familiar setup – a CEO, a board, and a management structure where every role is specified and every decision has an owner. In these firms, authority isn't spread thin – it's delegated. Leaders make decisions fast. Teams implement them without hesitation.

Single-point leadership lies at the heart of the corporate philosophy. There's someone who decides – and others who execute. That clarity lets you respond to market changes quickly and grab opportunities while they're still there.

CEOs like to draw the contrast. When a potential acquisition pops up, they run due diligence, assess synergies, and sign off within days. A partnership, they'll tell you, would still be debating it six months later.

Professional management is another defining strength. People trained for management handle the managerial roles – not by lawyers who've reluctantly accepted the job or treat it as a side hustle. Many firms now employ a CFO who used to work at McKinsey, or a head of operations poached from the Big Four. Partners, freed from admin work, can focus on what they do best – practicing law.

Scalability is where the corporate model really shines. Formalized hierarchy, clear reporting lines, and professional systems make growth not just possible but sustainable. One CEO proudly notes the firm went from 30 to 300 lawyers in five years – a pace few partnerships could survive.

Finally, there's the matter of risk. Limited liability protects shareholders from personal exposure. As one director explains, "If something goes wrong, we lose our investment in the firm – not our homes". It's a different kind of courage – the confidence that comes from structure, not faith.

The cost of hierarchy

Corporate efficiency has its price. The clarity that enables decisions to be made faster can, over time, make people feel smaller.

The first casualty? The sense of ownership. Once lawyers become employees – even highly paid ones – their motivation shifts. CEOs of corporate firms acknowledge the difference – partners work as if it's their own business, employees work as if it's someone else's. The incentives may be generous, but the emotional bond is weaker.

Formalization has its costs too. Structured approval chains and multiple reporting levels slow down anything unconventional. Senior associates admit that when a client requests something unusual, they have to navigate three layers of internal clearance. In a partnership, they'd just walk into a partner's office and sort it out within minutes.

The culture of collegiality fades as well. In corporate structures, people become more distant. Experienced lawyers observe that everyone seems to be running their own race. What once felt like a shared destiny now feels like a series of individual careers.

Short-termism poses another subtle risk. Professional managers, measured by annual results, may optimize for the quarter rather than the decade. Shareholders recall how one former CEO posted record profits three years running – until it became clear he'd achieved them by slashing investment in development. The recovery took years.

And finally, there's the risk of detachment. When lawyers have no say in shaping strategy, they begin to drift from the business itself. Senior partners in corporate firms admit they now learn about strategic changes from internal newsletters – decisions they once helped make.

Hierarchy, for all its order, carries a quiet loneliness. It builds systems that work – but not always communities that last.

Hybrid models – the search for balance

The question arises naturally: can you combine the collegial spirit of a partnership with the efficiency of a corporation?

Some firms are experimenting with what they call managed partnerships – keeping the partnership ownership structure but handing operational authority to a professional management team. The logic's straightforward – partners decide on strategy; managers handle execution.

Others pursue the reverse: a corporation with a partnership soul. Legally a company, culturally it stays close to the partnership ideal – broad participation in decisions, profit sharing, and long-term incentives that encourage people to think collectively.

A third approach is evolutionary transition. As partnerships grow, they gradually corporatize while trying to preserve the human fabric that once defined them. Many managing partners describe the same journey – what started as a tight group of five lawyers becomes a firm of 150 – and at that point, formal processes aren't optional anymore.

Scale and maturity

The choice between partnership and corporation often depends on your firm's size and stage of development.

Smaller firms – 20 to 30 lawyers – naturally lean toward the partnership model. It fits the scale and spirit. Everyone knows everyone, you can make decisions round the kitchen table, and personal relationships matter more than formal procedure.

Mid-sized firms – 50 to 150 lawyers – live in the most awkward zone. The partnership model doesn't work efficiently anymore, but corporate governance still feels alien. This is where hybrid models usually appear – not from theory, but from necessity.

Large firms – 200 lawyers and beyond – almost inevitably adopt corporate features. Scale demands formalization, specialized management roles, and professional executives who can coordinate complex systems.

Management consultants who advise law firms put it this way: "A partnership is like a family. When the family's small, everything works beautifully. But when it grows to a hundred relatives, you need rules and rituals to keep everyone functioning."

An honest conversation about values

In the end, the choice between partnership and corporation isn't about structure – it's about values.

What matters more to you – equality or efficiency? Collegiality or speed? Personal accountability or protection from risk?

If you believe in sharing every decision and carrying its weight – even risking your own assets – partnership may be your natural home. If the spirit of brotherhood matters more to you than managerial precision, if you prefer long discussions to quick directives, the partnership path will feel right.

If, on the other hand, you value clarity over consensus, if you see efficiency as a higher virtue than democracy, if you'd rather focus on practicing law than managing the business that delivers it – the corporate model may suit you better.

What matters most is understanding the price of every choice and resisting the temptation to grab all the benefits without accepting the accompanying costs.

And perhaps the hardest truth – there's no perfect model. There's only the one that matches your values, your scale, and your ambition.

Personal brands vs the corporate brand

Stars or systems?

Here's something prominent lawyers in corporate practice will often admit over a drink – clients call them personally, not the firm. The client isn't buying a service – they're buying a specialist. Their expertise, their reputation, their network.

Some partners have become brands in their own right. Their LinkedIn profiles pull in tens of thousands of followers. Their names carry more weight than the firm's logo on the door.

Managing partners of institutional firms see things differently. Sure, their lawyers are excellent – but none are stars. Clients choose these firms not because of one name, but because of a system – consistent quality, reliable processes, and a brand that stands for trust, not personality.

This tension between personal brands and corporate brand isn't just a marketing question. It reflects two fundamentally different philosophies of how you create value and sustain competitive advantage – through individual brilliance, or through collective design.

The nature of the legal business – why stars still matter

Before we dive into models, it's worth remembering that legal practice differs fundamentally from most other professional services. It's a titular, deeply conservative business where the individual still matters more than the institution.

Partners with decades of experience will tell you the same thing – clients don't buy a legal service. What clients actually buy – a lawyer. A person.

Even in the largest international firms, the first question a client asks isn't, "What team will handle my matter?" or "What systems do you use?" It's simply, "Who will be my lawyer?"

Personal responsibility in law isn't only professional but ethical. A lawyer's accountable not just through the firm's reputation but through their own license and name. As many partners put it, when you sign a document, you stand behind every word personally – no corporate structure can dilute that.

The conservatism of the client base reinforces this. Large corporates, family-owned businesses, private clients – they all prefer working with people they know and trust. Some partners tell stories of family enterprises now in their third generation – clients they've advised for 20 years. These clients will pay more, wait longer, even travel across the country to work with the lawyer who knows their business history inside out.

Even among the world's most institutionalized firms – the Magic Circle, the White Shoe elite, leading continental European networks – corporatization remains incomplete. Yes, there are standards, processes, quality-control systems. Yet clients still associate firms with names – with partners they can point to, whose reputations they recognize.

Legal marketing consultants often make the same observation – crack open a Linklaters or Freshfields pitch deck for a major client, and half the slides are devoted to biographies of specific partners – their achievements, credentials, deal history. Clients want to know who they'll be working with.

Regulation itself sustains personalization. In most jurisdictions, partners are required to take personal responsibility for client matters – to sign documents, appear in filings, be named on the record.

Cultural context amplifies these differences. In Germany or Switzerland, personal relationships with lawyers remain essential. In the Anglo-Saxon world, corporate structures are more advanced, yet even there, truly impersonal firms are rare.

Partners in major international firms will admit that the shift towards the corporate brand is real – but far from complete. For all the systems and standards, roughly 80 percent of new mandates still come through a partner's personal network.

The legal profession, for all its modernization, remains one of the last bastions where trust has a name – and a face.

The cult of personality – the power of the star

Given this reality, firms built around personal brands have a natural advantage. They're working with the grain of market expectations, not against it.

Managing partners of boutiques known for their star lawyers will explain their philosophy simply – they gather the best experts in every field. Each one's a recognized leader in their niche. Clients know them personally, trust them, are willing to pay a premium for the chance to work with them specifically.

Personalization of relationships becomes the key advantage. The client's not dealing with some faceless corporation – they're working with a specific person they know, value, trust. These partners tell you that their clients ring them on their mobile at any time of day, meet up outside work. The lawyers know their families, their hobbies, their plans for the future.

Premium positioning flows naturally from the star model. When clients are seeking out a specific individual, price stops being the main factor. Well-known arbitration lawyers note that their clients don't haggle – they understand they're paying not for hours worked, but for unique expertise they won't get anywhere else.

Flexibility in decision making works for the star system too. A star partner can make instant decisions on their projects, no need to check with committees or follow procedures. Partners give examples of a client asking them to start work immediately, they said "yes" and began that same day – in a large corporate firm, that would have taken weeks of approvals.

Innovation often runs higher in star firms. When your reputation's built on personal expertise, there's an incentive to constantly come up with new approaches and develop unconventional solutions. Leading IP lawyers explain that they can't afford to work from templates – their value lies in their ability to find solutions where others don't see them.

The cost of stardom

The star system carries undeniable risks – for both the firm and the stars themselves.

Dependence on key individuals is the most obvious vulnerability. When your business revolves around a few names, their departure can be catastrophic. Many firms have learned this the hard way – the leading M&A partner leaves for a competitor, takes 80 percent of the practice's clients, and a decade of work is lost in a month.

Scalability poses another challenge. You can't replicate or standardize stars. Managing partners will admit, "We've got a brilliant tax partner – but only one. He can't work with a hundred clients at once, and finding another of the same caliber? Almost impossible."

Internal competition can poison the atmosphere too. When several stars coexist in one firm, ego clashes are inevitable. Managing partners confess, sometimes half-jokingly, that two of their rainmakers can't even be in the same room – each convinced they're the brightest light in the firm. The result isn't just tension but toxicity.

Over time, the fragility becomes apparent. The star model works beautifully while the stars are shining. But what happens when they age, burn out, or simply lose interest? Partners recall founders who were once legends in their field but, by 70, could no longer lead – and the firm never learned to function without them.

And finally, there's reputational risk. When your firm's identity is tied to specific individuals, their personal crises become your firm's crises. Colleagues tell of a once-celebrated partner who got entangled in scandal – the firm spent months and vast resources rebuilding its reputation.

Stardom brings prestige, but it also concentrates fragility. The brighter the light, the deeper the shadows it casts.

Institutional strength – the quality machine

Firms built on strong corporate brands rest on a different philosophy. What matters isn't the individual lawyer, but the system – the processes, the institutional expertise, the collective discipline that ensures quality at scale.

Managing partners of major international networks will explain that their clients don't choose a specific partner – they choose the brand. They know that whoever handles the matter, the quality will be the same. The system guarantees it.

Predictability of quality is the central advantage here. Standardized processes, unified expectations of expertise, rigorous quality-control mechanisms – they deliver a consistent outcome, regardless of who does the work.

Operational partners can describe in detail how this works – for every type of transaction, there are procedures, checklists, templates, and knowledge databases. Any lawyer can pick up a matter and execute it to a high standard simply by following the firm's protocols.

Scalability follows naturally. When value is created by the system rather than individuals, growth becomes easier – new offices can open, teams can expand, culture stays coherent. Managing partners take quiet pride in this – five offices opened in three years, all running under the same processes, standards, and culture.

Resilience to personnel change is another advantage. Even losing a top lawyer is rarely fatal to a firm built on institutional strength. Colleagues will admit, "We were disappointed when our senior partner left – but the system kept working. The clients stayed."

Investment efficiency improves too. In institutional firms, resources spent on training, systems, and processes create value for the whole organization – not just for a few individuals.

The result is a different kind of excellence – one that relies not on brilliance, but on design.

The cost of impersonality

In institutional firms, personalization inevitably suffers. Clients may feel less valued when they're working not with a person, but with a system. Some clients of large firms will admit they sometimes feel like a case number – one lawyer handles the matter today, another tomorrow, no one truly knows their business in depth.

Flexibility gets constrained by standardization. Structured processes, while ensuring consistency, can inhibit unconventional thinking. Clients often observe that institutional firms have an answer to every typical question – but when something atypical crops up, the system hesitates. Exceptions don't fit easily into procedures.

Innovation may decline too. When everything runs by protocol, the incentive to search for new approaches weakens. As some lawyers in institutional firms will candidly admit, "Why reinvent the wheel when the template already works?"

Motivation can shift as well. When personal brands are irrelevant, the drive for individual growth and recognition fades. Senior associates sometimes reflect that in such firms you can be an excellent lawyer and remain completely invisible to the market – every success attributed to the firm, not the person behind it.

And finally, there's the risk of dehumanization. In the pursuit of efficiency and uniformity, it's all too easy to lose the human dimension of legal work – the empathy, intuition, and personal trust the profession was built on. Perfection of the system, pushed too far, risks perfection without soul.

Hybrid models – stars within the system

The natural question follows: can you design a system that supports its stars – without depending on them entirely?

Some firms are experimenting with what you might call managed stardom. They maintain a few visible partners who drive client acquisition and reputation, while a strong institutional backbone ensures consistent delivery. Managing partners describe it simply: "We've got three high-profile partners who speak at conferences, publish, bring in clients – but the work gets done by the whole team to the same standards. The stars set direction; the system delivers the result."

Another approach focuses on stars within niches. Here, the firm develops personal brands of partners in highly specialized areas, while keeping a system-driven approach in core practices. Colleagues give examples such as an IP partner who becomes a recognized public figure in their field, while the corporate department operates like a finely tuned machine.

A third model is next-generation stardom. The firm deliberately cultivates personal brands of younger partners – nurturing future leaders who can one day replace today's stars. This reduces dependence on individual names while preserving the advantages of personal connection and visibility.

In these hybrid models, reputation becomes distributed – the light no longer belongs to one star, but to a constellation.

A strategic choice

The balance between personal and corporate brands often gets determined by the nature of your firm's clients and the character of its work.

For complex, high-stakes matters – those depending on personal relationships and creative judgment – the star model can be more effective. Clients are willing to pay a premium for direct access to trusted experts.

For standardized, process-heavy services where predictability and scale matter more, the institutional model holds the advantage. Such clients value reliability and the efficiency of a system over the charisma of an individual.

Managing partners often explain their choices in practical terms. Their M&A clients expect to work with specific partners they know and trust; their corporate clients simply want recurring legal needs handled seamlessly and on time.

Size and maturity play their part too. Smaller firms naturally gravitate toward the star model – it's easier to build around a few strong personalities. Larger firms, by contrast, inevitably evolve toward institutionalization as they grow, needing systems to maintain coherence across people and offices.

An honest conversation about ego

In the end, the choice between personal and corporate brands is a choice between different kinds of ambition.

If you want your name known within the profession, if you're willing to take personal responsibility for your reputation, if you value direct relationships with clients more than systemic efficiency – the star model may be your path.

If, however, you aspire to build something larger than yourself, if you're ready to trade personal recognition for institutional strength, if you believe more in teams than heroes – the corporate brand may suit you better.

What matters most is clarity – understanding the limits and risks of each model. Don't try to grab the benefits of stardom without accepting its costs, or the advantages of institutionalization without conceding some personal influence.

In a world of growing transparency and increasing personalization, many firms seek a balance between the two. Yet pure models still work best – when you make the choice consciously and follow it consistently.

True leadership, after all, begins not with strategy, but with self-awareness.

Individual achievements vs team results

The partnership formula as an architectural choice

A partnership formula isn't a technical element of internal accounting. It's an architectural choice – one that defines partner behavior, shapes the firm's culture, and determines its capacity for growth. What the formula rewards becomes what partners prioritize. What it ignores gradually disappears from daily practice.

The decision between a system that rewards individual achievement and one that promotes collective performance profoundly affects how partners interact, how they treat clients, and how they resolve internal conflicts.

The culture of meritocracy – everyone for themselves

Formulas built on individual performance rest on a simple premise – the more you generate, the more you earn. In such firms, each partner becomes a business within the business – running their own practice, managing their own clients, competing for their own results.

The metrics are familiar and precise:

- Billing – the value of premium hours billed by the partner.
- Origination – the revenue generated by the clients they brought in.
- Client development – the growth of their client portfolio.
- Personal profitability – the margin achieved after deducting their own costs.

Together they form a transparent scorecard. Numbers don't argue – they reward exactly what they measure. Work more, earn more. Work better, earn better.

Advocates of this model praise its fairness and clarity. No one can complain about favoritism or politics when performance is visible, comparable, and directly monetized. The system seems almost self-regulating – elegant in its simplicity and merciless in its logic. Its motivational power is undeniable. Partners in meritocratic firms tend to operate at full capacity, pushing themselves harder than any manager could demand, because every extra effort translates into measurable reward. They thrive in an environment where the line between effort and outcome is perfectly straight.

Yet the same clarity that drives performance also defines the culture it creates. In a pure meritocracy, collaboration becomes optional, and solidarity – a luxury few can afford.

The cost of individualism

The culture of meritocracy carries hidden costs that rarely appear overnight but accumulate slowly over the years.

The first casualty is teamwork. When every partner is measured by their own numbers, collaboration turns from a virtue into a distraction. Why spend time helping a colleague if it brings no credit to your personal account? A familiar scene plays out in many firms – a client requests a complex, multi-practice transaction that requires a corporate lawyer, a tax specialist, and an employment expert. Each partner wants to be the lead counsel – and to receive the credit for origination. More time gets spent debating ownership than solving the client's problem.

The reluctance to invest in firm-wide activities follows naturally. Training younger lawyers, contributing to marketing, serving on committees – it all eats into billable time and reduces personal profitability. In an individualistic system, anything that can't be billed is seen as waste. Management roles become equally unattractive – heading a practice or leading a quality committee means hours of non-billable work, a direct financial loss under a formula that values only individual output.

Short-term thinking intensifies too. When the formula rewards immediate results, partners get tempted to sacrifice the future for the present, extracting more from existing clients instead of developing new areas or nurturing long-term relationships. Over time, the internal competition becomes corrosive. Instead of competing with other firms, partners begin competing with each other. Information gets withheld, contacts are guarded, cooperation turns political.

Ultimately, the risk of fragmentation becomes real. When every partner operates as a business of their own, the firm starts to lose its cohesion. Some leave, taking their clients and teams with them. What began as a partnership gradually unravels into a collection of disconnected enterprises. The irony of meritocracy is that it maximizes effort but erodes unity – it builds strong performers and weak institutions.

The culture of collaboration – shared success

Formulas based on collective performance rest on the opposite philosophy – the firm's a single organism, and its health matters more than any individual achievement. In collaborative firms, no one keeps a meticulous record of who brought in what. The focus lies on shared goals – total revenue, profitability, client satisfaction, and team development. All partners work toward these objectives and receive a fair share of the common result.

The underlying principles of such systems are straightforward. There's equality of base shares – partners at the same level earn comparable amounts. There are bonuses for contributions to the firm's collective success – leadership in practice development, mentoring, business growth. And there's a long-term orientation – performance is measured not only by what partners achieve today, but by the future value they help create.

Collaboration in such firms happens naturally and gets encouraged by design. When a complex project arrives, a team from multiple practices forms automatically. No one asks who will receive the credit. The only concern is solving the client's problem well.

The same logic promotes investment in the firm's future. Partners willingly take on management roles or mentoring responsibilities, seeing the firm's development as an extension of their own. The stronger the institution becomes, the more everyone benefits.

Stability is another reward of the collective model. Partner turnover tends to be minimal, and few see departure as the only path to higher income. In such firms, you can build not just a career, but a professional home.

The cost of collectivism

The collective model brings its own set of challenges. The first is the dilution of individual responsibility. When everyone receives roughly the same share regardless of personal contribution, the motivation to go the extra mile inevitably weakens. In every team-based firm there are partners who work 60 hours a week and those who work 40 – yet their compensation differs only marginally. It's hard to call that fair.

Assessing individual contribution is another perennial source of tension. How do you measure the value of mentoring or administrative work? How do you compare a partner who brings in one major client with another who serves a dozen smaller ones with equal dedication? Each year, debates over bonuses resurface, with no fully objective criteria to rely on. Sooner or later, subjective judgment steps in, and with it comes frustration.

The risk of complacency is also real. When income remains steady and predictable regardless of personal effort, the drive to improve can fade. Revenues in collaborative firms often grow more slowly than in their meritocratic counterparts – perhaps because they lack the hard edge of competition that pushes each partner to perform at their limit.

Finally, attracting star talent becomes harder. High-performing partners who thrive on individual results may balk at egalitarian formulas. Strong candidates sometimes walk away upon learning that their efforts would subsidize less productive colleagues. For them, equality feels less like fairness and more like restraint.

Practice and client dynamics

The choice between individual and collective formulas often depends on the nature of the firm's practices and its client base. Transactional areas such as M&A, banking, and capital markets naturally lean toward individualism. Contribution is easy to measure, projects have clear boundaries, and clients are often tied to specific partners. In M&A, the equation's simple – either you closed the deal or you didn't; either the client came through you or through someone else.

Litigation practices, by contrast, depend far more on teamwork. Disputes can last for years, involving multiple specialists whose success hinges on coordination and trust. A single case may engage a dozen lawyers at different levels – a senior partner designing the strategy, associates drafting pleadings, paralegals collecting evidence. How can anyone meaningfully separate their individual contributions?

The same applies to long-term client relationships such as corporate advisory, compliance, or tax planning. These areas favor collective systems built on stability and continuity. Corporate clients often stay with a firm for decades, working with dozens of lawyers over time. No one can claim full credit for a relationship that's been nurtured across generations of teams.

Firm size plays its part too. Small firms of 20 or 30 lawyers can succeed under almost any model – partners know each other personally, and individual effort is visible to all. As firms grow beyond a hundred lawyers, however, the balance tends to shift. Larger organizations often adopt more structured formulas, blending individual accountability with systemic fairness.

Hybrid approaches – balancing incentives

Most successful firms eventually arrive at hybrid formulas that combine elements of both philosophies. The simplest version divides profits between a shared base and an individual component – for example, 60 percent distributed equally among partners, and 40 percent allocated according to personal performance. This balance preserves a sense of fairness while maintaining motivation for individual achievement.

Another common approach is functional differentiation. Rainmaker partners earn more for business development, service partners are rewarded for excellence in delivery, and management partners for administrative leadership. Each contributes differently to the firm's success – one attracts new clients, another executes flawlessly, a third ensures that systems and people function smoothly. A well-designed formula recognizes and rewards all these forms of contribution.

Some firms take a temporal view, adjusting incentives over time. During periods of rapid growth, business development carries greater weight. In times of stability, operational excellence becomes the priority. In crises, the emphasis shifts to cohesion and collective resilience. The underlying idea is simple but powerful – a compensation system should evolve with the firm's own life cycle, reflecting not only what drives profit today but what sustains the institution tomorrow.

The evolution of partner formulas

Partnership formulas are never static – they evolve with the firm itself. Young firms often begin with simple equality. When there are only a few partners and everyone contributes more or less equally to growth, there's little need for complex mechanics. As the firm expands, differentiation naturally appears. Some partners excel at bringing in clients, others at management or technical expertise. The formula grows more sophisticated to reflect these differences.

At maturity, many firms circle back toward more collective models. Once reputation is established, the client base stable, and internal systems refined, the focus shifts to preserving culture and cohesion. Many firms trace a full cycle over time – they start with equality, move through strict meritocracy, and eventually return to a more team-oriented approach. At each stage, the formula mirrors the firm's priorities.

The hidden functions of the formula

A partner compensation system does more than motivate – it shapes the firm's entire ecosystem. Recruitment is one example. Individualistic firms tend to attract independent high-performers, while team-oriented ones appeal to collaborators. Many firms make a point of explaining their formula to candidates during the very first interview – better to know at once whether the culture fits.

Practice development follows the same logic. Individualist systems reward profitable practices, sometimes at the expense of strategically important ones. Collective models, by contrast, can afford to support investment areas using profits from more mature practices. The formula becomes an implicit policy tool – directing resources, attention, and talent.

Client relationships are influenced as well. In individualistic firms, loyalty attaches to specific partners; in collective firms, it attaches to the institution. And succession planning often reflects these dynamics too. Team-based formulas tend to foster the transfer of clients and knowledge across generations, while individualistic ones can make succession far more complicated.

In the end, a partner formula isn't just an economic equation. It's the most honest expression of what a firm truly values – growth or stability, independence or unity, the individual or the institution.

A candid conversation about fairness

In the end, the choice between individual and collective formulas reflects your own definition of fairness. Do you believe it's fair for those who work harder and deliver more to earn substantially more than their colleagues? Or is fairness, in your view, about equal opportunity and recognition of different forms of contribution?

Are you willing to tolerate internal competition for the sake of higher motivation? Or do you prefer collaboration, even if it means accepting lower individual output? What matters more to you – attracting and retaining stars, or preserving a sense of unity? Maximizing short-term results, or investing in long-term strength?

There are no universally correct answers – only those consistent with your values, your strategy, and your culture. A partner formula, in the end, defines the character of your firm. What you reward is what you'll get. If you want teamwork, pay for collective results. If you want individual excellence, reward personal achievement. But don't expect team spirit from an individualistic system, nor star performance from an equal distribution.

Structural constellations

How choices shape choices

The 14 dichotomies described in Appendix 11 form a complex web of interdependence. Philosophical choices at the level of meta-decisions determine the logic of every subsequent architectural decision. Your firm's design isn't a collection of independent switches – it's a constellation of interconnected elements that either reinforce one another or pull in opposite directions.

Understanding these relationships is essential to building an internally coherent architecture. Ignoring the logical links between choices inevitably leads to internal tension, cultural contradictions, and strategic drift.

Three strategic games

1. The Lone Wolf

Built on the philosophy of hunters, exploiters, and growth at any cost, the "Lone Wolf" model represents a highly efficient machine for extracting profit. Each partner is a combat unit of their own, pursuing personal maximization as the purest expression of success. When every partner hunts for the highest-value work, the market naturally drifts toward elite, high-stakes projects. Why handle routine matters when one million-dollar deal can outshine a dozen smaller ones? From this logic comes exclusivity – and, inevitably, the need to expand beyond local markets once they're exhausted. Governments impose limits – the Lone Wolf keeps its distance.

Innovation becomes a weapon in the competition for clients, and formal processes act as armor against the risks of high-stakes play. Each partner builds a personal brand – their ultimate competitive advantage. Individual achievement becomes the only fair basis for profit allocation.

Typical examples include leading international arbitration boutiques, elite M&A practices, and top-tier Silicon Valley IP firms. The strength of the Lone Wolf lies in the relentless motivation of every player. Yet with this power comes fragility – high turnover, internal rivalries, and dependence on stars. When the lead hunter leaves, half the prey leaves with them.

2. The Family

The opposite philosophy rests on a different triad – farmers, investors, and balance. These are stable organizations where team comfort matters more than maximizing profit. The Family focuses on what it knows best – a familiar market, a loyal client base, and time-tested methods. Routine work provides predictability – long-standing relationships with regional authorities or local businesses guarantee a steady flow of matters. Why reinvent the wheel when the old one's carried you safely for decades?

Personal relationships with clients matter more than systems. Most issues are resolved through conversation and trust rather than formal processes. The corporate brand outweighs personal fame – the firm must outlive any single partner. Success is measured collectively, because everyone contributes together.

Typical examples include regional leaders, long-established family practices, and conservative European partnerships. The Family's strength lies in its stability and deep roots – its weakness in a limited capacity for rapid growth and a certain vulnerability to market disruption.

3. The Corporation

A hybrid philosophy built on farmers, investors, and growth through systems. Ambitious goals, but achieved collectively – by constructing a machine that works flawlessly. The Corporation can operate in elite segments, but does so methodically – it can serve mass markets, yet on a global scale. Innovation isn't a burst of inspiration but a managed process, channeled through R&D units and implemented with precision. Formalization doesn't hinder growth – it enables it.

The corporate brand becomes the ultimate guarantee of quality. Team-based results encourage collaboration, while elements of individual recognition prevent the dulling effect of equality. Typical examples include the Magic Circle, major American networks, and emerging technological legal platforms.

The strength of the Corporation lies in its scalability and resilience. Its danger lies in bureaucracy – and in the gradual loss of the human touch that once inspired it.

See Table 10.1.

Table 10.1: Three strategic games

Dimension	The lone wolf	The family	The corporation
Core philosophy	Hunters, Renters, Growth at any cost	Farmers, Investors, Balance	Farmers, Investors, Systematic growth
Market focus	Elite, high-stakes matters. Exclusivity over volume.	Local market, loyal client base. Known territory.	Scalable across segments. Elite or mass, but systematically.
Geography	Global – local markets exhaust quickly	Regional – deep roots matter more than reach	Multi-jurisdictional – scalable systems enable expansion
Client model	Personal relationships with individual partners	Long-term relationships built on trust and familiarity	Institutional relationships – firm guarantees quality
Innovation	Weapon in competition for clients. First-mover advantage.	Tradition and proven methods. "If it works, why change?"	Managed process through R&D. Innovation via systems.

continued on next page

Dimension	The lone wolf	The family	The corporation
Formalization	Formal processes as armor against high-stakes risk	Informal – relationships trump systems	Highly formalized – systems enable scale
Brand	Personal brands – each partner is the brand	Corporate brand – firm outlives founders	Corporate brand as ultimate quality guarantee
Rewards	Individual achievement – eat what you kill	Collective success – shared prosperity	Team results with elements of individual recognition
Key strengths	• Extreme motivation • High margins • Attract stars • Market agility	• Stability • Deep roots • Client loyalty • Low turnover	• Scalability • Resilience • Consistency • Institutional strength
Key vulnerabilities	• High turnover • Star dependency • Internal competition • Fragility	• Limited growth • Market disruption risk • Comfort trap • Innovation resistance	• Bureaucracy • Loss of human touch • Slower decisions • Cultural dilution

Logical traps

Some combinations create contradictions that can't be resolved. Trying to be a hunter under a team-based profit system is like asking a sprinter to run a relay alone. Attempting to build personal, relationship-based trust inside a thousand-lawyer global corporation is like trying to host a family dinner in a football stadium.

Exploiters can't both squeeze maximum profit and pursue ambitious growth – expansion requires reinvestment. Lone Wolves, by their very nature, struggle to thrive in egalitarian environments built on shared rewards. Relationship-driven models can't be scaled across hundreds of lawyers and dozens of offices without losing their essence.

Architectural evolution

Successful firms rarely preserve a single architecture throughout their life. They evolve – but the successful ones do so logically and in sequence.

Start-ups of five lawyers often begin as Families – survival outweighs optimization, flexibility is critical, and equality feels natural. But once stars emerge and differences in productivity become visible, the structure reaches a crossroads – either move toward the individualistic logic of the Lone Wolf, or preserve a managed sense of family by consciously limiting ambition.

High-performing boutiques built on the Lone Wolf model eventually face the challenge of scale. Stars resist formalization, yet without systems there can be no growth. The transition toward a corporate structure is painful but inevitable. Mature Corporations, in turn, sometimes rediscover family values at a higher level – processes intact, but with a human face.

Architectural problems usually reveal themselves through behavioral symptoms. When partners refuse to collaborate, it often signals individualistic incentives beneath the surface of proclaimed teamwork. High turnover among talented lawyers points to a clash between personal brands and institutionalization. When clients complain about a lack of personal attention, it means formal processes have been imposed on relationship-driven expectations. Opening new offices becomes a headache when a relationship-based model can't handle geographic expansion. Young lawyers burn out quickly when a family-style culture collides with individualistic ambition. Conscious architectural navigation begins with honesty about motives. The first step is to make – the philosophical decisions that set the direction and then follow the logical sequence of the rest. No element can be changed in isolation. Moving toward elitism, for example, requires a full redesign of the motivational system.

Choosing a *modus vivendi*

The architecture of a law firm is, at its core, a choice of existence. Successful firms build internally coherent systems where every element reinforces the others – where the philosophy of partnership naturally leads to a certain strategy, the strategy shapes a corresponding service model, and that model dictates an organization aligned with both. There's no universally "right" architecture. There's only one that reflects your values, ambitions, and willingness to bear the consequences of your choices. The essential task is to understand the logic behind your decisions – and to follow it consistently, rather than trying to capture the advantages of all models at once. See Appendix 12.

Part V:
Decision-Making Timeline

Chapter 11:
Architectural decisions life cycle

Time and transformation – the map of the life cycle

Architectural choices aren't one-time decisions. They evolve with the firm, tracking through predictable growth crises, transformation moments, and strategic crossroads. What worked perfectly for three partners in Year One can become toxic for ten partners in Year 17.

Imagine a doctor indefinitely postponing a diagnosis. Or an architect who starts building a house without deciding how many floors it needs. Absurd? Yet this is exactly what many law firms do with their own architecture – deferring critical choices, hoping time will somehow sort everything out.

Architectural decisions follow their own rhythm. Some come with hard deadlines – postpone them, and the cost multiplies. Others can be safely pondered for years without serious consequences. A third category requires constant revision – yesterday's right answer can easily become tomorrow's structural problem.

Understanding this dynamic is one of the most important management skills. Firms that make the right decisions at the wrong time often lose to those that simply make timely ones.

Four types of foundational decisions

All architectural choices fall into four categories based on temporal urgency. Understanding this classification helps you avoid two opposite mistakes – delaying what can't wait, and rushing what can.

Day One decisions

Some architectural choices can't be postponed even for an hour. Without them, a firm either fails to launch or drifts into chaos from the very first steps. Most often, these are the fundamental agreements between partners on why they're in business together in the first place.

Hunters or farmers? This conversation can't wait, because it defines the logic of everything that follows. If one partner sees the firm as a community of strong individuals, each maximizing their own results, while another views it as a team working towards collective success, the first serious crisis turns into an existential conflict.

Without an honest discussion upfront, partners spend years speaking different languages. One wonders why the other refuses to share client contacts; the other wonders why individual credit gets demanded for team achievements.

Renters or investors? The partners' attitude towards the jointly created asset also demands immediate clarity. Will they extract maximum current profit or invest in long-term growth?

This isn't a philosophical question – it shapes every financial decision. Renters rent the cheapest offices, hire minimal staff, and spend on marketing only under pressure. Investors willingly limit current payouts to build competitive advantages. Mixing these approaches within one firm is a direct path to permanent conflict.

Serve or be served? This basic question of priorities also brooks no delay. Are the partners ready to subordinate personal interests to the firm's strategic goals – or will they limit the firm's ambitions to protect their own work–life balance?

The answer plays out in hundreds of daily choices – whether to take on a project requiring weekend work, whether to open an office in another city if it means constant travel, whether to hire an expensive specialist at the cost of partner payouts. Without shared understanding of priorities, every such decision becomes a debate.

Decisions at critical turning points

Some choices can be deferred, but only up to a certain point. Beyond that moment, delay becomes dangerous – the firm either misses opportunities or accumulates internal strain. Critical turning points usually coincide with changes in team size, scale of operations, or shifts in the external environment. See Table 11.1 below.

State or business? In the first months, a firm can work with almost anyone – private companies, state entities, or regulators. But within two or three years it must decide where it stands in relation to power. Proximity to the state opens some doors and closes others. Independence carries its own price and its own advantages.

Avoiding this choice creates confusion in positioning. Potential clients don't know who you are or whether they can trust you with sensitive matters. Private companies may doubt confidentiality if they see you advising regulators. State bodies may doubt your loyalty if most of your clients are private.

Formality or relationships? Once a firm grows beyond 20 or 30 people, a purely relationship-driven model begins to break down. Not everyone knows everyone else; important information gets lost in private conversations; key decisions get made without the right people in the room.

The classic symptoms are familiar. Employees learn about major changes by accident, through hallway gossip. Clients receive conflicting information from different lawyers. Partners discover that colleagues have taken decisions directly affecting their work – without ever being consulted.

Family or corporation? As partnerships grow beyond seven partners, consensus-based decision making slows to a crawl. Three people can discuss an issue for an hour and reach agreement. Ten will debate for days.

The problem isn't unwillingness to cooperate but simple mathematics of difference – ten people bring ten priorities, ten interpretations, and ten definitions of what "optimal" looks like. The result is often a compromise that satisfies no one.

Decisions that require periodic reassessment

The third category includes choices that must be revisited from time to time – not because they were wrong, but because the context has changed. What once worked for a team of ten may become an obstacle for a team of 50.

Innovation or tradition? Proven methods bring stability and predictability. Yet the world moves on, and what worked yesterday may fail tomorrow. Clients arrive with new expectations, technologies reshape delivery models, and regulation evolves faster than culture does.

Mature firms must balance respect for tradition with readiness to experiment. The challenge isn't to discard everything old in pursuit of fashionable novelties, but also not to cling to outdated practices out of fear of change.

The weight of process. Formal procedures tend to expand and complicate over time. What began as a simple checklist can turn, within a few years, into a multi-page manual filled with exceptions and disclaimers.

Firms must periodically perform a "spring cleaning" of their processes – which ones still add value, and which exist merely because "we've always done it this way".

Corporate brand or personal brands? In mature firms, tension often arises between institutional strength and individual ambition. Institutionalization brings stability, but may limit scope for personal recognition and growth.

How can talented partners develop and be visible without weakening the collective identity? How can individual motivation align with institutional purpose? These are questions that never stay solved for long – they must be managed continuously and with nuance.

Fluctuating decisions

Finally, there are choices that can be adjusted along the way without serious consequences. They give the firm room to experiment and adapt as circumstances change.

Specialization or breadth. Young firms often begin as generalists, taking on any work to survive – and that's both normal and sensible. As they mature, they can gradually focus on what they do best, without making abrupt moves. The reverse is also possible – a specialized boutique can evolve into a firm with three or four strong practice areas.

Local or global. Geographic focus can also shift over time. A firm may start on the local market, then expand outward – or, conversely, deepen its local expertise depending on opportunities and temperament.

Elite or broad-market. Positioning in the market can evolve too. A firm may begin with a wide client base and become more selective as its reputation grows – or, after establishing a name in a niche, widen its reach to attract a broader audience.

The key insight is simple – flexible decisions need periodic review but don't provoke crises when changed. They allow a firm to adjust to new realities without architectural upheaval.

Table 11.1: Decision Types Classification

Type	When to decide	Reversibility	Cost of delay
Day one Foundational philosophy	Before launch – cannot wait	Extremely hard to reverse	Years of friction, eventual breakdown
Critical turning points Scale-dependent	When triggered by growth or change	Very hard – requires restructuring	Missed opportunities, market confusion
Periodic reassessment Context-dependent	Every two to three years or when context shifts	Moderate – adjustable with planning	Slow drift from reality
Fluctuative Adaptable	When opportune – flexible timing	Easy – reversible without disruption	Minimal – room for experimentation

More examples and a prioritization framework are available in Appendix 13.

The timeline of key decisions

Once you understand the types of architectural choices, you can build a timeline for making them. Each stage of development brings certain decisions to the surface and sets the timing for revisiting others.

The first three years – laying the foundations

The start-up stage is deceptive. Treating it as a warm-up for "real" decisions later is one of the most common strategic mistakes.

It feels natural to focus on operations – finding clients, hiring people, sorting out office space – and postpone structural questions until you've got "time to think". Yet these first years are precisely when you make decisions that define the firm's trajectory for decades.

All Day One decisions need settling before launch. You can't improvise the meta-choices behind your partnership philosophy. Either the partners understand each other from the outset, or they're in for years of friction.

By the end of Year One, you should already see the direction of your flexible choices. You don't need full specialization yet, but patterns should be emerging. Which projects bring the most satisfaction? Which clients pay premium rates? In which areas do your peers already recognize your strength?

By Year Three, the critical-point decisions affecting reputation can't wait any longer – your stance towards the state, your basic market positioning, your geographic focus. Delay them, and you'll only create confusion about who you are and what clients can expect.

Internal matters can stay open for now. With a small team, the relationship-based model still works, partnership democracy runs efficiently, and corporate branding feels premature.

Three to seven years – adapting to scale and the leadership crisis

Firms that survive the start-up period face the growth paradox – what brought you success can become the obstacle to more of it. Informal methods that worked brilliantly for a small team start failing as you scale.

This stage brings your first serious transition crisis – the leadership crisis. Founders who successfully launched the firm through sheer enthusiasm and personal charisma often prove ineffective at managing a growing organization. Informal leadership either professionalism or makes way for new leaders with actual management competencies.

Critical organizational decision points hit when your team exceeds 25-30 lawyers and the purely relationship-based model starts breaking down. Once partner numbers cross seven, partnership democracy becomes painfully inefficient.

The solution isn't abandoning human relationships for soulless bureaucracy or ditching partnership values for corporate hierarchy. It's adapting your working principles to the new scale.

Flexible early-stage solutions now demand clarity. Specialization versus full-service stops being about survival and becomes strategic choice. Universality can flip from advantage to liability – you risk staying mediocre at everything while excelling at nothing.

Meta-choices need refining, not revising – the basic philosophy stays the same but needs adapting to new circumstances. How do you preserve a farmer culture when partners with hunter instincts have joined? How do you maintain investment logic under mounting pressure for current profitability?

New architectural choices become relevant when personal brands start working against the corporate brand, individual achievements against team results. These questions simply didn't exist in a small team but become critical as you grow.

Seven to 15 years – maintaining living architecture and the autonomy crisis

Mature firms face the success paradox – the architectural decisions that brought you here can become the obstacles to staying here. Formal processes calcify into bureaucracy. Proven methods harden into dogma. Successful culture ossifies.

This stage brings the autonomy crisis. Partners and senior lawyers, accustomed to independence, start resisting process formalization and tighter controls. You're balancing coordination needs against preserving entrepreneurial spirit.

Your main task? Keep the architecture alive. Most decisions requiring regular review become especially urgent at this stage. Systems you created for efficiency start living their own lives. Moving forward demands regular spring cleaning.

Preparing for generational change becomes crucial when architectural decisions known only to the founders need passing to the next generation of leaders. The firm's basic philosophy often exists at an intuitive level – it needs articulating and institutionalizing.

Cultural continuity demands special attention. You're constantly expanding the team while trying to maintain cultural codes. New people need to understand not just what to do but how it's done at this particular firm.

Mature firms must constantly balance innovation and tradition. Respect for proven methods mustn't turn into fear of change. The world shifts, and your architecture needs shifting with it.

See Table 11.2.

Table 11.2: Firm Lifecycle Timeline

Years	**Phase**	**Key decisions**	**Typical crisis**
0-3	**Foundations**	Day One decisions: Hunters/farmers? Renters/investors? Philosophy and values	Survival
3-7	**Scale**	Critical turning points: Formality/relationships? Family/corporation? Structure and governance	Leadership crisis (founders become bottleneck)
7-15	**Maturity**	Periodic reassessment: Process review, cultural continuity, generational transition	Autonomy, bureaucratization, or relevance crisis

More information on crisis diagnostics and navigation strategies is available in Appendix 14.

When the system stops working

Transitions between development stages rarely happen smoothly. Usually they're preceded by crises – painful periods when old solutions stop working and new ones haven't been found yet. These crises are unpleasant but inevitable and even useful. They signal that the firm has outgrown its current architecture and needs adapting.

Each crisis has its own anatomy – warning symptoms, peak phase, and resolution paths. Understanding this logic helps you not just survive the crisis but use it as a catalyst for necessary change.

Leadership crisis – when founders become the bottleneck

This crisis strikes growing firms and stems from basic human capacity limits. Founders who successfully launched the firm through sheer enthusiasm and personal charisma often prove ineffective at managing a growing organization.

First symptoms are barely noticeable. Founders start complaining about time shortage, constantly work overtime, postpone strategic questions because they're drowning in operational details. Decisions happen more slowly because every important question flows through them. Staff wait for instructions on trivialities that used to sort themselves out.

Peak phase arrives when founders physically can't keep up with all the processes. Clients start complaining about delays. Talented staff leave because they've got no autonomy. Partners quarrel from overload and exhaustion. You get the sense that the firm's working on survival, not development.

Resolving the crisis demands open (and perhaps painful) acknowledgement – what brought you success at start-up can become the obstacle to growth. Informal leadership either professionalizes or makes way for new leaders with actual management competencies.

Successful exit strategies include delegating authority, hiring professional managers, and creating clear procedures for routine decisions. The hardest thing for founders? Delegating tasks rather than doing everything themselves.

Autonomy crisis – rebellion against the system

This crisis typifies the transition to maturity, when the firm starts actively formalizing processes. Partners and senior lawyers, accustomed to independence, resist the tightening controls and new standards.

Symptoms show up as growing dissatisfaction with "bureaucratization". Experienced lawyers complain about needing to fill in forms, get approvals, or follow procedures. You hear phrases like, "We used to just do the work, now we waste time on reports". Nostalgia emerges for "the good old days" when everything felt simpler.

Peak phase hits when resistance to formalization starts actually harming the work. Partners ignore new procedures, creating chaos and confusion.

Conflicts erupt between the "old guard" and new staff who expect structured systems. Efficiency drops through deliberate system sabotage.

Resolution demands delicate balance between coordination needs and preserving entrepreneurial spirit. Successful firms formalize only the critically important processes, leaving maximum autonomy on creative matters. They explain the logic behind changes and involve the sceptics in developing new procedures.

The system should serve the people, not vice versa. Any procedure must have clear justification and deliver obvious benefit to those executing it.

Bureaucratization crisis – when system devours meaning

This crisis strikes mature firms where formal processes and procedures, created to ensure quality and efficiency, transform into self-serving bureaucracy.

Symptoms accumulate gradually. Simple tasks start requiring multiple approvals. Staff spend more time filling in forms than doing actual work. Procedures for procedures' sake appear – rules nobody can explain but everyone must follow.

Peak phase arrives when the system becomes more important than the result, and rule compliance more important than client satisfaction. The firm loses flexibility and ability to react quickly to changes. Talented people leave because they feel like cogs in a machine. Clients complain about formalism and the absence of personal touch.

Resolving this crisis demands radical spring cleaning of procedures. Every procedure must pass a necessity test – does it add real value or exist purely through inertia? Successful firms regularly simplify processes, automate routine tasks, and restore the human dimension to formal systems.

Any procedure should make work easier, not harder. If a rule creates more problems than it solves – scrap it.

Relevance crisis – when the world changed but the firm didn't

This is the most serious crisis that can strike long-lived firms. Successful models from the past stop working under radically changed conditions. A new generation of clients has different expectations, technology transforms the very nature of legal services, competitors offer fundamentally different approaches.

Symptoms show up as gradual competitiveness loss. Young clients increasingly choose other providers. Talented candidates prefer more modern firms.

Traditional advantages – experience, reputation, connections – get valued less than speed, tech-savviness, or innovativeness.

Peak phase arrives when the firm realizes its basic model has become obsolete. Cosmetic change attempts don't help – you need deep transformation. But years of investment in existing architecture make changes painful and risky.

Resolving this crisis demands courage to acknowledge the need for fundamental change and wisdom to preserve what's valuable in what you've created. The trickiest part? Identifying the unchanging core of values and principles that must survive any transformation.

Exit strategies vary in radicality – from evolutionary adaptation to revolutionary transformation. Choice depends on how deep the required changes go and the firm's readiness for risk.

Principles for navigating through crises

Every crisis is simultaneously threat and opportunity. Firms that successfully navigate through crises emerge stronger and more adaptive. Those who ignore signals or try solving new problems with old methods risk losing competitiveness or even ceasing to exist.

Consider the key principles for successfully navigating crises – early symptom recognition, honest problem acknowledgement, readiness for painful changes, preserving cultural continuity while transforming architecture.

It's crucial to understand that attempts to avoid crises often intensify them. It's better to prepare in advance and use them as catalysts for necessary change. Crisis isn't architectural failure – it's a signal that evolution time has arrived.

Managing architectural decisions over time is the art of balancing numerous conflicting demands. You need to develop flexibility for adapting to changes, yet maintain stability to preserve identity.

The timeliness principle demands understanding each architectural decision's calendar. When must it be made? When must it be reconsidered? When can you wait? Make a decision too early, you create unnecessary constraints. Too late – you miss opportunities and accumulate problems.

The coherence principle reminds you that architectural decisions don't exist in isolation. Changing one element affects all others. You can't transition to formal processes while preserving an entirely relationship-based culture. You can't build corporate brand while rewarding only individual achievements.

The smooth transitions principle emphasizes that radical architectural changes prove painful and risky. It's better to prepare for transitions in advance, gradually introducing new model elements while discarding obsolete elements of the old.

The cultural continuity principle stresses the importance of preserving core values whatever the changes. The firm can change structure, processes, even strategy. But losing cultural identity means creating a new organization on the old one's ruins.

The honesty about price principle requires understanding that every architectural choice carries costs. No decisions deliver only advantages. The task isn't finding the perfect variant but choosing the one whose price matches your capabilities and priorities.

Firms that grasp these principles and consistently apply them can do more than merely survive in a changing world. They use change as a source of competitive advantage, transforming adaptation's inevitability into development opportunity.

Chapter 12:
The real time of decisions

When decisions should happen – and how to prepare for them

Picture an international firm with a financial year beginning in July. In May, formally, this is the end of the financial year – time for taking stock, distributing profits, making fateful decisions about partnerships. But outside it's May, clients are planning summer holidays, universities are hosting graduation ceremonies, and the partners themselves are mentally already on the beach.

Now picture a local European firm in December. According to the financial cycle, this is just a regular month in the fourth quarter. But psychologically? It's time for summing up, holiday parties, making decisions about next year's work. Clients are rushing to close deals before the holidays, the team's working flat out, and managing partners understand – it's now or never.

Here's the paradox: lawyers – rational professionals who make decisions based on facts – find themselves hostage to three different rhythms that often contradict each other.

The calendar year sets the basic pulse of human life, regardless of business logic. January will always be a month of new plans and resolutions, May – a time of spring energy and university graduations, August – a month of holidays and slowing pace, December – a period of summing up and holiday lull. This rhythm is embedded in human psychology at the level of archetypes and cultural codes.

A partner can tell themselves as much as they like that "June is just a regular working month" but their brain has already switched to summer mode. They can schedule serious strategic sessions for 28th December, but the team will be thinking about New Year's gifts, not firm development.

The calendar rhythm affects not only partners' internal state but also their environment. Children start summer holidays, and meeting schedules have to adjust for family circumstances. A new school year begins, and fresh university graduates appear on the candidate market. New Year approaches, and everyone wants to "close issues before the holidays".

But the legal services market lives by its own laws, which only partially align with calendar cycles. Corporate clients plan budgets for legal services at different times. Some – in October-November, others – in March-April, still others are tied to industry cycles. In banking, peak activity falls during regulatory reporting periods. In retail – pre-holiday months. In real estate – spring and autumn. In tech – during venture rounds and IPOs.

International deals have their own seasonality – in summer, many slow down due to European holidays, in December – due to American holidays. Court cases follow procedural deadlines that don't consider lawyers' convenience.

Partners find themselves needing to make internal decisions about firm development precisely when main forces are concentrated on servicing client activity peaks. Or conversely, when the market has frozen but the firm's internal development logic requires intensive work on strategy.

And the third rhythm – the firm's own financial cycle, creating a formal framework for making key decisions. It determines when to sum up work results, when to distribute profits, when to plan investments for the next period. For firms with a calendar financial year (January-December), this rhythm coincides with cultural cycles. But for many international firms, the financial year begins in other months: 1 July for many American and international firms, 1 May for a number of British firms, 1 October for some consulting companies, 1 April for firms in Asian jurisdictions.

The choice of financial year start date is often driven by wanting to avoid overlap with stressful periods in the firm's key practices. But this creates misalignment with natural psychological and cultural cycles.

Human psychology becomes the mechanism trying to integrate all three rhythms into a unified decision-making system. And this is where the main contradictions arise. The financial cycle may require intensive strategic work during a period when people are psychologically tuned for rest. Or conversely – force artificial restraint of spring energy for change because "now is not the time for new initiatives".

Partners must focus on internal firm development issues precisely when market conditions demand maximum attention to clients. Or spend mental energy on year-end reviews when the market's opening new opportunities. Each partner lives in their own personal rhythm – some have peak productivity in the morning, others in the evening; some recover quickly, others need more time. But decisions in a partnership get made collectively, and you must find a common denominator for different personality types and life rhythms.

Representatives of different decision-making archetypes react differently to cyclicality and rhythm contradictions.

- *Rational archetypes* (Logical Seer, Insightful Advisor, Creative Architect) try to rationalize chaos by creating detailed plans and cycle management systems. They're least subject to emotional fluctuations associated with calendar periods, but may underestimate their impact on others.
- *Intuitive archetypes* (Creative Architect, Visionary Improviser, Logical Seer, Sensitive Confidant, Thoughtful Delayer) read patterns in cyclical chaos and sense when rhythms are shifting, but under time pressure may act on incomplete pattern recognition.
- *Dependent archetypes* (Methodical Diplomat, Empathic Ally, Insightful Advisor) suffer most from cycle misalignment, as they strive to consider all factors and find consensus. Contradictory signals from different rhythms create additional complexity for them.
- *Avoidant archetypes* (Cautious Procrastinator, Thoughtful Delayer) may use cyclicality as justification for postponing decisions: "Now is not the right time", "Let's wait until the new quarter begins", "Things will be clearer after the holidays".
- *Spontaneous archetypes* (Instinctive Impulsive, Visionary Improviser, Responsive Supporter) adapt best to changing rhythms, quickly switching between different work modes, but they also make impulsive decisions more often under time pressure.

Successful partnerships learn to create their own meta-rhythm that accounts for all three basic cycles but doesn't become hostage to them. This meta-rhythm includes understanding the features of each cycle and their intersection points, planning key decisions with consideration of psychological and market factors, flexibility in adapting formal procedures to real circumstances, communication with the team about the logic and reasons for choosing timing for decisions, and support systems for making quality decisions during non-optimal periods.

What does that meta-rhythm actually look like in practice? That's what we'll tackle next – the practical tools for planning decisions, dividing responsibility, and keeping quality high even when the timing's far from perfect.

The decision calendar in a partnership firm

In any law firm, dozens of decisions get made daily, but not all are equally important. To understand the logic of calendar planning, you need to divide decisions along two dimensions – how tied they are to the calendar and what kind of impact they have.

Rigid calendar vs flexible planning

Rigidly calendar-bound decisions must be made at a specific time for objective reasons. Profit distribution happens at the end of the financial year when final results are known. Mass employee evaluations are tied to the annual cycle. Strategic planning syncs with the budget process. You can't arbitrarily move these decisions to another time – they're dictated by the logic of financial cycles and corporate governance.

Flexible decisions can be made at any moment, but practically they depend on rigidly calendar-bound decisions. Implementing a new CRM system is technically possible year-round, but it's actually tied to the budget cycle and strategic priorities. Hiring a specialized partner can be discussed anytime, but can only be financed after budget approval. Launching a new practice area conceptually doesn't depend on the time of year, but requires resources allocated in annual planning.

This creates frustration. Partners want to be flexible in operational matters but constantly run into calendar cycle constraints. "I want to launch a new practice area right now" collides with "The budget's already allocated through year-end".

Four types by nature of impact

1. *Strategic decisions* shape the firm's long-term vision. This includes development planning, selection of priority practice areas, strategic initiatives for entering new markets, and formation of long-term partnerships. These decisions determine where the firm will be in three to five years, what competencies need developing, and which directions should be abandoned.
2. *Financial decisions* transform strategic plans into concrete resource frameworks. Budgeting, profit distribution among partners, investment decisions, service pricing, establishment of financial goals and performance indicators – all of this determines what resources will be directed toward strategy implementation.
3. *Personnel decisions* form the team to achieve set goals within allocated financial capabilities. Hiring and termination, promotions to partner, employee performance evaluation, creation of motivation systems,

training and personnel development programs – these decisions determine who will execute the strategy and with what motivation.

4. *Operational decisions* ensure the firm's daily functioning. Business process optimization, implementation of new technologies, client relationship management, operational efficiency improvements – all of this creates the conditions for strategy implementation.

Theory vs practice

Theoretically, these four types of decisions should be made in strict sequence – first strategy determines goals, then finance allocates resources, personnel decisions form the team, and operational decisions fine-tune processes. But in practice? Everything happens differently.

Here's what actually happens – the financial year runs everything, and decisions concentrate in specific periods. In the third quarter, preliminary preparation begins – analysis of current results, initial adjustment of strategic goals, operational preparation for the intensive year-end finale.

The fourth quarter becomes the critical phase when most fateful decisions get made. Here financial decisions take priority – you need to sum up the year and distribute profits. In parallel, strategic plans for the next year get finalized and key personnel decisions are made.

The first quarter transforms into the implementation phase. Mass personnel decisions – employee evaluations, bonus payments, hiring new people – implement plans adopted in the fourth quarter. Operational decisions adapt processes to new goals.

The second quarter becomes a time for adjustments. Initial results show where plans diverge from reality and where financial corrections are needed – budget revisions, operational decisions to eliminate bottlenecks.

Hidden interconnections

The main complexity lies not in the sequence but in the interconnections between types of decisions. These connections create both synergy and conflicts. See Figure 12.1 overleaf.

Strategy determines finance, but limited resources may require revision of ambitious plans. A decision to develop a new IT practice requires investment in hiring specialized lawyers and marketing, but if the budget doesn't allow it, the strategy will have to be adjusted.

Finance constrains personnel, creating tension between wanting to motivate the team and needing to maintain profitability. The size of the bonus pool directly affects the number of possible promotions, but overly strict economies can demotivate key employees.

Personnel determines operations. Hiring an experienced project manager can dramatically improve project management systems, but if the team lacks people ready for new processes, even the best systems won't work.

Operations influence strategy. Implementation of an effective CRM system can free up partners' time to develop new business directions, while automation of routine processes can reduce the need to hire junior lawyers.

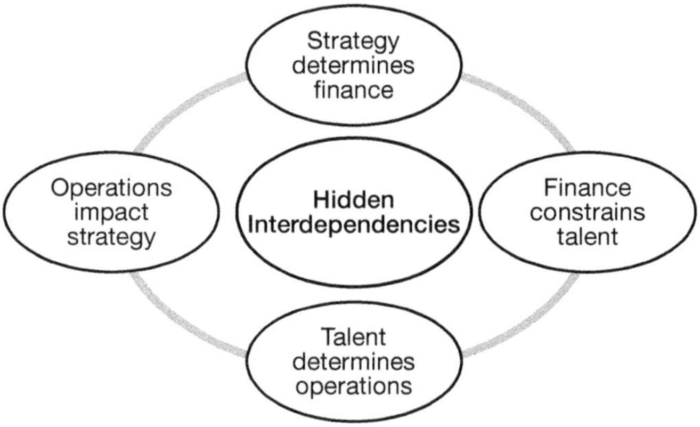

Figure 12.1: The decision interdependency cycle

Critical conflict nodes

These interconnections create critical conflict nodes where problems most often arise.

- *Finance-Strategy Node (Q4).* Partners must simultaneously distribute earned profits and plan investments in the future. The balance between rewarding past results and investing in development requires complex compromises.
- *Personnel-Finance Node (Q4-Q1).* Personnel decisions get made after financial ones but dramatically affect the possibilities of their execution. It's difficult to motivate the team if the bonus pool has already been distributed without considering people's real merits.
- *Operations-Strategy Node (Q1-Q2).* Operational adjustments may require revision of strategic plans when it becomes clear that real processes don't match underlying assumptions.

See Table 12.1 overleaf.

Partners with different decision-making archetypes react differently to these critical nodes. The Logical Seer strives to analyze each connection in detail, which can slow down the process during intensive periods. The Instinctive Impulsive rushes decisions, risking failure to account for all interconnections. The Methodical Diplomat tries to find consensus on every issue, which is especially difficult when interests conflict. The Empathic Ally focuses on human consequences, sometimes at the expense of financial logic. The Cautious Procrastinator prefers to postpone complex issues, which can lead to problem accumulation. The Sensitive Confidant intuitively foresees the human and relational consequences of nodal decisions but needs to discuss and validate these concerns with partners before acting, which can delay critical choices.

Table 12.1: The annual decision calendar

Quarter	Primary focus	Key decisions	Conflict node
Q3 **Preparation**	Strategic Planning	Analyze results, initial strategic adjustments, scenario planning	Minimal conflict – exploratory phase
Q4 **Critical phase**	Financial + Strategic	Close year, distribute profits, approve budget, finalize strategy, key personnel decisions	⚠⚠⚠ Finance-Strategy Node Distribute earnings vs invest in future
Q1 **Implementation**	Personnel + Operations	Annual reviews, distribute bonuses, execute hiring plan, launch initiatives	⚠ Operations-Strategy Node Real processes may not match assumptions
Q2 **Adjustment**	Operational + Financial	Review Q1 performance, identify variances, adjust budgets if needed, fix operational issues	Moderate conflict – reality check on plans

More information on the cycle of partnership decisions, conflict resolution strategies and management principles is available in Appendix 15.

Practical management principles

Successful management of the decision calendar requires understanding interconnections and conscious planning of critical nodes.

Divide strategic planning into a conceptual phase in the third quarter and detailed elaboration in the fourth. This helps reduce the burden on the most intensive period of the year.

Create buffer time between financial and personnel decisions. This allows better consideration of the human factor in reward distribution.

Reserve the second quarter for adjustments without radical strategy revision. This maintains plan stability.

For each type of decision, it's worth appointing clear "owners", creating conflict escalation procedures, and implementing systems to track the impact of decisions on each other. It's important to consider archetypes: involve, for example, the Logical Seer in strategic-financial matters, engage the Empathic Allie in personnel decisions, use the Methodical Diplomat to find compromises, and activate the Instinctive Impulsive when quick adjustments are needed.

Decision-making matrix – who decides what and when

Division of roles – leadership and management

Before discussing who makes decisions, partners need to clearly distinguish between two concepts – leadership within the firm and business management. This distinction becomes the foundation for building an effective decision-making system.

Some firms prefer to assign functional responsibilities, such as executive oversight of human resources functions, to partners. Other firms create committees for various internal issues – a business development committee, a legal-tech committee, or a diversity committee. These have been useful and welcome for many years. The only reservation? These approaches work best when professional managers collaborate on management decisions rather than having decisions imposed on them.

Clearly a functional partner isn't an arbitrator or a decision-making machine, but rather a pilot through the world of partnership decision-making, translating the decisions and their implications into actions in terms that the business staff understand practically.

Five key areas of joint work between partners and managers

There are five key areas where partners and professional managers cooperate:

1. *Strategic planning and execution.* Partners determine the direction of movement, while managers develop paths to achieve goals and monitor plan execution.
2. *Monitoring the effectiveness and efficiency of the firm's operations.* A system of indicators and regular evaluation of results requires joint efforts – partners understand the business context, managers possess measurement tools.
3. *Shaping the firm's business support functions and supervising those activities.* Decisions about what functions the firm needs and how they should be organized get made jointly, but managers are responsible for their professional execution.
4. *Risk management and mitigation.* Partners see legal and reputational risks better, managers see operational and financial risks. Only together can they create a comprehensive risk management system.
5. *Being a positive role model for the firm's business management and administrative teams.* Both partners and top managers serve as role models for the entire firm team in matters of business culture and work standards.

Four levels of involvement in decisions

It's important to distinguish four sectors within each of the above-mentioned areas, where:

1. Equity partners make the final decision, but don't take part in its implementation (e.g., approval of the company's annual budget).
2. Partners are involved in both the decision making and implementation processes (e.g., mid-year budget review or other budget amendments).
3. Partners aren't involved in decision making, but they're direct participants of a business process (e.g., a firm's billing cycle).
4. Partners distance themselves from both decision making and implementation (e.g., the calculation and payment of taxes).

Decision-making matrix – a practical example

To avoid gray areas in dividing duties or overlapping responsibilities that could impact the effectiveness of the management system, you need to create a firm-wide decision-making matrix.

Mapping your key business processes along with responsible actors gives you a clear and useful matrix. This is the firm-wide decision matrix. Table 12.2 below shows an example from my recent practice. The client is a leading local firm (full-service, ten years in the market, 120+ employees, and described as tech-savvy).

The main business processes of the company and their specifications are represented below:

- Strategic planning: strategy development, budgeting, pricing.
- Strategic execution: business continuity, budget execution, new projects, risk management.
- Knowledge and business development: knowledge management, business development, marketing strategy.
- Client relations: client care, quality control, conflict management.
- Human resources: hiring and integration, remuneration, learning and development, evaluation and promotions, separation.
- Communication: external and internal.
- Information technologies: new services, release management, investments, problem solving.
- Assets management: office premises, fixed assets.
- Monitoring and control: quality control, firm-wide reporting (monthly basis), annual reporting.
- Adjustments and improvements: strategy/goals amendments, budget execution.

The firm's management structure includes functional directors, the head of operations (as a senior management role) and practice leaders. The highest managerial body is the equity partners committee.

Let's examine how accountability is distributed in the management team of such a firm when developing and making decisions.

To monitor the performance of a particular function, you need to introduce key performance indicators for the main expected results by time periods (a quarter / a year) or by a specific project. This approach will motivate partners and top management not to fall into micromanagement, but to judge success or failure in accordance with an agreed matrix.

Partners and professional managers, each within their areas of authority and responsibility, contribute through their activities to the functioning of the firm as an integrated organism. This organism has its own dynamics, external and internal. These dynamics have to be carefully observed and analyzed. The results of ongoing changes should be measured and considered as possible indicators for further improvements.

But the question arises: How should you distribute efforts and share responsibility in such a complex situation?

Table 12.2: Firm-wide decision matrix

Strategic execution					
		Equity partners	**Practice leaders**	**Head of operations**	**Functional directors**
Business continuity	FW operations			X	
	Practices		X		
	Business support			+	X
Budget execution	Corrections (within approved budget) – Legal Practices		X		
	Corrections (within approved budget) – Business Support			X	
	Carry forwards within the annual budget – Legal Practices		X		+
	Carry forwards within the annual budget – Business Support			X	+
	Excess over annual budget	X			
New projects	Launches within approved annual budget			X	
	Launches over approved annual budget	X			
Risk management	Conflict check	X			
	Security	X		+	
	Emergencies	X		+	
		(X) role in charge, (+) in coordination with			

Zones of authority intersection and potential conflicts

Clear distribution of authority exists more in theory. In practice, many decisions require coordination between levels, which creates zones of intersection and potential conflicts.

Strategy and operations intersection arises when strategic initiatives of equity partners require operational changes for which the head of operations is responsible. If operational capabilities don't match strategic ambitions, a conflict emerges between "what we want" and "what we can do".

Practices and functions intersection manifests when practice leaders want to change processes in their areas, but these processes are managed by functional directors. For example, a practice wants to implement specialized software, but this affects the IT architecture of the entire firm.

Budget and ambitions intersection is a source of constant tension. Practice leaders want to develop their areas, functional directors see opportunities for improvements, but budget constraints established by equity partners require prioritization.

Evolution of the matrix with firm growth

The authority matrix isn't static – it evolves as the firm grows and develops.

- In small firms (up to 20 lawyers), most decisions are made by equity partners, often informally. A head of operations may be absent, and functional directors combine several roles.
- In medium-sized firms (20-150 lawyers), specialization appears. Practice leaders gain more autonomy, a head of operations emerges, and functional directors become professionalized.
- In large firms (200+ lawyers), the matrix becomes more complex. Intermediate management levels appear, some decisions are delegated to committees, and decision-making procedures become formalized.
- In international firms, a geographic dimension is added. Regional heads receive authority similar to practice leaders, but in a geographic context.

Understanding this matrix helps partners interact effectively, avoid authority conflicts, and ensure decisions are made at the right level. But the matrix is only a structure. How it works in practice depends on the decision-making archetypes of the people who occupy key positions.

From matrix to structure – how to organize interaction

The decision-making matrix shows you who's responsible for what, but it doesn't answer another fundamental question – how exactly should this interaction be organized? It's one thing to understand that the head of operations is responsible for budget execution for business support, and quite another to build an organizational structure where this responsibility will be implemented effectively.

Practice shows that successful implementation of the decision-making matrix directly depends on how well reporting and coordination relationships are structured in the firm. An incorrectly chosen organizational model can nullify the most carefully thought-out responsibility matrix, creating authority conflicts and functional duplication.

Moreover, the decision-making matrix itself evolves with the firm's growth. What worked for a team of 30 people may prove ineffective for a firm with 120 employees. Therefore, choosing an organizational structure isn't a one-time decision, but a strategic process that must consider not only the firm's current needs but also its development plans.

The choice of a specific model for interaction between partners and managers depends on the firm's size, market specifics, and the partnership's management philosophy. But most importantly – it must correspond to the decision-making matrix the firm has defined for itself. In reality, the choice is limited and there are three models worth considering for organizing the interaction between the partnership and hired managers for effective decision-making and managing their firm.

Model 1: Released Managing Partner (CEO) + Chief Operating Officer (COO)

This model is preferable when problem-solving and managing partnership relationships constitute the main part of the managing partner's workload.

The position of chief operating officer in the firm's management structure can be both an advantage and a disadvantage. The advantage arises if the managing partner and COO complement each other in management abilities and personal characteristics.

The combination of strengths in a tandem of two people can significantly strengthen the firm's internal management structure.

The disadvantage manifests if the COO acts as an intermediary between the managing partner and other members of the administrative team, becoming an extra link in the management communication chain.

Partners often rotate the managing partner position every two to three years to minimize the impact on the managing partner's legal practice. In such a scheme, the specific role of the COO also consists of providing effective support to the newly elected managing partner during their adaptation period to the new position. See Figure 12.2.

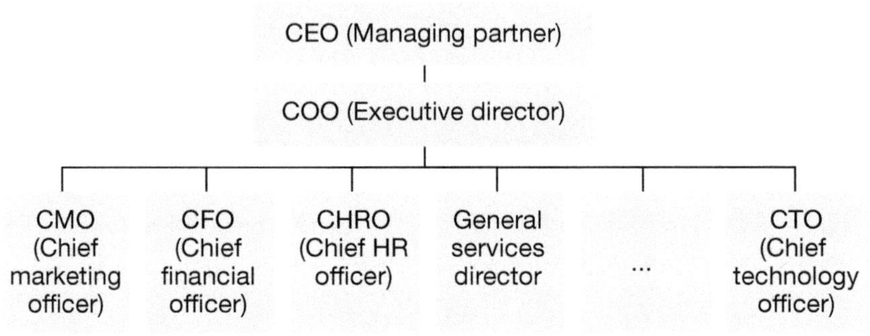

Figure 12.2: Business support functions are supervised by COO

Model 2: Practicing Managing Partner (CEO) + Chief Operating Officer (COO)
Engaging a COO in the presence of a practicing managing partner in most cases creates additional competitive advantages for the firm.

The main efforts of the COO in this scheme can focus on one of two areas:

1. *Execution* – a management function aimed at achieving goals set by the partnership. The most effective way to accomplish this task would be direct reporting of the functional C-suite team to the COO.
2. *Change management* – a leadership function requiring the professional manager to be an agent of change. The ideal condition for implementing this function would be direct reporting of all C-suite team members to the managing partner.

Additional value for the partnership and firm will be brought by the COO performing an adaptation function alongside the management or leadership function – introducing laterally hired partners to the business; raising partners' awareness of the status of changes occurring in the business; helping young, recently promoted partners adapt to new roles and find their unique niche in the existing partnership. See Figure 12.3 overleaf.

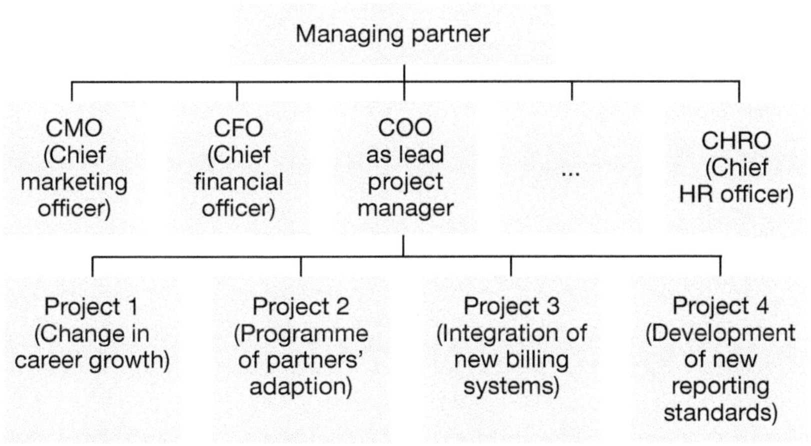

Figure 12.3: COO focused on coordination and implementation of firm's projects

Model 3: Managing Partner (CEO and COO) + Functional Managers

Regardless of whether a released or practicing partner manages the firm, a model can be chosen in which all functions (including operational ones) are linearly aligned with each other and report directly to the managing partner. See Figure 12.4.

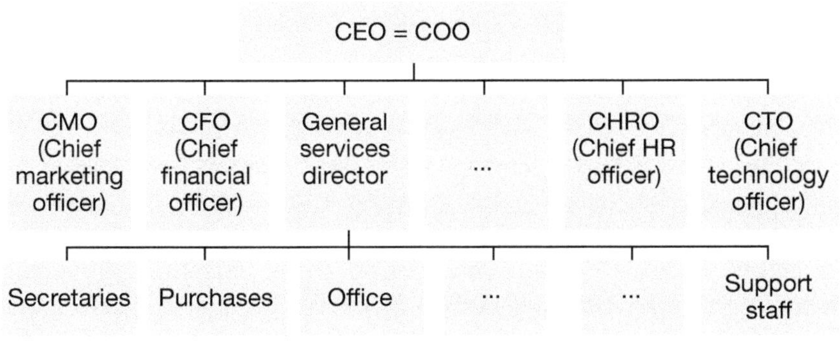

Figure 12.4: General services director covers essential office management functions

The business support team may include a chief operating officer, or, more likely, an administrative director. The role of this director will most likely focus on mentoring or direct implementation of specific projects important for the firm's development at this stage.

Monitoring the firm's compliance with policies and procedures, tracking their relevance, and proposing, when necessary, further improvement or radical change should also be the exclusive competence of the chief operating, executive, or administrative director.

Monitoring system effectiveness

To monitor the performance of a particular function, you need to introduce key performance indicators for the main expected results by time periods (a quarter / a year) or by a specific project. This approach will motivate partners and top management not to fall into micromanagement, but to judge success or failure in accordance with an agreed matrix.

Partners and professional managers, each within their areas of authority and responsibility, contribute through their activities to the functioning of the firm as an integrated organism. This organism has its own dynamics, external and internal. These dynamics have to be carefully observed and analyzed. The results of ongoing changes should be measured and considered as possible indicators for further improvements.

Speaking the language of decision-making styles

If you thought having a rational decision-making style was your golden ticket to the partners' table, think again. Sure, 59 percent of lawyers overall favor a rational approach, and among partners, that number climbs to 62 percent. But let's be honest – that's hardly a game-changing difference. It seems the secret to making partner lies less in your decision-making style and more in knowing how to effectively use its strengths while working with different styles to drive results.

Among law firm partners, the rational and intuitive styles dominate by a wide margin. This doesn't mean other styles are absent, but they're less common. For example, picture a situation where two partners – one rational, the other intuitive – are discussing bonus payouts. The rational partner will focus on numbers: "Let's look at the firm's revenue and each lawyer's KPIs." The intuitive partner might say, "I feel we need to support the team, even if the numbers aren't perfect".

It gets even more interesting when three partners with different styles are involved in the discussion. The rational partner insists on data analysis, the avoidant partner suggests delaying the decision to "let everyone cool down", and the dependent partner seeks a compromise, considering everyone's opinions. Such differences can create both conflict and synergy, depending on how the process is managed.

Information as the key to understanding

Decision-making style doesn't just determine how a person approaches choices – it also influences how they perceive and process information. Some need detailed data and clear structure, others prefer vivid imagery and intuitive cues, while others seek support and feedback from colleagues.

Understanding these needs allows you to prepare information in a way that's most useful and easily digestible for partners with different styles.

Key hints for representatives of each decision-making style:

- *Rational style – detail and structure.* People with a rational style prefer a systematic approach and thorough data analysis. They need to understand the logic and cause-and-effect relationships. For example, when discussing a new strategy, provide the rational partner with a detailed report including market analysis, financial forecasts, and a step-by-step action plan.
- *Intuitive style – imagery and holistic perception.* Intuitive partners rely on internal feelings and intuition. They prefer overall impressions and "images" based on experience. For example, when discussing a new project, show the intuitive partner a presentation with vivid visuals and examples of successful cases.
- *Dependent style – meetings and feedback.* Dependent partners strive for consensus and prefer to receive advice and support from others before making decisions. Before making a decision, for example, about implementing a new compensation system, hold a meeting with all stakeholders and provide a report with expert opinions.
- *Avoidant style – clarity and simplicity.* Avoidant partners tend to postpone decisions, especially in stressful situations. They need to minimize complexity and risk. When discussing a new project, provide the avoidant partner with a clear action plan, including deadlines and responsibilities.
- *Spontaneous style – speed and visuals.* Spontaneous partners prefer to make quick decisions based on intuition and immediate impressions. When discussing a new opportunity, show the spontaneous partner a chart with key metrics and examples of successful decisions.

Creating an environment for effective decision making

To create an environment where each partner can make decisions effectively based on their style, provide your partners with the following:

- *For rational partners:* Ensure they have access to detailed data and analytical tools. Support their need for structured information.

- *For intuitive partners:* Provide information in the form of images and metaphors. Use visualizations and brief overviews to help them quickly grasp the essence.
- *For dependent partners:* Organize meetings and discussions so they can receive feedback and support from colleagues.
- *For avoidant partners:* Simplify the decision-making process by providing clear instructions and minimizing complexity.
- *For spontaneous partners:* Prepare materials that allow them to quickly assess the situation and make decisions without lengthy discussions.

See Table 12.3.

Table 12.3: Overview of decision-making style information needs

Style	Preferences	Presentation methods
Rational	Detailed, structured information – charts, reports.	Graphs, detailed reports, statistical analysis.
Intuitive	Imagery, metaphors, brief visualizations.	Presentations, success stories.
Dependent	Feedback, discussions, team opinions.	Meetings, group discussions, consultations.
Avoidant	Simple, concrete information – step-by-step instructions.	Checklists, straightforward guides.
Spontaneous	Minimal constraints – task requiring immediate action.	Charts, diagrams, key points without unnecessary details.

Turning decision-making styles into a competitive advantage

A law firm is a complex organism where each partner and employee contributes uniquely to overall success. Understanding decision-making styles and their impact on firm management isn't just a theoretical exercise but a powerful tool for increasing efficiency and reducing stress.

Instead of striving for a single "ideal" style, it's important to develop flexibility. Lawyers who can combine different approaches are more resilient to stress and more effective in their work. For example, the rational style helps with data analysis and long-term planning, while the intuitive style is useful in crisis situations requiring quick action. The dependent style is beneficial for building consensus, and the spontaneous style is effective for quick decisions under tight deadlines.

The key task for law firm leaders is to create an environment where each style can leverage its strengths. For example, rational lawyers can take on strategic planning, intuitive lawyers can manage crises, and dependent lawyers can foster teamwork. It's important not to try to "fix" someone's style but to help each lawyer develop additional skills that complement their natural tendencies.

Key takeaways

1. *Diversity of styles is a strength.* Rational, intuitive, dependent, avoidant, and spontaneous styles – each brings something valuable to the table. The leader's task isn't to change a partner's style but to create an environment where those strengths can shine.
2. *Flexibility drives resilience.* Lawyers who can adapt and combine different decision-making styles are more effective under pressure and better equipped to handle uncertainty. Cultivate this adaptability within your team to build a competitive edge.
3. *Tailored information is essential.* Preparing data in ways that align with different styles – whether through charts, discussions, or concise overviews – helps partners make decisions faster and with confidence.
4. *Stress management is crucial.* Decision making under pressure affects everyone differently. Acknowledging these differences and creating supportive mechanisms can transform the firm's culture.

A law firm that understands this DNA has the power to turn diversity into its greatest strength. It's not just about managing differences – it's about embracing them, leveraging them, and creating a culture where collaboration and flexibility thrive.

The future of your firm doesn't depend on uniformity but on harmony – the right mix of styles, the ability to adapt, and the courage to think differently. By starting with small, intentional steps – like understanding the decision-making archetypes in your partnership – you can set your firm on a path to resilience, innovation, and long-term success.

Appendices

Appendix 1: Complexity navigation checklist

Before making decisions in multi-layered partnerships, consider the following.

Have you:

1. Geographic filter
   - Identified all affected offices?
   - Consulted local leadership in each jurisdiction?
   - Considered time zone and cultural differences?
   - Mapped regional regulatory variations?

2. Practice filter
   - Got sign-off from all relevant practice areas?
   - Identified practices with conflicting interests?
   - Considered cross-practice implications?
   - Assessed impact on practice autonomy?

3. Committee filter
   - Routed through all relevant committees?
   - Understood committee mandates and authority?
   - Avoided parallel committee decision making?
   - Scheduled realistic timeline for committee review?

4. Informal channels
   - Mapped key influencers and opinion leaders?
   - Conducted preliminary soundings?
   - Identified potential blocking coalitions?
   - Built support before formal process?

5. Partnership level

- Prepared for full partnership scrutiny?
- Developed communication strategy?
- Anticipated questions and objections?
- Planned for implementation after approval?

The more complex your partnership structure, the more critical this checklist becomes.

Appendix 2: Decision cost calculator

Making abstract costs tangible – what every decision really costs

Cost type	What to measure	Typical blind spots
Financial cost	Direct expenses, revenue impact, opportunity cost of capital	Hidden costs, maintenance expenses, full lifecycle cost
Time cost	Partner hours, management attention, implementation timeline	Meeting time, rework cycles, decision fatigue
Political cost	Relationships strained, trust depleted, coalitions shifted	Long-term resentment, cultural damage, invisible grudges
Opportunity cost	What else could resources accomplish? What doors close?	Strategic alternatives, capability building, market positioning
Reversibility cost	How hard to undo? What gets locked in? Exit costs?	Reputation damage, contractual obligations, cultural momentum

Practical application:

- What is the total financial outlay (not just year one)?
- How many partner hours will this actually consume?
- Who will this alienate and does that matter?
- What are we NOT doing if we commit to this?
- How painful would it be to reverse this decision?

Most decisions fail not because of wrong choice, but because costs were underestimated.

Appendix 3: Decision maturity self-assessment

Where is your partnership on the maturity spectrum? Rate each dimension.

Dimension	Immature partnership	Mature partnership
Level awareness	Treats every decision the same way	Consciously matches decision to appropriate level
Role clarity	Role conflicts remain unacknowledged	Partners navigate role tensions consciously
Authority mapping	Nobody knows who really decides	Clear authority assignment at each level
Informal channels	Backroom deals dominate or are denied	Acknowledged and integrated constructively
Complexity	Drowning in layers with no navigation	Deliberate structures with clear routing
Partner-manager	Mutual suspicion and turf wars	Collaborative authority and genuine partnership
Client pressure	Automatic compliance or resistance	Strategic evaluation and conscious choice
Competition	FOMO-driven panic moves	Deliberate assessment against strategy

Score yourself honestly. Maturity is not about perfection – it is about awareness and intentionality.

Appendix 4: Red flags

Warning signs that your decision making is broken.

1. Decision-making illusions
   - Partners say "We need to decide" but nothing changes for months.
   - Every discussion resurfaces the same debates as if memory has been erased.
   - Formal votes happen but informal power determines outcomes.
   - People claim consensus while harboring fundamental disagreements.

2. Decision-making journey
   - Partners debate operational details in partnership meetings.
   - Strategic questions get deferred with "not now" indefinitely.
   - Nobody can explain who has authority to decide what.
   - Role conflicts erupt into personal conflicts regularly.
   - Backroom deals completely replace formal processes.
   - Every decision requires navigating a bureaucratic maze.
   - Partners and managers operate in parallel universes.

3. External and internal forces
   - Client requests trigger automatic compliance without assessment.
   - The firm matches every competitor move out of panic.
   - Partners know a decision is needed but nobody wants to pay the cost.
   - Discussions about change focus on who loses, not what is gained.
   - The partnership treats every external pressure as existential.

If you recognize three or more red flags, your partnership needs honest diagnosis before any solutions.

Most dysfunctional decision making has a common root – avoiding difficult conversations. When partnerships defer hard choices, dodge role conflicts, ignore political realities, or pretend external pressures do not exist, decisions become performative rather than real. The cure is not better process – it is greater honesty about what is actually happening.

Appendix 5: The 16 types of legal decision makers

There are 16 distinct ways lawyers make decisions, and most of us have never stopped to think about which camp we're in. Each type blends different approaches – some rely on hard data, others trust their gut, some need the team's blessing, others avoid decisions like the plague, and a few just wing it entirely.

If you're curious about your own style (and let's face it, who isn't?), there's a quick assessment at https://surveymonkey.com/r/9LY9JTV. Here's what each type looks like in practice:

1. The Logical Seer (Data + Gut Feel)

These lawyers dig deep into the facts first, then let intuition guide them to the right answer. They're the ones who can crunch numbers all morning and still trust that nagging feeling something's not quite right.

2. The Creative Architect (Gut Feel + Data)

They know the answer almost immediately, then spend time proving they're right. Quick off the mark but clever enough to back up their hunches with solid reasoning.

3. The Insightful Advisor (Data + Team Input)

Thorough researchers who won't pull the trigger without checking with colleagues first. They've done their homework but need that reassuring nod from the team.

4. The Methodical Diplomat (Team Input + Data)

Always starts with "What does everyone think?" then filters the responses through cold, hard logic. Collaborative but nobody's fool.

5. The Sensitive Confidant (Gut Feel + Team Input)

Knows instinctively what to do but can't move forward without peer approval. Brilliant insight, but confidence wavers without backup.

6. The Empathic Ally (Team Input + Gut Feel)

Seeks consensus first, then uses intuition to seal the deal. Draws strength from group support and reads situations like a book.

7. The Thoughtful Delayer (Gut Feel + Avoidance)

Sees the right path clearly but gets paralyzed by overthinking. Has excellent instincts but lets doubt creep in and delay action.

8. The Cautious Procrastinator (Avoidance + Gut Feel)
Knows exactly what needs doing but keeps putting it off. Waits for the "perfect moment" that rarely comes.

9. The Visionary Improviser (Gut Feel + Quick Action)
Acts fast on instinct and rarely looks back. Thrives on change and makes snap decisions that somehow usually work out.

10. The Instinctive Impulsive (Quick Action + Gut Feel)
The ultimate "shoot first, ask questions later" type. Lives by gut feelings and adapts on the fly – exhausting to watch but oddly effective.

11. The Hesitant Conformist (Team Input + Avoidance)
Desperately wants group agreement but dreads taking responsibility. Passes decisions around like a hot potato.

12. The Compliant Seeker (Avoidance + Team Input)
Asks everyone's opinion to avoid making the call themselves. Masters of "What do you think we should do?"

13. The Expressive Adherent (Team Input + Quick Action)
Checks with colleagues but then acts on impulse anyway. Wants approval but won't wait around for it indefinitely.

14. The Responsive Supporter (Quick Action + Team Input)
Makes fast decisions but needs teammates to say "Good call." Decisive when backed up, wobbly when flying solo.

15. The Unpredictable Escapist (Avoidance + Quick Action)
Puts off decisions until absolutely forced, then makes sudden, surprising choices. Think careful deliberation followed by apparent madness.

16. The Erratic Drifter (Quick Action + Avoidance)
Procrastinates brilliantly until deadline pressure forces wild improvisation. Somehow always lands on their feet, though nobody knows how.

There you have it – 16 ways legal minds work when the pressure's on. Recognizing your type isn't about putting yourself in a box; it's about understanding how you naturally operate so you can play to your strengths and shore up your weak spots.

Appendix 6: Perfect duos and trios

High-performing archetype combinations for partnership success.

Perfect Duos: When two become one superpower

Combination	How they work together	What they achieve
Creative Architect + Insightful Advisor	Architect paints the big picture through intuitive vision. Advisor validates it through rigorous analysis and builds team buy-in. Architect spots strategic opportunities; Advisor identifies implementation obstacles. Architect crafts the vision; Advisor turns it into an executable plan.	Strategic vision grounded in analysis. Innovation with full partnership support. Change that sticks because it's both visionary and validated.
Methodical Diplomat + Logical Seer	Diplomat builds consensus through structured processes. Seer ensures decisions are grounded in solid analysis. Diplomat understands what the partnership will support; Seer calculates what will actually work. Diplomat creates alignment; Seer provides analytical foundation.	Well-analyzed decisions with full buy-in. Strategy that's both rigorous and embraced. Complex initiatives that partnerships actually execute.
Logical Seer + Visionary Improviser	Seer analyzes data and spots patterns. Improviser translates insights into immediate action. Seer identifies what's strategically sound; Improviser senses the right moment to move. Seer guards against analytical blindness; Improviser prevents analysis paralysis.	Speed without recklessness. Opportunism grounded in analysis. Market advantages captured before competitors act.
Empathic Ally + Insightful Advisor	Ally reads the room and senses resistance. Advisor provides rational frameworks to address concerns. Ally understands why people hesitate; Advisor identifies what data or consultation would build confidence. Ally builds emotional buy-in; Advisor creates intellectual justification.	Consensus that lasts. Decisions with both emotional and rational support. Change management that actually works.

These duos work because each partner compensates for the other's natural blind spots.

Optimal Trios: Three-dimensional problem solving

Purpose	The trio	Roles and dynamics	Outcome
Innovation	Innovation Trio: Creative Architect + Sensitive Confidant + Instinctive Impulsive	Architect generates the concept. Impulsive finds ways to test it immediately. Confidant intuitively senses how the team will respond. Architect paints vision; Impulsive creates momentum; Confidant prevents resistance from derailing progress.	Bold innovations that move fast without breaking team cohesion. Ideas that are both ambitious and implementable.
Execution	Execution Trio: Logical Seer + Methodical Diplomat + Empathic Ally	Seer plans with analytical rigor. Diplomat organizes the process and builds consensus. Ally ensures the team doesn't buckle under pressure. Seer guards against oversights; Diplomat keeps everyone aligned; Ally reads morale and prevents burnout.	Complex projects delivered on time without breaking the team. Difficult initiatives executed successfully.
Adaptation	Adaptation Trio: Visionary Improviser + Insightful Advisor + Empathic Ally	Improviser spots shifts in the market and senses when change is needed. Advisor analyzes what changes mean and validates direction. Ally helps the team embrace new approaches. Improviser provides speed; Advisor provides validation; Ally provides acceptance.	A firm that adapts swiftly to new conditions without losing its people. Change that happens fast but doesn't create casualties.

Why three is better than two – the third member acts as a catalyst, preventing the pair from getting trapped in their own logic.

True teamwork isn't everyone doing the same thing – it's each person doing what they do best. These combinations work because they create resonance – small, well-directed efforts from each archetype create outsized impact when perfectly synchronized.

Appendix 7: Navigating style conflicts

Common partnership conflicts decoded – recognition patterns and resolution strategies

These conflicts feel personal but they are procedural. Partners are not disagreeing about what to decide – they are disagreeing about how to decide. The dispute is about form masquerading as substance.

Type 1: Speed Conflicts

When partners disagree about how fast decisions should be made.

Clash	Recognition pattern	What each side misunderstands	Resolution strategy
Spontaneous vs Avoidant	Repeated phrases: "We're running out of time" vs "We need more information" Body language: One tapping fingers impatiently, other pulling back physically Meeting pattern: One pushes for immediate vote, other suggests forming committee	Spontaneous thinks: "They are stalling to avoid responsibility" Avoidant thinks: "They are rushing without considering consequences" Reality: Both managing risk – one sees delay as dangerous, other sees speed as dangerous	Acknowledge different risk tolerances explicitly Separate "What do we decide?" from "When do we decide?" Create decision deadlines with built-in analysis time Example: "We decide by Friday, but spend Monday to Wednesday analyzing risks you've identified"
Spontaneous vs Rational	Phrases: "The answer is obvious" vs "We need to model this properly" Frustration about: timing (not substance) One creates urgency, other creates process	Spontaneous thinks: "They're overthinking to seem smart" Rational thinks: "They want to decide before understanding the problem" REALITY: Different confidence thresholds – one needs gut check, other needs data validation	Fast-track analysis on key factors only Spontaneous: identify the three factors that matter most Rational: analyze Only those three, not everything Compromise: Quick analysis on critical issues, skip the rest

Type 2: Authority Conflicts

When partners disagree about who should make decisions and why.

Clash	Recognition pattern	What each side misunderstands	Resolution strategy
Intuitive vs Dependent	Phrases: "I know what needs to happen" vs "We need to consult everyone" Conflict about: process legitimacy One cites expertise, other cites fairness	Intuitive thinks: "They're turning this into endless committee debate" Dependent thinks: "They're being autocratic and dismissing valid concerns"	Reality: Different sources of legitimacy – expertise vs consensus Separate decision from implementation Intuitive: makes the strategic call Dependent: designs implementation with team input Example: "You decide what office to open, we decide how to staff it together"
Rational vs Dependent	Phrases: "The data clearly shows..." vs "But what does the team think?" Conflict about: what makes decisions stick One trusts facts, other trusts buy-in	Rational thinks: "Facts don't care about feelings – why are we polling people?" Dependent thinks: "They're ignoring that people won't support this" Reality: Both want decisions to stick – via different mechanisms	Use data to inform consultation Rational: presents analysis first Dependent: gathers reactions and concerns Synthesis: "Data says X, team concerns are Y and Z, here's how we address Z while doing X"

Type 3: Information Conflicts

When partners need different types of information to feel confident.

Clash	Recognition pattern	What each side misunderstands	Resolution strategy
Rational vs Intuitive	Phrases: "Where's the evidence?" vs "I can see the pattern" Conflict about: what counts as valid information One speaks in data, other speaks in precedents	Rational thinks: "They're making reckless decisions without analysis" Intuitive thinks: "They're paralyzed by analysis while opportunities disappear" Reality: Language barrier – both gathering information, just different types	Translate between languages Intuitive: articulate the pattern you see Rational: find data that confirms or refutes the pattern Synthesis: "My experience says X, your data shows Y – what explains the gap?"

Type 4: Confidence Conflicts

When partners have different levels of certainty tolerance.

Clash	Recognition pattern	What each side misunderstands	Resolution strategy
Intuitive vs Avoidant	Phrases: "I'm confident this is right" vs "But what if we're wrong?" Conflict about: acceptable risk levels One focuses on opportunity cost, other on error cost	Intuitive thinks: "They see the problem but refuse to act – irresponsible!" Avoidant thinks: "They're too confident – what if they're wrong and I get blamed?" Reality: Different psychological comfort with uncertainty	Make uncertainty explicit and shared "We're 70 percent confident – is that enough?" Create reversibility: "If we're wrong, here's how we reverse this decision in three months" Share risk: "We decide together, we own outcome together"

Master framework: Diagnosing any stylistic conflict

When partners are clearly clashing, ask these diagnostic questions:

1. What are they arguing about?
If it's process/timing/authority ➡ Stylistic conflict

2. Who is frustrated?
If frustration is personal ("Why is HE so difficult?") ➡ Stylistic conflict

3. When did it escalate?
If it escalated when discussing HOW to decide ➡ Stylistic conflict

4. Where is common ground?
If they agree on outcome but not process ➡ Stylistic conflict

Universal resolution protocol

Once you've identified a stylistic conflict:

Name it: "I think we agree on opening the office. We're debating whether to analyze first or move quickly."

1. Separate it: "Let's confirm: do we all believe this is strategically necessary? Good. Now separately: what process gives us confidence?"

2. Validate both: "You're right, we need analysis. You're right, timing matters. How do we honor both?"

3. Test it: "If I agreed to your timeline, would you support the decision? If I agreed to analyze, would you support opening?"

The maturity marker

Junior partnerships conflate substance and style, turning every strategic debate into a meta-argument about whose decision-making philosophy is superior.

Senior partnerships separate them, having vigorous debates about what to decide, then calm discussions about how to decide it.

The substance gets resolved. The style gets managed. The partnership survives.

What's really happening when styles clash

Common partnership conflicts decoded – what each side perceives vs what is actually happening

Clash	What side A thinks	What side B thinks	What is actually happening
1. Rational vs Intuitive	"They are making reckless decisions without proper analysis. Where is the evidence?"	"They are paralyzed by analysis. We will miss opportunities while they build spreadsheets."	Language barrier: One speaks in data, the other in patterns. Neither is wrong – they need different information to feel confident.
2. Rational vs Dependent	"The data clearly shows the answer. Why are we still polling people?"	"They are ignoring legitimate concerns. Everyone needs to be heard."	Legitimacy dispute: One derives authority from facts, the other from consensus. Both want the decision to stick – just via different routes.
3. Rational vs Avoidant	"The analysis is complete. Why are we still debating alternatives?"	"Their analysis might be wrong. We need to explore other options before committing."	Certainty conflict: One believes thorough analysis eliminates risk, the other believes analysis can miss hidden dangers. Both seek safety – through different means.
4. Rational vs Spontaneous	"They want to decide before we even understand the problem properly."	"They are overthinking. The answer is obvious – just act!"	Preparation conflict: One sees analysis as procrastination, the other sees speed as recklessness. Neither has engaged with the actual decision yet.
5. Intuitive vs Dependent	"They are turning this into a committee debate. I already know what needs to happen."	"They are being autocratic. Why are we not consulting everyone?"	Process conflict: One needs consensus to feel legitimate, the other needs autonomy to act decisively. Neither cares about substance yet.

continued on next page

Clash	What side A thinks	What side B thinks	What is actually happening
6. Intuitive vs Avoidant	"They see the problem but refuse to act. This is irresponsible!"	"They are too confident. What if they are wrong and I get blamed?"	Confidence gap: One trusts their judgment, the other fears the consequences of any choice. The decision is hostage to psychological comfort levels.
7. Intuitive vs Spontaneous	"They are acting on impulse without understanding the deeper patterns. This is reactive, not strategic."	"They are overthinking and missing the moment. By the time they see the pattern, the opportunity is gone."	Timeframe conflict: One operates on recognition of long-term patterns, the other on immediate situational reads. Both are reading signals - just on different timescales.
8. Dependent vs Avoidant	"We have consulted everyone. Why can they not commit to a decision?"	"Just because everyone agrees does not mean it is the right choice. What if we are all wrong?"	Validation conflict: One finds confidence in collective agreement, the other fears groupthink. Both want to avoid mistakes – one through consensus, the other through skepticism.
9. Dependent vs Spontaneous	"They keep deciding without consulting the team. This creates resistance."	"By the time we finish consulting everyone, the opportunity will be gone."	Inclusion conflict: One believes buy-in is essential for execution, the other believes speed is essential for success. Both want the decision to work – through different mechanisms.
10. Avoidant vs Spontaneous	"They are rushing into things without considering consequences. Slow down!"	"They are stalling and avoiding responsibility. Just make a decision already!"	Timeline conflict: One sees delay as risk, the other sees speed as risk. Both are managing risk – just different types.a

Appendix 8: Team composition optimizer

Use this tool when forming practice groups, management committees, deal teams, or any group that needs to make complex decisions together. The goal is not to have one of everything, but to match archetype strengths to the specific challenges your team will face.

Step 1: Define your team's primary mission

Mission Type	Critical archetypes needed	Why these matter
Innovation Developing new services, entering new markets	• Creative Architect • Instinctive Impulsive • Sensitive Confidant	Architect provides vision, Impulsive tests quickly, Confidant senses team response and prevents resistance
Strategic planning Long-term direction and resource allocation	• Creative Architect • Logical Seer • Insightful Advisor	Architect generates strategic vision, Seer validates it through rigorous analysis, Advisor ensures the strategy has partnership buy-in and addresses real concerns.
Execution Delivering complex projects on time	• Logical Seer • Methodical Diplomat • Empathic Ally	Seer plans with analytical rigor, Diplomat organizes process and builds consensus, Ally maintains team cohesion under pressure
Client Management Building and maintaining relationships	• Insightful Advisor • Empathic Ally • Methodical Diplomat	Advisor reads client needs and provides analytical frameworks, Ally builds trust, Diplomat ensures consistent delivery
Crisis Response Handling urgent, high-stakes situations	• Instinctive Impulsive • Logical Seer • Insightful Advisor	Impulsive acts quickly, Seer calculates risks and validates direction, Advisor manages stakeholders
Transformation Major strategic or cultural change	• Visionary Improviser • Empathic Ally • Methodical Diplomat	Improviser spots opportunities and senses when change is needed, Ally helps team embrace change, Diplomat structures the process
Adaptation Responding to market shifts and new conditions	• Visionary Improviser • Insightful Advisor • Empathic Ally	Improviser spots shifts in the market and senses when change is needed, Advisor analyzes what changes mean and validates direction, Ally helps team embrace new approaches

Pay attention to:

If your team has no...	You will likely suffer from...	Mitigation strategy
Rational archetype (Logical Seer, Insightful Advisor, Creative Architect)	Decisions based on enthusiasm rather than analysis. Missed risks. Financial surprises. "We should have seen that coming."	Mandate external analysis for major decisions. Require business cases. Build decision checklists.
Intuitive archetype (Creative Architect, Visionary Improviser, Logical Seer)	Analysis paralysis. Missed opportunities. Slow response to market shifts. "By the time we decided, it was too late."	Set decision deadlines. Create "fast track" process for time-sensitive opportunities. Trust pattern recognition.
Dependent archetype (Methodical Diplomat, Empathic Ally, Insightful Advisor)	Poor implementation. Resistance you did not anticipate. "The decision was right but no one supported it."	Build formal consultation into process. Conduct stakeholder analysis. Test decisions with key influencers first.
Spontaneous archetype (Instinctive Impulsive, Visionary Improviser, Responsive Supporter)	Slow execution. Missed windows of opportunity. Competitors move faster. "We are always one step behind."	Empower quick decisions on defined criteria. Create "bias toward action" for low-risk choices. Reduce approval layers.
Avoidant archetype (Cautious Procrastinator, Thoughtful Delayer)	Preventable mistakes. Insufficient contingency planning. "We never thought about what could go wrong."	Conduct pre-mortem analysis. Assign someone to play devil's advocate. Build scenario planning into major decisions.

Step 2: Run the balance check

Once you have identified core team members, assess for critical gaps and dangerous imbalances.

Decision speed

- Do you have at least one Spontaneous archetype (Instinctive Impulsive, Visionary Improviser, Responsive Supporter) to drive momentum?

- Do you have at least one Rational archetype (Logical Seer, Insightful Advisor) to prevent reckless choices?
- ⚠ Red flag: All fast decision-makers OR all slow decision-makers

Analytical depth

- Do you have at least one Rational archetype (Logical Seer, Insightful Advisor, Creative Architect) for rigorous analysis?
- Do you have at least one Intuitive archetype (Creative Architect, Visionary Improviser, Logical Seer) to spot patterns data might miss?
- ⚠ Red flag: No one comfortable with detailed analysis OR no one who trusts instinct

People dynamics

- Do you have at least one Empathic Ally or Sensitive Confidant to read the room?
- Do you have at least one Methodical Diplomat to manage consensus building?
- ⚠ Red flag: All task-focused with no people specialists

Courage to decide

- Do you have decision-makers who will actually make calls, not just discuss?
- Is someone willing to own decisions even when consensus is unclear?
- ⚠ Red flag: Multiple Avoidant archetypes (Cautious Procrastinator, Thoughtful Delayer) with no counterbalance OR all Spontaneous with no brake

Complementary tension

- Do you have productive tension (different styles that push each other)?
- Have you avoided toxic combinations (see conflict matrix)?
- ⚠ Red flag: Everyone thinks exactly alike OR constant unproductive conflict

Step 3: Balance team size

Ideal team size: three to seven members

- Below three: Insufficient diversity of perspective
- Above seven: Coordination costs exceed diversity benefits

Team size	Best for	Watch out for
Two people (Duo)	Specific projects with clear scope. Client relationship management. Rapid decision making.	Can get stuck in their own logic. No tiebreaker for disagreements. Limited perspective.
Three people (Trio)	Complex initiatives needing multiple perspectives. Balanced decision-making. Innovation and execution.	Can form 2-against-1 dynamics. Requires active facilitation.
Four to six people (Committee)	Strategic decisions needing broad buy-in. Diverse expertise required. Firm-wide initiatives.	Slower decision making. Risk of endless discussion. Needs strong chair.
Seven+ people	Consultation and input gathering (not decision making).	Ineffective for actual decisions. Diffusion of responsibility. Meetings become performances.

Rule of thumb: The more people involved, the more process you need. Teams over five require explicit facilitation.

Step 4: Balance team composition

Balanced team formula:

- At least one rational archetype (for analytical grounding)
- At least one intuitive archetype (for pattern recognition)
- At least one dependent archetype (for consensus building)
- Either spontaneous or avoidant (for tempo management)

Avoid homogeneous teams

- Teams of similar archetypes amplify weaknesses:
  All Rational: Analysis paralysis. Endless data gathering. Missed opportunities. "We are still studying it."

- *All Spontaneous:* Constant firefighting. Insufficient planning. Preventable errors. "We keep fixing the same problems."
- *All Dependent:* Decisions by committee. Vague compromises. Slow execution. "Everyone had input but nothing happened."
- *All Avoidant:* No decisions ever get made. Perpetual exploration of alternatives. Strategic drift. "We are considering our options."

Perfect balance is impossible. The goal is to ensure critical perspectives are present for your specific mission, avoid dangerous blind spots, and leverage archetype strengths strategically.

Step 5: Leverage universal connectors
Some archetypes work well with almost anyone. Use them as "glue" in your team:

Logical Seer: Balances analysis with intuition. Can connect with both data-driven and pattern-driven thinkers. Ensures quality without blocking speed.

Empathic Ally: Creates psychological safety. Helps archetypes understand each other emotionally. Essential for any team at risk of interpersonal conflict.

Insightful Advisor: Analytical enough for rational types, consultative enough for dependent types. Asks questions that help others articulate positions.

Step 6: Prevent predictable conflicts
Before the team starts working, establish ground rules that acknowledge different decision-making styles:

For Rational archetypes (Logical Seer, Insightful Advisor, Creative Architect): Agree on information requirements upfront - what analysis is "enough"

For Intuitive archetypes (Creative Architect, Visionary Improviser, Logical Seer): Create space for pattern-based insights without requiring full justification immediately

For Dependent archetypes (Methodical Diplomat, Empathic Ally, Insightful Advisor): Define consultation scope – who needs to be involved and when

*For Avoidant archetypes (Cautious Procrastinator, Thoughtful Del*ayer): Set decision deadlines and clarify that silence = consent after cutoff

For Spontaneous archetypes (Instinctive Impulsive, Visionary Improviser, Responsive Supporter): Identify which decisions can be made quickly vs which need deliberation

For everyone: Separate process debates from substance debates – meta-discuss HOW you will decide before arguing WHAT to decide

Step 7: Monitor team dynamics and adjust

Dimension	Healthy pattern	Warning signs
Decision velocity	Decisions happen at appropriate speed for their importance	Everything takes forever OR everything is rushed
Conflict pattern	Disagreements are about substance and get resolved	Same people clash repeatedly over process
Participation	Everyone contributes their expertise; no one dominates	One archetype dominates OR some never speak up
Decision quality	Decisions stick and produce expected outcomes	Frequent reversals or unexpected consequences
Team morale	Members value each other's different approaches	Frustration with "how people think" rather than "what they think"

After three to six months, assess how the team is actually functioning.

When to intervene:

- If you spot warning signs, do not change team composition immediately.
- Make the implicit explicit – facilitate a discussion about different decision-making styles.
- Establish clearer process protocols that honor different approaches.
- Consider adding a complementary archetype rather than replacing someone.

- If conflicts persist despite process fixes, then consider composition changes.

Remember: The goal is not a team of identical thinkers. The goal is a team that leverages different thinking styles productively.

The three non-negotiables

Match to mission: Different challenges need different archetype combinations

Balance without blandness: Tension is productive; homogeneity is death

Process before people: Most "personality conflicts" are actually process conflicts in disguise

A well-composed team is not one where everyone gets along – it is one where different decision-making styles combine to produce results none could achieve alone.

Appendix 9: Ten distortions of consensus

Which fake consensus are you experiencing? A diagnostic guide.

Type	What it looks like	When it works	When it breaks
1. False consensus	"Everyone agrees" only because no one wants to speak first. Silence is mistaken for consent.	Decision is genuinely sound and partners avoid debating the obvious.	Half the room has serious doubts but each assumes they are the only sceptic.
2. Polite consensus	Partners remain silent from exhaustion, overload, or not wanting to create problems.	Social lubrication that keeps group functioning on minor issues.	End of lengthy meetings or complex issues when minds are already elsewhere.
3. Coerced consensus	"Agreement" from authority pressure, not reasoning. Dissent has consequences.	Rapid decisions amid uncertainty when senior judgment is genuinely superior.	Senior emphasizes team loyalty over proposal merits; doubts get disguised as "questions".
4. Consensus pause	Temporary agreement to postpone conflict, not resolve it.	Wise strategy to cool emotions, gather information, wait for better moment.	"Deferred" list grows for years, becoming cemetery of unresolved issues.
5. Consensus as cover	"Unified position" serves as camouflage for hidden agendas.	Advancing unpopular but necessary moves; saves months of unproductive debate.	Becomes manipulation tool for personal benefit rather than firm good.
6. Performative democracy	Decision already made but everyone invited to speak "for show".	Leader genuinely hopes for new arguments; occasionally uncovers overlooked points.	Partners perform advisory roles whose contributions no one values.

continued on next page

Type	What it looks like	When it works	When it breaks
7. No-consensus culture	No one agrees with anyone, yet partnership pretends to function.	Diverse opinions spark innovation; internal competition drives growth.	Exhausts participants; accumulated tensions explode when conditions deteriorate.
8. Consensus through abdication	All silently agree to avoid taking responsibility.	Reduces conflict, speeds decisions, shares blame for failures in stable periods.	No one feels ownership or advocates for implementation.
9. Emotional consensus	"Agreement" secured through emotional pressure: "Disagree and you are against the team".	Unity during genuine crises when firm must unite against external threats.	Becomes critical-thinking inhibitor; defending against accusations is impossible.
10. Symbolic consensus	Everyone supposedly agrees, yet no one plans to act.	Discussion process matters more than outcome; partners release frustration.	Six months later nothing has changed; time and energy wasted.

How to use this diagnostic

Step 1: Identify the pattern
When a decision feels "off" but you cannot explain why, scan the list above. Which description matches what you are experiencing?

Step 2: Check the conditions
Look at the "When it works" column. Are those conditions present? If yes, you might be experiencing the productive version. If not, you are in the danger zone.

Step 3: Intervene before it breaks
The "When it breaks" column shows the warning signs. If you see them emerging, address the underlying issue before the fake consensus collapses.

These patterns are not inherently good or bad – context determines whether they are tools or obstacles. The danger lies in using them unconsciously or in the wrong situations. Once you recognize the pattern, you can decide whether to lean into it or break out of it.

Appendix 10: Four phases of consensus life

The natural lifecycle of partnership consensus – where are you now?

Phase	Characteristics	Opportunities	Risks and warning signs
Phase 1 Formation (Honeymoon period)	Optimism and enthusiasm Easy, quick decisions Minimal formal procedures Maximum financial transparency Conflicts rare and quickly resolved	Build foundation of trust Establish core values Create positive precedents Develop personal relationships	Assuming harmony will last forever Not preparing for inevitable conflicts Accepting too many commitments Unrealistic expectations
Phase 2 Institutionalization (Establishing framework)	Written procedures emerge Committees and working groups form Decisions require more discussion Precedents gain importance Stability and predictability increase	Create sustainable structures Clarify authority and responsibility Document decision-making processes Build institutional memory	Rules become objectives themselves Bureaucracy slows decisions Initiative constrained by formalities System becomes inflexible
Phase 3 Erosion (Building contradictions)	Growing gap between formal rules and reality Informal networks gain power Cynicism about "official" processes Unresolved tensions accumulate Trust gradually deteriorates	Opportunity to reform before crisis Identify what needs updating Address festering issues Prevent full breakdown	Ignoring warning signs "This is how we have always done it" Key people planning exits Talent retention problems Client service deterioration

continued on next page

Phase	Characteristics	Opportunities	Risks and warning signs
Phase 4 Crisis or renewal (The fork in the road)	Consensus breaks down completely Open conflicts emerge Fundamental questions resurface Partnership faces existential choice: ? Dissolve ? Transform ? Renew	Complete reset possible Address root causes, not symptoms Build new consensus from scratch Emerge stronger if handled well	Attempting cosmetic fixes to deep problems Blaming individuals vs examining systems Choosing dissolution by default Missing renewal window

What triggers phase transitions?

Formation ➡ Institutionalization

- First serious conflict that cannot be resolved "amicably"
- Firm growth makes informal arrangements unworkable
- External factors (clients, regulators) require formalization

Institutionalization ➡ Erosion

- Rules designed for past problems prevent adaptation to new challenges
- Key assumptions underlying consensus prove false
- External environment changes faster than internal processes
- New partners join with different expectations

Erosion ➡ Crisis

- Major external shock (economic downturn, key client loss, regulatory change)
- Internal breaking point (partner departures, public conflict, financial stress)
- Accumulated small violations reach critical mass

Crisis ➡ Renewal (or Dissolution)

- Partners choose honest reckoning over blame and defensiveness
- Leadership willing to fundamentally rethink partnership model
- Enough trust remains to attempt rebuilding
- External conditions allow time and resources for transformation

Where is your partnership now?

Ask yourself these questions to identify your current phase:

- How long does it take to make decisions? (Fast = Formation; Moderate = Institutionalization; Slow/Stuck = Erosion)
- How do partners talk about "the old days"? (Fondly = Formation ending; Nostalgically = Erosion; Bitterly = Crisis)
- Are formal processes respected or routinely bypassed? (Respected = Institutionalization; Bypassed = Erosion)
- How often do you revisit fundamental questions about partnership? (Never = Formation/Institutionalization; Constantly = Erosion/Crisis)
- What is the emotional temperature in partner meetings? (Warm = Formation; Professional = Institutionalization; Tense = Erosion; Explosive = Crisis)
- Are younger partners enthusiastic or disillusioned? (Enthusiastic = Formation/Institutionalization; Disillusioned = Erosion/Crisis)

Strategic guidance by phase:

- *Formation:* Enjoy the honeymoon but build foundations for harder times. Document decisions and establish conflict resolution mechanisms while goodwill is high.
- *Institutionalization:* Strike balance between structure and flexibility. Create processes that serve the partnership, not bureaucracy that constrains it.
- *Erosion:* This is your last chance for preventative action. Address gaps between formal rules and reality before they become unbridgeable. Honest diagnosis now prevents crisis later.
- *Crisis:* Choose transformation over blame. This is painful but potentially transformative. Partnerships that navigate crisis well often emerge stronger than before.

The cycle is inevitable:

Consensus follows natural patterns as predictable as seasons. What succeeds in Formation fails in Erosion. Strategies that work in Institutionalization backfire during Crisis. Partnership wisdom lies in recognizing where you are and adapting leadership to the current phase – not fighting the cycle, but navigating it intelligently.

Appendix 11: The 14 strategic dichotomies

Your firm's DNA – map your choices to understand your architecture.

Layer 1: meta-choices (Partnership philosophy)

Choice	Option A	Option B	What it determines
1. Core model	*Hunters:* Individual fighters, personal mastery, internal competition	*Farmers:* Collective wisdom, synergy, coordination	Collaboration vs competition, decision centralization, leadership style
2. Time horizon	*Renters:* Maximize current income, high distributions	*Investors:* Build long-term value, reinvest profits	Growth capacity, infrastructure investment, partner wealth model
3. Information	*Transparent:* All partners know everyone's income	*Confidential:* Each knows only own figures	Trust dynamics, conflict patterns, compensation flexibility
4. Ambition	*Aggressive growth:* High intensity, ambitious targets	*Work–life balance:* Quality of life, stable rhythm	Work intensity, strategic pace, partner lifestyle expectations
5. Purpose	*Serve the firm:* Institutional thinking, strategy first	*Be served:* Partners come first, firm serves them	Sacrifice willingness, succession planning, institutional vs personal focus

Layer 2: Strategic positioning (market identity)

Choice	Option A	Option B	What it determines
6. Market focus	*Exclusivity:* Elite clients, high-stakes matters	*Volume:* Many clients, standardized products	Pricing model, expertise depth, scalability, margin structure
7. Geography	*Local:* Deep roots, home advantage	*Global:* Multi-jurisdictional reach	Complexity, overhead, cultural diversity, market size
8. Power relations	*State-aligned:* Proximity to power, insider position	*Independent:* Proud distance from government	Client access, constraints, reputational dynamics, risk profile

Layer 3: Service model (delivery approach)

Choice	Option A	Option B	What it determines
9. Scope	*Specialisation:* Narrow expertise, deep knowledge	*Full-service:* Universal soldiers, one-stop shop	Market size, expertise depth, cross-sell potential, hiring complexity
10. Trust model	*Formal:* Reproducibility, systems, predictability	*Relationships:* Trust through culture, personal touch	Scalability, consistency, partner leverage, cultural requirements
11. Change stance	*Innovation:* Cutting edge, first-mover advantage	*Tradition:* Proven methods, conservatism	Risk profile, investment needs, market positioning, client expectations

Layer 4: Organizational Model (Internal Structure)

Choice	Option A	Option B	What it determines
12. Governance	*Partnership:* Brotherhood of equals	*Corporation:* Clear hierarchy, accountability	Decision speed, accountability, scalability, cultural identity
13. Brand focus	*Personal brands:* Stars – each partner is the brand	*Corporate brand:* Systems – firm guarantees quality	Exit risk, marketing approach, succession, institutional strength
14. Compensation	*Individual:* Eat what you kill	*Team results:* Shared success	Collaboration incentives, internal dynamics, knowledge sharing, cultural tone

How to use this map

Step 1: Map your current position

For each of the 14 dichotomies, honestly assess where your firm sits today. Mark Option A, Option B, or somewhere in between. Do not describe where you wish to be – describe reality.

Step 2: Check for coherence

Look for contradictions. Are you Hunters (meta-choice 1) but with Team compensation (choice 14)? Renters (choice 2) but trying to build Corporate brand (choice 13)? Relationship-based (choice 10) but scaling Globally (choice 7)?

Step 3: Identify which strategic game you play

Compare your pattern to the three strategic games. Lone Wolves tend toward Option A on most choices. Families lean toward Option B or middle ground. Corporations are selective but systematic in their choices.

Step 4: Decide – commit or fix

Either commit to your pattern and accept its tradeoffs, or identify which choices must change to achieve coherence. Remember: you cannot change everything at once, and deeper layers are harder to shift.

Warning:
The most dangerous position is the mushy middle on everything. Firms that try to be "a bit of both" on all 14 choices end up being nothing distinctive to anyone.

Successful firms make clear choices on meta-decisions and strategic positioning (Layers 1-2), then align everything else. Failing firms drift through tactical compromises that accumulate into incoherence.

Choose your battles. You cannot optimize for everything.

Appendix 12: Architectural coherence checker

Common logical traps – what combinations do not work.

Incompatible combination	Why it fails	Typical symptoms
Hunters + Team compensation	Hunters are motivated by individual achievement. Team-based rewards kill the very incentive that makes hunters effective.	Top performers leave, internal competition becomes toxic, or compensation system gets ignored in practice.
Renters + Aggressive growth	Growth requires reinvestment. Renters maximize current distributions. Cannot do both simultaneously.	Chronic underinvestment, deteriorating infrastructure, strategic plans without funding.
Exclusivity + Volume economics	Elite positioning requires low client numbers, high touch, premium pricing. Volume requires opposite.	Market confusion, pricing pressure, inability to deliver premium service at scale.
Relationships + Global scale	Personal relationship model cannot scale across hundreds of lawyers and dozens of offices without losing essence.	Client service deterioration, partner frustration, cultural fragmentation across offices.
Personal Brands + Corporate governance	Stars resist hierarchy and accountability. Corporate structure requires both. Fundamental clash.	Governance paralysis, star departures, or corporate structure exists on paper only.
Specialization + Full partnership equality	Specialists in hot markets earn multiples of those in declining niches. Lockstep compensation creates resentment.	Profitable practice partners subsidize unprofitable ones, top earners defect, or equality abandoned.
Innovation + Risk aversion	Innovation requires tolerance for failure and investment without guaranteed returns. Risk aversion prevents both.	Innovation theatre – pilot projects that never scale, committees that study but never act.

continued on next page

Incompatible combination	Why it fails	Typical symptoms
Local focus + Premium talent	Best talent wants global opportunities and exposure. Purely local firms cannot retain them long-term.	Talent drain to international firms, inability to compete for ambitious associates.
Farmer Culture + Eat-what-you-kill rewards	Farmers need collaborative incentives. Individual-focused compensation creates hunters regardless of stated culture.	Knowledge hoarding, refusal to cross-sell, internal competition despite collaboration rhetoric.
State-Aligned + Independent positioning	Cannot simultaneously be seen as government insiders and fiercely independent. Market will not believe it.	Reputational confusion, losing clients from both segments, credibility erosion.

Coherence diagnostic questions

Ask yourself these questions to test your architectural coherence:

Philosophy-strategy alignment

- Do our market positioning choices logically flow from our partnership philosophy?
- If we are Renters, are we pursuing strategies that require long-term investment?
- If we are Hunters, are we in markets that reward individual excellence?

Strategy-service alignment

- Does our service model enable our strategic positioning?
- If we claim exclusivity, do we have the expertise depth to justify it?
- If we claim scale, do we have systems that deliver consistency?

Service-organization alignment

- Does our organizational model support our service delivery?
- If we rely on relationships, do we have governance that preserves them?
- If we need innovation, do we have structures that reward experimentation?

Compensation-culture alignment

- Do our compensation systems reinforce or undermine our stated culture?

- If we want collaboration, do we reward it financially?
- If we celebrate individual achievement, does compensation reflect that?

Brand-reality alignment

- Can we actually deliver on our market promises?
- Do our internal capabilities match our external positioning?
- Are we who we say we are, or who we wish to be?

What to do when you find incoherence

If you discover...	Your options
Minor misalignment (1-2 contradictions)	Fix at the execution level. Adjust processes, systems, or practices to align with deeper choices. Relatively straightforward.
Moderate incoherence (3-4 contradictions)	Choose which layer to change. Either adjust strategy/service model to match philosophy, or acknowledge philosophy has shifted and formalize it.
Severe incoherence (5+ contradictions)	Full architectural redesign required. Accept that you are essentially building a new firm. Expect partner departures, revenue disruption, multi-year transition.
Fundamental philosophy split	Partners hold incompatible visions. Either force resolution through governance, or accept that partnership dissolution may be healthier than perpetual conflict.

The coherence imperative:
Incoherence is not always fatal in the short-term – many firms survive for years with contradictory architectures. But incoherence creates constant friction – partners arguing past each other because they hold different mental models, strategic initiatives that fail because they clash with underlying culture, talent that leaves because "something just feels off".

The firms that thrive over decades are not necessarily the ones that made perfect initial choices. They are the ones that built internally coherent systems and had the courage to revise those systems when circumstances changed – rather than pretending contradictions did not exist.

Architectural coherence is not a one-time achievement. It is a discipline of continuous alignment between what you believe, what you promise, and what you actually do.

Appendix 13: Decision types classification matrix

Understanding urgency, timing, and flexibility – what can wait and what cannot.

Decision type	Urgency level	When to decide	Reversibility	Cost of delay
Day one decisions Foundational philosophy	*Critical* Cannot wait	*Before launch* Literally Day One	*Extremely hard* Changing requires rebuilding everything	*Catastrophic* Years of friction, eventual breakdown, partnership dissolution
Critical turning points Scale-dependent choices	*High* Window of opportunity	*When triggered* By growth, team size, or market shift	*Very hard* Requires significant restructuring	*Severe* Missed opportunities, internal strain, market confusion
Periodic reassessment Context-dependent reviews	*Moderate* Scheduled reviews	*Every two to three years* Or when context shifts significantly	*Moderate* Adjustable with proper planning	*Accumulating* Slow drift from reality, gradual irrelevance
Fluctuative decisions Adaptable choices	*Low* Flexible timing	*When opportune* Can evolve gradually	*Easy* Reversible without major disruption	*Minimal* Room for experimentation and learning

Examples of each decision type

Type	Specific examples
Day one	• Hunters or farmers? • Renters or investors? • Transparent or confidential compensation? • Aggressive growth or work–life balance? • Serve the firm or be served by it?
Critical turning points	• State or business alignment? (by Year Three) • Formality or relationships? (when team exceeds 20-30) • Family or corporation governance? (when partners exceed seven) • Personal brands or corporate brand? (growth dependent)
Periodic reassessment	• Innovation or tradition balance • Process weight ("spring cleaning") • Personal vs corporate brand tension • Generational knowledge transfer • Cultural continuity maintenance
Fluctuative	• Specialization or full-service (can evolve) • Local or global geographic focus (gradual expansion) • Elite or broad-market positioning (can shift over time) • Service delivery model adjustments

How to prioritize competing decisions

When multiple decisions demand attention, use this prioritization framework:

- *Step 1:* Identify the decision type: Day One > Critical Turning Points > Periodic > Fluctuative
- *Step 2:* Check the window: Has the window for a Critical Turning Point already arrived? Are you past the optimal timing?
- *Step 3:* Assess interdependencies: Which decision is prerequisite for others? (e.g., meta-choices before strategic positioning)
- *Step 4:* Evaluate cost of delay: What breaks if you wait another quarter? Another year?
- *Step 5:* Consider implementation capacity: Can you actually execute on this decision now, or do other prerequisites need addressing first?

Common prioritization mistakes

Mistake	Why it fails
Postponing day one decisions "until we have time"	There is never "time later". Every month of delay embeds dysfunction deeper. These decisions cannot wait.
Treating all decisions as equally urgent	Leads to decision fatigue and paralysis. Fluctuative decisions can wait – focus energy on what truly matters.
Missing the window on critical turning points	Waiting too long makes the decision much harder. Formality at 50 people is far more painful than at 25.
Never revisiting periodic decisions	Context changes but decisions do not. Slow drift from reality until crisis forces painful correction.

The art of timing

Partnership decision making is not just about making the right choices – it is about making them at the right time.

Day One decisions demand immediate clarity. Delay creates permanent friction.

Critical turning points have windows. Miss the window and the decision becomes exponentially harder. Periodic Reassessment requires discipline. Set review schedules and honor them. Fluctuative Decisions offer freedom to experiment. Use this flexibility strategically.

The firms that master timing do not make better decisions than their competitors – they make the same decisions at moments when they are easier, clearer, and less costly. Timing is strategy.

Appendix 14: Firm lifecycle timeline

The 15-year journey – when architectural decisions must be made and crises emerge.

Period	Phase name	Critical decisions	Typical crisis	Key challenge
Years zero to three Foundations	Laying the foundations Start-up stage	Day One decisions (immediate): • Hunters or Farmers? • Renters or Investors? • Transparent or Confidential? • Serve or Be Served? By Year Three: • State or Business? • Market positioning • Geographic focus	Survival crisis Cash flow, client acquisition, team building	Making foundational choices while fighting for survival. Most firms postpone philosophy discussions - fatal mistake.
Years three to seven Scale and Growth	Adapting to scale Growth paradox	Critical turning points: • Formality or Relationships? (20-30 people) • Family or Corporation? (7+ partners) • Specialization clarity First reviews: • Refine meta-choices • Innovation vs Tradition • Process formalization	Leadership crisis Founders become bottlenecks. Informal methods fail at scale.	What brought success now prevents growth. Profession-alizing leadership or replacing founders.

continued on next page

Period	Phase name	Critical decisions	Typical crisis	Key challenge
Years seven to 15 Maturity	Maintaining living architecture Institutionalization	Periodic reassessment (ongoing): • All flexible decisions • Process "spring cleaning" • Personal vs Corporate brand balance • Weight of bureaucracy Generational transition: • Passing architectural knowledge • Cultural continuity • Succession planning	Autonomy crisis Resistance to formalization Or: Bureaucratization crisis Systems devour meaning. Or: Relevance crisis World changed, firm did not.	Keeping architecture alive while preserving entrepreneurial spirit. Balancing innovation and tradition.

Decision urgency guide

Type	Timing
Day one decisions	Cannot be postponed even for an hour. Decide before launch or face permanent friction.
Critical turning points	Can be deferred, but only to a specific moment. Beyond that, delay becomes dangerous.
Periodic reassessment	Must be revisited regularly as context changes. Set review schedule.
Fluctuative decisions	Can be adjusted along the way without serious consequences. Maximum flexibility.

Crisis points: warning signs and resolution paths

Crisis type	When it hits	Warning signs	Resolution path
Leadership crisis	Years three to seven Rapid growth phase	• Founders drowning in operational details • Decisions slow to crawl • Staff waiting for instructions on trivia • Client complaints about delays	• Delegate authority • Hire professional managers • Create clear procedures • Professionalize or step aside
Autonomy crisis	Years seven to 15 Formalization phase	• Complaints about "bureaucratization" • Partners ignore new procedures • Nostalgia for "good old days" • Sabotage of systems	• Balance coordination and entrepreneurship • Formalize only critical processes • Involve sceptics in procedure design • Explain logic behind changes
Bureaucratization crisis	Years ten to 15 Over-mature systems	• Procedures exist for their own sake • Compliance trumps results • Innovation stifled by approvals • Talented people leave	• Process "spring cleaning" • Kill procedures that no longer add value • Empower front-line decision making • Inject entrepreneurial energy
Relevance crisis	Any mature stage External disruption	• Market shifting faster than firm • Clients demanding new capabilities • Competitors using new models • Revenue stagnation despite effort	• Strategic reset • Revisit positioning decisions • Invest in new capabilities • Accept painful architectural changes

Principles for navigating the lifecycle:

1. *Crises are inevitable:* They signal outgrown architecture, not failure. Firms that never experience crisis are not growing.

2. *Timing matters:* Day One decisions cannot wait. Critical turning point decisions have windows. Missing the window creates years of dysfunction.

3. *Architecture evolves:* What works for five partners fails for 50. Successful firms consciously adapt their architecture at each stage.

4. *Forward planning:* You can see crises coming. Leadership crisis hits at 25-30 people. Autonomy crisis follows formalization. Prepare rather than react.

5. *Cultural continuity:* As you grow, architectural decisions known intuitively by founders must be articulated and institutionalized for the next generation.

Where are you now? Use this timeline to identify your current stage, anticipate upcoming decision points, and prepare for predictable crises before they arrive.

Appendix 15: The annual decision calendar

The quarterly cycle of partnership decisions – understanding the rhythm and managing conflict nodes.

Quarter	Primary focus	Key decisions	Conflict nodes	Critical actions
Q3 Preparation	Strategic Planning Analysis and Initial Concepts	• Analyze current results • Initial strategic adjustments • Conceptual phase of planning • Market positioning review	Minimal conflict Exploratory phase	• Review performance data • Identify strategic gaps • Begin scenario planning • Consult practice leaders
Q4 Critical phase	Financial + Strategic Most Intensive Period	• Sum up financial year • Distribute profits • Finalize strategic plans • Make key personnel decisions • Approve budget	⚠⚠⚠ Finance-strategy node Distribute earnings vs invest in future ⚠⚠ Personnel-finance node Bonus pool already set	• Close financial year • Partner profit distribution • Approve next year budget • Finalize strategic initiatives • Key hiring decisions • Partner promotions

continued on next page

Quarter	Primary focus	Key decisions	Conflict nodes	Critical actions
Q1 Implementation	Personnel + Operations Executing Approved Plans	• Mass personnel decisions • Employee evaluations • Bonus payments • New hires onboarding • Adapt processes to new goals	⚠ Operations-strategy node Real processes may not match assumptions	• Annual reviews • Distribute bonuses • Execute hiring plan • Launch new initiatives • Adjust workflows
Q2 Adjustment	Operational + Financial Course Corrections	• Initial results review • Budget revisions if needed • Operational bottleneck fixes • Mid-year check-ins • Process optimizations	Moderate conflict Reality check on plans	• Review Q1 performance • Identify variances • Adjust budgets if needed • Fix operational issues • Maintain plan stability

The decision flow across quarters

How decision types cascade through the year:

Q3: Strategic planning
Sets direction and priorities for next year
⬇
Q4: Financial decisions
Allocates resources to execute strategy
⬇
Q4-Q1: Personnel decisions
Forms team within financial constraints
⬇
Q1-Q2: Operational decisions
Optimizes processes for new goals
⬇
Q2-Q3: Feedback loop
Results inform next cycle of strategic planning

Managing the three critical conflict nodes

Conflict node	When it occurs	The tension	Management strategy
Finance-strategy node	Q4 Year-end closeout	Must simultaneously: • Distribute earned profits (reward past) • Plan investments (build future) Partners want high distributions *and* ambitious growth	• Separate discussions: profit distribution first, then investment • Create buffer time between decisions • Use three-year planning to show ROI • Consider phased investment approach
Personnel-finance node	Q4-Q1 Bonus and hiring season	Personnel decisions made *after* financial ones. Bonus pool already set before evaluating individual merit. Difficult to motivate when money already allocated	• Reserve contingency in bonus pool • Make preliminary personnel assessments in Q3 • Create merit-based distribution framework before Q4 • Allow flexibility for exceptional performers
Operations-strategy node	Q1-Q2 Implementation reality check	Operational realities may not match strategic assumptions. Processes cannot support ambitious plans. Need strategy revision or operational overhaul	• Build operational assessment into Q3 planning • Pilot test strategic initiatives in Q4 • Reserve Q2 for adjustments, not radical pivots • Use feedback to inform next cycle

Practical calendar management principles

1. Divide strategic planning into phases: Conceptual work in Q3, detailed elaboration in Q4. Reduces burden on most intensive period.
2. Create buffer time between decision types: Do not make financial and personnel decisions on same day. Allow time for human factor consideration.
3. Reserve Q2 for adjustments only: Minor corrections acceptable, radical strategy revision destabilizes the year.
4. Appoint clear decision owners: Each decision type needs an owner. Each conflict node needs escalation path.
5. Consider decision-making archetypes: Logical Seer for strategic-financial planning, Empathic Ally for client management and team cohesion, Methodical Diplomat for finding compromises, Instinctive Impulser for Q2 adjustments.
6. Track decision interdependencies: Every choice affects others. Map connections and monitor cascade effects.

The calendar is your friend

The annual decision calendar is not a constraint – it is a rhythm. Firms that fight the calendar exhaust themselves making the same decisions repeatedly. Firms that master the calendar make each decision once, at the right time, with the right preparation.

The most dangerous mistake is treating all quarters as equivalent. Q4 is inevitably intense – trying to distribute that load evenly across the year creates confusion. Better to accept the rhythm, prepare for the crunch, and use Q2-Q3 strategically for the work that cannot happen during crisis mode.

Your calendar reflects your values. If Q4 is only about distributing money, you are renters. If Q4 balances rewards with investment, you are investors.

About Globe Law and Business

Globe Law and Business was established in 2005. From the very beginning, we set out to create legal books that are sufficiently high level to be of real use to the experienced professional, yet still accessible and easy to navigate. Most of our authors are drawn from Magic Circle and other top commercial firms, both in the United Kingdom and internationally. Our titles are carefully produced, with the utmost attention paid to editorial, design and production processes. We hope this results in high-quality publications that are easy to read and a pleasure to own.

In 2021, we were very pleased to announce the start of a new chapter for Globe Law and Business following the acquisition of law books under the imprint Ark Publishing. Our law firm management list is now significantly expanded with many well-known and loved Ark Publishing titles.

We are also pleased to announce the launch of our online content platform, Globe Law Online, which allows for easy access across firms. Details of all titles included can be found at www.globelawonline.com. Email glo@globelawandbusiness.com for further details and to arrange a free trial for you or your firm.

We'd very much like to hear from you with your thoughts and ideas for improving what we offer. Please do feel free to email me on sian@globelawandbusiness.com. Happy reading and thank you for your time.

Sian O'Neill
Managing director
Globe Law and Business
www.globelawandbusiness.com